Hiking Kansas

Hiking Kansas

A Guide to the State's Greatest Hiking Adventures

Seth Brooks

FALCONGUIDES

ESSEX, CONNECTICUT

To Mom and Dad, for always encouraging me to explore

FALCONGUIDES®

An imprint of Globe Pequot, the trade division of
The Rowman & Littlefield Publishing Group, Inc.
4501 Forbes Blvd., Ste. 200
Lanham, MD 20706
www.rowman.com

Falcon and FalconGuides are registered trademarks and Make Adventure Your Story is a trademark of The Rowman & Littlefield Publishing Group, Inc.

Distributed by NATIONAL BOOK NETWORK

Copyright © 2024 The Rowman & Littlefield Publishing Group, Inc.
Photos by Seth Brooks.
Maps by Melissa Baker and The Rowman & Littlefield Publishing Group, Inc.

British Library Cataloguing in Publication Information available

Library of Congress Cataloging-in-Publication Data

Names: Brooks, Seth (Conservationist), author.
Title: Hiking Kansas : a guide to the state's greatest hiking adventures /
   Seth Brooks.
Description: Essex, Connecticut : FalconGuides, [2024] | Includes index. |
   Summary: "Hiking Kansas introduces hikers of all abilities to the
   greatest hiking adventures across the state"—Provided by publisher.
Identifiers: LCCN 2023051933 (print) | LCCN 2023051934 (ebook) | ISBN
   9781493077724 (paperback) | ISBN 9781493077731 (epub)
Subjects: LCSH: Hiking—Kansas—Guidebooks. | Trails—Kansas—Guidebooks. |
   Kansas—Guidebooks.
Classification: LCC GV199.42.K2 B76 2024 (print) | LCC GV199.42.K2
   (ebook) | DDC 796.5109781—dc23/eng/20231107
LC record available at https://lccn.loc.gov/2023051933
LC ebook record available at https://lccn.loc.gov/2023051934

∞™ The paper used in this publication meets the minimum requirements of American National Standard for Information Sciences—Permanence of Paper for Printed Library Materials, ANSI/NISO Z39.48-1992.

Contents

The Hikes

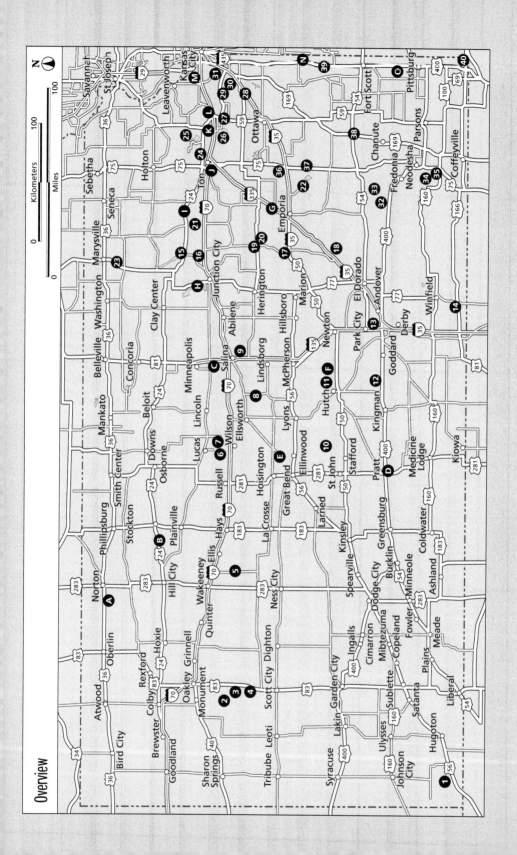

Overview

Acknowledgments

Numerous people helped bring this book to publication. Thank you to all the hikers, outdoor recreationists, and travelers who were curious about my project and shared my passion for the state of Kansas. I hope this book introduces more like-minded people to the natural beauty and cultural wealth the Sunflower State offers.

First, I must thank everyone at Globe Pequot and FalconGuides. Mason Gadd, thank you for offering guidance, answering my questions, and encouraging me during this project. I am honored that you entrusted me to write FalconGuides' first hiking guidebook for the state of Kansas.

A hearty thank you to the following park managers, rangers, biologists, naturalists, administrators, and inspirations who shared their knowledge to improve the accuracy of this guidebook or helped spark my curiosity: Jared Wilson, US Army Corps of Engineers, Clinton Lake; Jennifer Rader, the Southeast Kansas Nature Center; Joshua Standridge, Elk City State Park; Scott McCrone US Army Corps of Engineers, Fall River Lake; Barbara Van Slyke, the Konza Prairie Biological Station; Elizabeth Scrimsher, Wyandotte Lake County Park; Amy Isenburg, the Ernie Miller Nature Center; Kyle Goldwater, US Army Corps of Engineers, Melvern Lake; Paige Harman, Tuttle Creek State Park; Kyle Broockerd, US Army Corps of Engineers, Perry Lake; Blake Keith, Milford State Park; Brandi Coker, Cheney State Park; Jacob Riley, El Dorado State Park; David McGuire, Pawnee Prairie Park; Shawn Silliman, Chaplin Nature Center; Brenda Dean, Kansas Department of Wildlife & Parks; Ellen Rader and Willis Ohl, Wilson State Park; Nolan Fisher, US Army Corps of Engineers, Lucas Park and Minooka Park; Amber McLaughlin, Cedar Bluff State Park; the staff at Smoky Hills Audubon Sanctuary; and Tom Parker, Alcove Spring Historic Park.

Finally, and most importantly, I must thank my parents, Betty and Lloyd, for always encouraging me to explore. Thank you for all your support during this journey. Without your help, this book would not have been possible. I could not have done this without you. I love you.

Meet Your Guide

Seth Brooks has been interested in travel and the natural world since an early age. Family trips were common growing up, including trips to Fort Robinson State Park in western Nebraska, a road trip to California, and visits to Wrigley Field in Chicago to root on the Cubs, among many other adventures. Seth frequently accompanied his father on business trips to Alaska, where the two braved the high seas to fish halibut and the giant mosquitoes on wild Alaskan rivers while fishing for king salmon.

Seth called the rainy, mystical region of Galicia in northwestern Spain home for seven years and currently resides in his home state of Nebraska. He has worked in environmental education, conservation, outdoor recreation, and rural tourism since returning to the United States in late 2020. Seth enjoys spending time with his partner, Chelle, in the Loess Hills of western Iowa and exploring with his dog, Jasper.

To follow Seth on his adventures and see photography of his travels, you can find him on Instagram, @sethfromsomewhere, and his website, sethfromsomewhere.com.

Monument Rocks.

Introduction

"If I went West, I think I would go to Kansas." If Abraham Lincoln had traveled the American West, he may have changed his answer. Most travelers would think about the Rockies, the Grand Canyon, or, inspired by the words of John Muir, the Sierra Nevada. Anyone who has read *PrairyErth* by William Least Heat-Moon, however, will have been inspired by the beauty of the prairie. Anyone who has visited Kansas, traveling its backroads like Least Heat-Moon in his seminal work on Chase County, will have seen the beauty of the Sunflower State. Once the traveler ventures off I-70 and I-35, away from the Kansas City metro, they can find peaceful prairies to hike, sandstone canyons to explore, and rugged river bluffs to traverse.

The problem, however, is land. Along with its Midwestern neighbors Iowa and Nebraska, Kansas ranks in the bottom three in the United States in publicly accessible land. Land in Kansas is overwhelmingly private property. This is what happens when much of your state is covered by rich topsoil. However, shortsighted thinking

Butterfly weed.

1

in southwestern Kansas led to much of that topsoil being blown away, resulting in the Dust Bowl of the 1930s. The worst environmental disaster in our nation's history left farmers bankrupt and families devastated. The federal government bought back land in Morton and Stevens Counties, two of the most devastated counties in the Dust Bowl area. That land is now the Cimarron National Grassland, home to the Santa Fe Companion Trail, one of the best historical hikes in Kansas. Point of Rocks, overlooking the dry Cimarron River, is the only landmark, but you will be awed by the never-ending horizon and "sublime simplicity" of the prairie, as Dan Flores eloquently described the shortgrass prairie in his book *American Serengeti*.

The High Plains and Smoky Hills, which together cover much of the western half of Kansas, have several areas open to the public that will challenge your stereotypes of the Sunflower State. A sunset hike at Little Jerusalem Badlands State Park will have you saying "we're not in Kansas anymore" to your canine companion. If you're lucky, as this author was in January 2023, you'll track another canine, a coyote, on Smoky Valley Ranch's Long Loop. The canyons and water crossings at Kanopolis State Park will challenge the most seasoned hiker.

If you look at a map of where the hikes in this guidebook are located, you will notice that most of the hikes are located in the eastern half of the state. Effort was made by the author to provide an equitable geographical balance, but the reality of land in Kansas is that publicly accessible land is more prevalent where most of the state's population lives. For those living in eastern Kansas, this is convenient. The Flint Hills, where most of the remaining remnant tallgrass prairie is found, is within reasonable driving distance from Wichita, Manhattan, Topeka, Lawrence, and Kansas City. Konza Prairie, for example, is minutes from Manhattan. Tallgrass Prairie National Preserve, located in Chase County, is just a short drive from those metro areas and provides hikers the closest wilderness experience you can find in the state. The Kansas City metro is full of parks with hiking trails, many of them around tranquil lakes. Shawnee Mission Park is the busiest park in the state; the South Shore Trails are hiking only and, while still popular, offer a quieter escape than the trails on the north shore.

In the southeastern corner of Kansas, hikers will be mistaken if they think they are in the Ozarks of neighboring Missouri. The Ozark Plateau reaches into the far southeastern corner, where you can visit Schermerhorn Cave, home to several endangered species of salamanders. The Osage Cuestas make up most of eastern Kansas south of the Kansas River. The best hiking in the state is found here. The Elk River Hiking Trail is one of the most challenging hikes in the Midwest. For those without the time or energy to hike its entire 15 miles, Table Mound Trail in nearby Elk City State Park is a 5-mile hike that packs in dramatic views atop cliffs and scrambles over large boulders.

Weather and Seasons

Every season in Kansas presents challenges to hikers, but every season also rewards hikers with great experiences. Spring in the Midwest is unpredictable, and Kansas is no exception. A snowstorm in May is rare but not impossible, followed by a heat

Historic Lake Scott State Park.

wave reaching into the 90s. What can be counted on, however, is that Kansas begins to thaw by April, and woodland wildflowers like Dutchman's breeches in the eastern hardwood forests signal that summer is ahead. Spring in Kansas is highlighted by the awesome spectacle of migratory birds making their way north via the Central Flyway to their breeding grounds in Canada, Alaska, and Siberia. Cheyenne Bottoms, Quivira National Wildlife Refuge, Flint Hills National Wildlife Refuge, to name a few, are excellent destinations for birding and hiking during the spring migratory season. Please be respectful of birds during this time, however, as they are exposed to numerous stresses on their immense and arduous journey north.

Summers in Kansas are hot and humid. Ticks are abundant and thunderstorms are frequent. These factors complicate hiking excursions from June through August, but the lure of wildflowers should be enough to entice hikers to explore the prairies of the state throughout the summer. Temperatures reach into the triple digits in summer, however, and the lack of shade and water on many prairie trails in Kansas presents challenges for the hiker. The arrival of fall brings milder temperatures and brilliant colors—from the reds, yellows, and browns of eastern Kansas's hardwood forests to the copper big bluestem, towering 6 feet and taller on the tallgrass prairie in the Flint Hills. Autumn also means the beginning of hunting season, and hikers would be wise to wear blaze orange when they hit the trails. Winters can be bitter and long in

Konza Prairie.

the Sunflower State, but cold days are often accompanied by blue skies, so if you are willing to bundle up and brave the cold, you will find quiet trails and prime birding, especially along rivers, lakes, and reservoirs, as bald eagles have spectacularly recovered in the state.

Flora and Fauna

Before it was a state, prairie covered most of Kansas. Today, less than 4 percent of the tallgrass prairie ecosystem remains in North America, and most of it lies within the Flint Hills of Kansas, spared the plow because of the flint, chert, and sandstone in the soil. The land is better suited to grazing than farming, and cattle now roam the grasslands in place of the bison that once roamed the Great Plains. You can still see bison at several places in Kansas, notably the Tallgrass Prairie National Preserve near Cottonwood Falls. The preserve is one of several areas in Kansas that protect the remaining remnant tallgrass prairie; Konza Prairie near Manhattan is another example. Wildflowers bloom from spring through the end of summer, from shooting stars in April to asters in October. Grassland birds such as dickcissels, meadowlarks, and scissor-tailed flycatchers are frequent sightings on the Kansas prairie.

The tallgrass prairie gives way to mixed-grass and shortgrass prairie in the western half of the state. The southwestern corner of Kansas was one of the hardest hit areas during the 1930s Dust Bowl. Unrelenting winds buried houses in windblown top-soil, leaving bankrupt farms in their wake. The Cimarron National Grasslands were cobbled together from land bought back by the federal government from bankrupt and broken farming families. Those who didn't succumb to the "brown plague" of dust pneumonia left the area after having given everything to scratch out a living.

Decades later, born out of the tragedy, is the possibility of "rewilding" this sparsely populated corner of Kansas. A herd of elk reportedly roams the Cimarron, but you'll be incredibly lucky to spot the elusive ungulates.

Eastern Kansas is home to the westernmost reaches of the eastern hardwood forests. Pecan groves can still be found, if you try hard enough, along the Missouri River north of Kansas City. The northeast corner of Kansas is known as the Glaciated Region, as at least two glaciers inched their way into this corner of the state during the last ice age. The rich loess soil left as the glaciers retreated is perfect for farming. Sioux Quartzite boulders left behind by the glaciers are the only remaining remnants of their presence. The woodlands provide hikers a different experience than the prairie and badlands of the western half of the state.

Great blue heron at Baker Wetlands.

Beware, however, of hiking in July and August, as ticks are abundant along woodland trails during these months. The author's dog had a traumatic encounter with a nest of seed ticks in late July; he is fine, but it was an unpleasant experience for both dog and owner.

Wilderness Restrictions/Regulations

Land Ownership

Native Lands

Native American tribes have lived in present-day Kansas for thousands of years. Tribes have come and gone over the centuries, following wildlife, pushed out by other tribes, or forced out by White settlers and the US government. The federal government recognizes four tribes in Kansas: the Sac & Fox Nation of Missouri in Kansas and Nebraska; the Kickapoo Tribe in Kansas; the Prairie Band Potawatomi Nation; and the Iowa Tribe of Kansas and Nebraska. These tribes, and their ancestors, are the

Meadowlark at Konza Prairie.

original stewards of these lands. Allegawaho Memorial Heritage Park was established and dedicated on April 20, 2002, by the Kaw Nation. On the occasion, Kaw Nation park director Betty Durkee said, "This officially marks the return of the Kanzas to the state that bears their name." The Kanza were forcibly removed from Kansas in 1873.

State Parks

The Kansas Department of Wildlife & Parks (KDWP) manages twenty-eight state parks in the Sunflower State. If you include Lehigh Portland, which was established as the newest state park in 2023, the total rises to twenty-nine. The state parks span the entire state, but most are in the easternmost half of Kansas. A valid park entry permit is required for all entrance to state parks. A permit can be purchased at the parks themselves but also at local vendors or online at ksoutdoors.com.

Most of the parks managed by the KDWP have hiking trails in one form or another. Some parks have well-maintained trails with signage that helps hikers navigate the trail system. Other parks, however, lack information at either the trailhead or on the trails themselves, with little to no waymarking or navigational directions at major junctions. Park maps, available at park headquarters or online, provide guidance for hikers. The maps included in this guide use the state parks as reference but also information gathered on the ground by the author and solicited from the manager of the respective state park.

Hunting is allowed at some state recreation areas and state parks. Check hunting season dates if you are hiking in the fall and winter. Always wear blaze orange when you hike during these months; two items of clothing with blaze orange are recommended, and don't forget to dress your dog appropriately.

County, Municipal, and Natural Resources District Parks

Rules and regulations for parks owned and managed by counties, municipalities, universities, and other entities vary. Check with the land manager before visiting to inquire about the state of trails. Many county and municipal parks have well-maintained trails, many of them ADA-accessible on paved paths.

National Parks, National Forests, and National Wildlife Refuges

National parks, national forests, and national wildlife refuge areas are the most protected and therefore have the most rules and regulations. They also typically have the best-maintained trails, with excellent waymarking and information at the trailhead for most hikes. Pets are mostly allowed on federal land, but check before bringing your four-legged friends. Always stay on designated trails, pack out what you pack in, and be respectful of wildlife.

Private Land and Nature Preserves

There are several nonprofit organizations that allow public access to their land. Notable organizations include The Nature Conservancy and several local chapters of the National Audubon Society; both organizations manage multiple reserves throughout Kansas. Like county and municipal parks, rules and regulations vary at each reserve. Dogs may be allowed at one place but not be permitted at another. Check the site's website or contact the manager to inquire about regulations.

Monument Rocks.

Before You Hit the Trail

Hiking Kansas focuses on some of the most scenic day hikes in Kansas. This guide-book is not comprehensive, however, as it was not possible to include every scenic trail in the state. *Hiking Kansas* aims to provide a survey of the best trails in the state while balancing geography, difficulty, accessibility, and ecology. Effort was made not to saturate one area of the state at the expense of others while including hikes in different ecosystems, from the High Plains and Smoky Hills in western Kansas and the singular Flint Hills to the unique Osage Cuestas in southeastern Kansas. The hikes are organized into five sections based on the Kansas physiographic regions established by the Kansas Geological Survey. The fifty-five hikes covered in this book vary in difficulty to engage novice as well as experienced hikers. Use the overview map to locate the hikes nearest you. Detailed information is provided for each of the trails as follows.

Start: The starting location for the hike.

Elevation gain: Elevation is generally the most important factor in determining a hike's difficulty. Total elevation gain in feet is listed, as well as the highest and lowest points reached on the hike. While the stereotype of Kansas is a flat state with little topographical variation, hikers will be surprised by elevation gain on several hikes in this guide.

Distance: The round-trip distance from the trailhead to the end of the route and back (one way in the case of point-to-point hikes). Hike lengths have been determined by using the author's GPS (Global Positioning System) unit. Some variability is to be expected between this measurement and those by the land manager or your own GPS device; however, any discrepancies should be minimal.

Difficulty: Assessing a hike's difficulty is very subjective. Elevation, elevation change, and distance all play a role, as do trail conditions, weather, and the hiker's physical condition. The abundance of trail markers, or lack thereof, can also significantly affect a trail's difficulty. Trails that require constant navigation due to a lack of waymarking, such as at Wyandotte County Lake Park, will be more difficult than a trail that has waymarking at every junction and important navigational point. The remoteness of a hiking area can also increase a trail's difficulty. For example, the trails at Little Jerusalem Badlands State Park are not difficult, but if a hiker experiences an emergency, the increased response time due to remoteness could be problematic. Difficulty is subjective and unique to each hiker and each hike. With that said, the author's subjective ratings will provide some idea of difficulty.

Hiking time: This is a rough estimate of the time it will take the average hiker to complete the hike. Very fit, fast-moving hikers will be able to complete it in less time. Slow-moving hikers or those preoccupied with activities such as photography or field identification may take longer. To arrive at hiking time, the author estimated that most people hike at 2.5 miles per hour and always rounded up to take into account water breaks, photography, and other activities that add time to a hike. Factors such as a rough trail or significant elevation changes were also considered. Carrying a backpack for overnight trips will add significantly to the time required.

Seasons/schedule: When the trails are open to the public. Most trails in Kansas are open year-round from sunset to sunrise, but some are closed on holidays or at specific times. Always contact the land manager or visit their website to verify the status of the trails, not only for opening hours but also current conditions. Some trails are closed during deer rifle season or important migration periods. Additionally, some agencies use prescribed burns to manage their land. Most prescribed fires occur in the spring (late April to early May), but they can occur throughout the year.

Moth cocoon on Pioneer Nature Trail.

Contact the land manager or check their website for updates and trail closures. In the Kansas City area, check the Rainout Line's website (rainoutline.com/search/dnis/9132040204) or call (913) 204-0204 for trail closures after inclement weather.

Sometimes, the best time to hike the trail is listed here. This advice is subjective but based on such factors as bird migrations, wildflower blooms, and other events that will enhance your hike. Hiking a prairie in winter or early spring does not compare to the summer when wildflowers are blooming or late fall when native grasses grow nearly 10 feet tall. There is great variety throughout the summer, as different wildflowers bloom at different times. However, summer is not always the best time to hike in Kansas. Extreme temperatures and an abundance of ticks and insects can make summer hiking unpleasant. Spring is a good time to hike, but snow and cold temperatures can linger into the spring. Fall is an excellent time to hike, perhaps the best season in Kansas. Temperatures are cooler, insects are less prevalent, and leaves begin to change. Winter is often overlooked as a hiking season, especially with the popularity of hunting in Kansas. However, there are great benefits to hiking in winter; bird-watching is easier due to the lack of foliage, and there is a complete absence of ticks and insects. It is imperative, however, that you be aware of hunting seasons and that you wear appropriate clothing for yourself and any pets that hike with you.

Ideally, two items of blaze orange clothing (a hat and vest, for example) are appropriate during hunting season.

Fees and permits: Valid park entry permits are required for state parks, state historical parks, and state recreation areas managed by the Kansas Department of Wildlife & Parks. These can be obtained at the park entrance, at kiosks located in each park, or at licensed vendors near the park. Permits can also be obtained online. Check ksoutdoors.com for regulations, prices, and places to obtain permits. An annual park entry permit is also available, allowing yearlong entrance to all parks in the KDWP system. Some of the areas managed by the USDA Forest Service and National Parks Service require passes, while others are free to the public. In general, organizations like The Nature Conservancy, the National Audubon Society, and other nonprofits do not require an entrance fee; however, always check before you visit to avoid an unexpected entrance fee.

Trail contact: The name, address, phone number, and website of the managing agency for the lands through which the trail passes. Call, write, or check the website for current information about the hike. Sometimes the address listed is not the physical address of the park or area where the hike and trailhead are located; rather it is the office or mailing address of the land manager.

Dog-friendly: Whether dogs are allowed on the trail. Generally, dogs need to be leashed when they are allowed. Please be courteous and pick up dog waste and dispose of it properly.

Trail surface: The material that makes up the trail. Most commonly it is simply a dirt path consisting of the native materials that were there when the trail was built. Occasionally gravel is added or the trail may be paved. In a few instances the hike follows a paved road, dirt road, or primitive doubletrack road.

Land status: The type of property or the agency, usually federal or state, that manages the land in which the trail lies. In this book, the Kansas Department of Wildlife & Parks, USDA Forest Service, US Fish & Wildlife Service, and National Park Service are the most common land managers, along with county, municipal, and private organizations.

Nearest town: The closest city or town to the hike's trailhead that has at least minimal visitor services. The listed town will usually have gas, food, and limited lodging available. In small towns and villages, the hours these services are available may be limited.

Maps: The maps in this guide are as accurate and current as possible. When used in conjunction with the hike description and the additional maps listed for each hike, you should have little trouble following the route.

Generally, two types of maps are listed. Most of the state parks have park or trail maps available free at the entrance station, park headquarters, or online. Some of the park maps have a rudimentary map of trails; other parks have more detailed maps. The USDA Forest Service offers two types of maps. The motor vehicle use map shows the different types of roads within the national forests. They do not, however,

Check before you hike if dogs are allowed on the trail.

show trails and are not topographical maps. Printable versions of these maps are available on the Forest Service's website; digital maps are also available for download on the Avenza Maps app. The Forest Service website also has color, foldable brochures available for purchase. These are excellent maps that show forest roads as well as hiking trails. They are not topographical, however.

USGS topographic quadrangles are generally the most detailed and accurate maps available of natural features. With some practice, they allow you to visualize peaks, canyons, cliffs, rivers, roads, and many other features. With a little experience, a topographic map, and a compass, you should never become lost. All the USGS maps noted in this guide are 7.5-minute quads. USGS quads are particularly useful for little-used trails and off-trail travel. Unfortunately, some of the quadrangles, particularly for less-populated parts of the state, are out of date and do not show many newer man-made features such as roads and trails. However, they are still useful for their topographic information. Most of the more developed hikes in this guide do not require a topo map. The state park maps, Forest Service maps, or maps available from other land managers will suffice on most trails.

GPS units, particularly those with installed maps, can be very useful for route finding when used in conjunction with paper maps. However, anyone who enters the backcountry should have at least basic knowledge in using a paper map and compass. Batteries die and GPS units get dropped, so it's best not to be completely dependent on them. A GPS unit with maps installed can be particularly helpful on off-trail hikes.

USGS quads can usually be purchased at outdoor shops or ordered directly from USGS at http://store.usgs.gov or from online companies such as mytopo.com or topozone.com. To order from USGS, know the state, the number desired of each map, the exact map name as listed in the hike heading, and the scale. You can also download USGS quads at https://apps.nationalmap.gov/downloader/#/ and print them yourself.

Other trail users: The other users you might encounter on the hike. Mountain bikers, equestrians, and hunters are the most common. On multiuse trails, bikers and hikers must yield to equestrians, while bikers must also yield to hikers.

Special considerations: Unique elements of this trail that require extra preparation. These might include water availability, drastic temperature changes, sun exposure, or extreme crowding.

Amenities: Restroom availability, running water, shelter, first aid, vending machines, ramps, etc.

Maximum grade: A good indication of how hard the hardest part of the hike gets. This will tell you how steep the trail gets, as well as how long the steepest sections last.

Cell service: It's important to know if you can, or cannot, count on cell service before you head to the trail. If you are traveling with anyone with mobility or disability considerations, make sure all are aware of the communication channels available. If no cell service is available, make extra sure to read the directions carefully and don't

Bison at Tallgrass Prairie National Preserve.

assume you'll be able to follow your GPS. If you use your mobile phone for maps or to follow GPX tracks, download them before hiking to use them offline.

Finding the trailhead: Here you'll find detailed directions to the trailhead. With a basic current state highway map or GPS unit, you can easily locate the starting point from the directions. In general, the nearest town or interstate exit is used as the starting point.

Distances were measured using Google Maps. Be sure to keep an eye open for the specific signs, junctions, and landmarks mentioned in the directions, not just the mileage. The map services available on cell phone GPS systems are often inaccurate or nonexistent in remote areas, so use them with care. In addition, many require decent cell service to work, further lessening their value. A current map is your best option for finding the trailhead.

Most of this guide's hikes have trailheads that can be reached by any type of vehicle. A few, as noted, require a high-clearance or four-wheel-drive vehicle. Rain or snow can temporarily make some roads impassable. Before venturing into the country, check with the land manager or other local services for current road conditions. On less-traveled back roads, particularly in the High Plains, you should carry basic emergency equipment such as a shovel, chains, water, a spare tire, a jack, blankets, and some extra food and clothing. Make sure your vehicle is in good operating condition with a full tank of gas.

Try not to leave any valuables in your car; if you must, lock them out of sight in the trunk. If I have enough room, I usually put everything in the trunk to give the car an overall empty appearance. In my many years of parking and hiking at remote trailheads, my vehicle has never been disturbed.

Trail conditions: Not all hikes are created equally. Some hikes are well-maintained and well-marked with trail signs, markers, and more that make navigation easy. Other hikes have nonexistent trail infrastructure that can frustrate even the most experienced hiker and make your hike unexpectedly long or, worse, cause you to get lost. This section addresses trail infrastructure such as waymarking, trail signage, and other helpful navigational assistance created by land managers and volunteers. This section also lists potential hazards you may encounter on your hike. Sun exposure, ticks, and thunderstorms are the most common hazards you will encounter while hiking in Kansas. Finally, an estimate of the foot traffic the hike receives is given to give you an idea of how popular the trails are in the area where the hike is located.

The Hike: All the hikes selected for this guide can be done by people in good physical condition. Scrambling may be necessary for a very few hikes, although none require any rock-climbing skills. A few of the hikes, as noted in their descriptions, travel on very faint trails. You should have an experienced hiker, along with a compass, USGS quad, and GPS unit, with your group before attempting those hikes.

The waymarking on trails depends on the agency that manages the land where the hike is located. There is no uniform trail waymarking used by the Kansas Department of Wildlife & Parks; each state park or recreation area uses different types of trail markers and signage. Most of the time the paths are very obvious and easy to follow, but trail markers help when the trails are little-used and faint or when there are numerous intersecting trails throughout the park. Fresh snow can obscure footpaths, so always know the type of trail markers used where you are hiking, and bring a map, compass, and GPS unit with fresh batteries. Do not add your own trail waymarkings—they can confuse the route. Leave such markings to the official trail workers.

Possible backcountry campsites are often suggested in the descriptions. The state parks and recreation areas do not allow backcountry camping, but some do have hike-in campsites. Check with the land manager regarding camping fees, registration, regulations, and other information.

After reading the descriptions, pick the hike that most appeals to you. Go only as far as ability and desire allow. There is no obligation to complete any hike. Remember, you are out hiking to enjoy yourself, not to prove anything.

Miles and Directions: To help you stay on course, a detailed route finder sets forth mileages between significant landmarks along the trail. The mileage may differ from official mileages of the land manager or your own personal GPS device. The author used both a mobile phone and GPS watch to track mileage; they rarely showed the same mileage but were usually within 0.5 mile of each other.

Trail Finder

Best Hikes for Families

9. Marty Bender Nature Trail, *Marty Bender Nature Area*

20. Kanza Heritage Trail, *Allegawaho Memorial Heritage Park*

24. Iliff Commons

Best Hikes for Epic Views

3. Overlook and Life on the Rocks Trails, *Little Jerusalem Badlands State Park*

7. Rocktown Trail, *Lucas Park*

17. Scenic Overlook Loop, *Tallgrass Prairie National Preserve*

Best Hikes for Wildlife

2. Long Loop, *Smoky Valley Ranch*

22. Dove Roost Trail, *Flint Hills National Wildlife Refuge*

27. Baker Wetlands, *Baker University Wetlands and Discovery Center*

Best Hikes for Wildflowers

16. Godwin Hill Loop, *Konza Prairie Biological Station*

21. Mount Mitchell Historical Trail, *Mount Mitchell Heritage Prairie Park*

30. Olathe Prairie Center, *Olathe Prairie Center*

Best "Kansas Isn't Flat" Hikes

8. Buffalo Tracks, Horsethief Canyon, and Red Rock Canyon Loop, *Kanopolis State Park*

28. Bull Creek Loop, *Big Bull Creek Park*

35. Table Mound Trail, *Elk City State Park*

Best Hikes for History

1. Santa Fe Companion Trail, *Cimarron National Grassland*

23. Alcove Spring, *Alcove Spring Historic Park*

39. Prairie, Creek, and Nature Trails, *Mine Creek Civil War Battlefield State Historic Site*

Best Hikes for Backpacking

25. Old Military Trail, *Perry Lake*

26. George Latham Trail, *Woodridge Primitive Park*

34. Elk River Hiking Trail, *Elk City Lake*

Map Legend

Municipal

≡70≡ Interstate Highway

=83= US Highway

=95= State Road

──── Local Road

==== Gravel Road

Trails

▬▬▬ Featured Trail

------ Trail

Water Features

Body of Water

River/Creek

Spring

Waterfalls

Rapids

Symbols

Bridge

■ Building/Point of Interest

▲ Campground

Gate

P Parking

▲ Peak

▲ Primitive Campground

Restroom

Scenic View/Overlook

|||||| Stairs

○ Town

1 Trailhead

? Visitor/Information Center

Land Management

Park/Preserve/Natural Area

High Plains and Smoky Hills

The High Plains and Smoky Hills extend over more than half of the entire state of Kansas. The High Plains covers the westernmost third of the state, with a portion also reaching into south-central Kansas. Although the highest part of the Sunflower State, you will hardly know it, as the surrounding countryside is largely flat or rolling hills. Mount Sunflower, the highest point in the state, is a nondescript hill near the border with Colorado. The extreme southwestern corner of Kansas was the epicenter of the Dust Bowl. The Cimarron National Grassland was cobbled together after the federal government bought back land from landowners who went broke during that disaster. Point of Rocks in Cimarron, the Arikaree Breaks, and the area around Historic Lake Scott State Park provide the only topographic relief in the High Plains. Hikers can retrace the steps of traders who made the Sante Fe Trail famous on the Santa Fe Companion Trail in Cimarron National Grasslands.

The Smoky Hills encompass a vast region of sandstone, limestone, and chalk deposits. The area was periodically covered by large inland seas millions of years ago. Later, rivers and streams and erosion carved the sandstone, limestone, and chalk into impressive formations. Chalk bluffs, badlands, pinnacles, spires, and other rock formations found nowhere else in Kansas make hiking the Smoky Hills a singular experience in the Sunflower State. Life on the Rocks Trail at Jerusalem Badlands State Park is worth the drive for the sunsets alone. The state park and US Army Corps of Engineers parks around Wilson Lake provide some of the best hiking trails in Kansas. The extensive trail system at Kanopolis State Park will challenge experienced hikers with deep stream crossings, isolated canyons, and short scrambles out of the canyon bottoms. Red Rock Canyon at Kanopolis requires multiple difficult stream crossings, but the canyon is unique in the state and worth wet hiking boots.

Mount Sunflower.

1 Santa Fe Companion Trail

Located within the Cimarron National Grassland, the Santa Fe Companion Trail is a 19-mile point-to-point trail that allows hikers the opportunity to see what traveling the famous nineteenth-century wagon trail was like. This hike on a portion of the trail passes Point of Rocks, a major landmark on the route that was a welcome sight to thirsty travelers. Begin at Middle Spring Picnic Area, an oasis in the dry, sun-drenched prairie, and hike through the epicenter of the 1930s Dust Bowl.

Start: Middle Spring Picnic Area
Elevation gain: 3,432 feet (trailhead) to 3,502 feet
Distance: 9.3 miles out and back
Difficulty: Moderate to difficult, depending on the length of your hike
Hiking time: About 4 hours
Seasons/schedule: Open daily year-round; best in spring and fall
Fees and permits: None
Trail contact: Pike-San Isabel National Forests and Cimarron and Comanche National Grasslands, 2840 Kachina Dr., Pueblo, CO 81008; (719) 553-1400; fs.usda.gov/recarea/psicc/recarea/?recid=12404
Dog-friendly: Yes, on leash
Trail surface: Grass and dirt

Land status: Cimarron National Grassland (US Forest Service)
Nearest town: Elkhart, 12 miles to the south; Hugoton, 36 miles to the east
Maps: USGS Elkhart North, KS; maps available online at fs.usda.gov/main/psicc/maps-pubs
Other trail users: Cyclists and equestrians
Special considerations: Bring and drink plenty of water; there is no shade along the trail. Maintain a safe and respectful distance from cattle.
Amenities: Vault toilets and hand pump for water at Middle Spring Picnic Area and Murphy Trailhead
Maximum grade: 5%
Cell service: Adequate coverage along the trail

Finding the trailhead: From Elkhart, Kansas, take US 56 east approximately 7 miles. Turn north onto CR 16 and continue approximately 6 miles. Cross the Cimarron River; turn east on FR 600.1 for approximately 3 miles then travel north 2 miles on FR 615. GPS: N37°6.782' / W101°55.604'

Trail conditions: The Companion Trail is marked with Carsonite trail markers; stay on the designated route. Limestone posts mark the Santa Fe National Historic Trail where hiking is allowed. Afternoon thunderstorms are common. Watch for rattlesnakes and low-lying cacti. The terrain is primarily flat but has gradual inclines across dry drainages and near Point of Rocks. There is no shade except at Middle Spring Picnic Area.

The Hike

Cimarron National Grassland is the largest area of public land in Kansas, covering 108,175 acres of shortgrass and sandsage prairie. It was born out of the 1930s Dust Bowl, the worst ecological disaster in American history. Natural causes (severe drought) and human activity (wet farming methods on the dry prairie) combined to bring Morton County farmers to ruin; the county was the most severely affected in

Approaching Point of Rocks from the east on the Santa Fe Companion Trail.

the entire Dust Bowl area. The federal government bought back land from destitute farmers, and in 1954 the USDA Forest Service assumed management.

The grassland lies in the extreme southwestern corner of Kansas, where the Cimarron River enters the state. The Cimarron Valley is the traditional hunting ground of the Comanche and Kiowa, and the region's human history dates back to perhaps the Folsom and Clovis cultures. In the sixteenth century, Francisco Vázquez de Coronado passed through the region in his quest to find Quivira. More recently, the Santa Fe Trail brought travelers from Missouri on their way to New Mexico in the 1800s.

The Sante Fe Companion Trail parallels the original route through today's Cimarron National Grassland. Hikers can traverse the 19-mile trail from the Conestoga Trailhead to the Murphy Trailhead to experience the journey across the sun-drenched prairie. This hike begins at Middle Spring Picnic Area, passes underneath Point of Rocks, and follows limestone trail markers through sand sagebrush to the Murphy Trailhead. If you have two vehicles, you can park one at each end of the hike for a more manageable 4.65-mile trek.

Middle Spring Picnic Area is a developed recreation area in the national grassland. The timber and year-round water are attractive to both wildlife and human visitors. The area has picnic tables, drinking water, vault toilets, and a short nature trail. The Santa Fe Companion Trail runs parallel to FR 600, and Middle Spring Picnic Area provides easy access to the trail. It heads southwest and reaches Point of Rocks after

Santa Fe Companion Trail

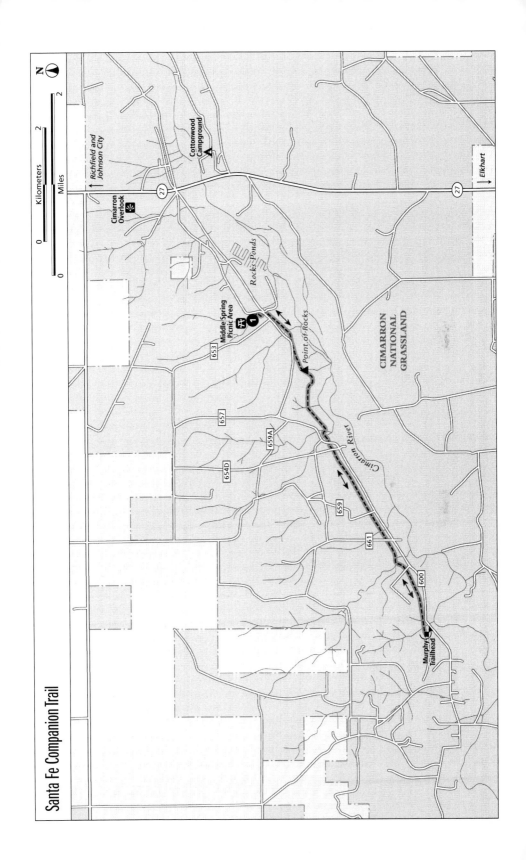

1.2 miles. The trail itself runs along the bottom of the bluff; however, intrepid hikers can climb to the top for views of the cottonwood-lined Cimarron River winding its way through the treeless prairie.

Point of Rocks would be a logical turnaround spot for those looking for a short hike. Otherwise, continue hiking southwest, following the limestone trail markers that dot the path. The trail crosses three forest roads until reaching Murphy Trailhead at 4.65 miles; the trailhead has vault toilets and drinking water but no shade. If you only have one car, consider beginning your hike at Murphy Trailhead—the shade of Middle Spring Picnic Area would be an ideal spot to rest before hiking back to your vehicle.

Additional hikes: For those looking for additional hiking in Cimarron National Grassland, the Turkey Trail System totals more than 10 miles, with motorized and nonmotorized sections from the Cottonwood Picnic Area to Cimarron Recreation Area, Wilburton Pond, and ending at KS 51. The Santa Fe Companion Trail runs parallel on the north side of the river. Before leaving Cimarron National Grassland, make sure you stop at the Cimarron River Overlook, which is on the north side of the river on KS 27.

Miles and Directions

0.00 Start at Middle Spring Picnic Area, next to the interpretive sign, and head south toward the road.

0.20 Cross FR 600 then turn right (southwest) onto Santa Fe Companion Trail.

1.20 Point of Rocks.

2.10 Cross FR 600 and continue southwest on Santa Fe Companion Trail.

3.00 Cross FR 659 and continue southwest on Santa Fe Companion Trail.

3.40 Cross FR 661 and continue southwest on Santa Fe Companion Trail.

3.80 Continue southwest.

4.65 Reach the Murphy Trailhead; turn around and return to Middle Spring Picnic Area.

9.30 Arrive back at Middle Spring Picnic Area.

2 Long Loop

In western Kansas, about 80 percent of the native prairie has been converted to some other use. Thanks to The Nature Conservancy, the 17,920-acre Smoky Valley Ranch is open to hikers and equestrians to experience its scenic views and history. Dramatic Niobrara Chalk breaks, rolling native prairie, an ancient bison kill site dating back 10,000 years, and more-recent homesteader history are some of the attractions of Smoky Valley Ranch. The location is remote, but that makes the hiking splendid and the wildlife viewing opportunities excellent.

Start: Southeast corner of parking area
Elevation gain: 2,877 feet (trailhead) to 2,923 feet
Distance: 5.48-mile loop (1.0-mile short loop option)
Difficulty: Moderate due to length and sun exposure
Hiking time: 2–3 hours
Seasons/schedule: Open daily year-round, sunrise to sunset
Fees and permits: None
Trail contact: The Nature Conservancy in Kansas, 2420 NW Button Rd., Topeka 66618; (785) 233-4400; nature.org/kansas; email: kansas@tnc.org
Dog-friendly: Yes, on leash
Trail surface: Grass and dirt
Land status: Smoky Valley Ranch (The Nature Conservancy)
Nearest town: Oakley, 25 miles to the northeast; Scott City, 37 miles to the south
Maps: USGS Russell Springs NE, KS, and USGS Elkader NW, KS; trail map available at the kiosk in the parking area and on the ranch's website
Other trail users: Equestrians
Special considerations: Collecting anything from the ground is not allowed. The ranch is remote and far from services; plan and pack accordingly. There is no restroom or potable water available.
Amenities: None
Maximum grade: 7%
Cell service: Weak and spotty

Finding the trailhead: From Oakley, head south on US 83 for 13 miles. Turn west onto Quail Road; after 7 miles, turn south onto CR 370. Continue for 1 mile, then turn west onto Plains Road. After 1 mile, turn south onto CR 350; continue for 2 miles to reach the Smoky Valley Ranch parking lot on the east side of CR 350. GPS: N38°53.258' / W101°1.096'

Trail conditions: Signage is still being developed with the use of temporary markers in some places. There are rattlesnakes in this area, so wear boots and watch where you walk, especially in the early morning and late evening. The trail receives light traffic.

The Hike

The purchase of Smoky Valley Ranch in 1999 was the largest land acquisition for conservation in state history. The Nature Conservancy manages it as a working ranch, utilizing rotational grazing, prescribed burns, and scientific research to maintain this important ecosystem.

Niobrara Chalk formations from the long loop trail.

Chalk bluffs overlooking the Smoky Hill River.

The trail begins on the south end of the parking lot. Both the short and long loops can be completed in either direction; you'll have a nearly 100-foot climb at the end of your hike regardless of which direction you choose. This description follows the long loop counterclockwise, so keep right after passing through the gate.

Counterclockwise is the preferred direction because the trail immediately comes up to the rim of eroded breaks that characterize this area of the Smoky Hills. The golden Niobrara Chalk bluffs are particularly striking in summer when contrasted with the green prairie grasses. The views are great year-round, however. The trail follows a footpath worn into the prairie over the years. In winter the trail was relatively easy to make out and follow. Wayfinding may be more difficult in summer with vegetation growth, but most hikers should have no problem following the path, especially if you carry a GPS device. The Nature Conservancy has placed milestone markers at each mile interval to help you stay on the trail.

After passing two sections of breaks, reach the junction of the short and long loops at 12-Mile Creek. If you prefer a short jaunt through the prairie, keep left to complete the 1.0-mile short loop. Otherwise, keep right (east) at 0.74 mile to continue on the long loop, which continues southeast, crossing the ranch.

MOUNT SUNFLOWER

At 4,039 feet, Mount Sunflower is the highest natural point in the state of Kansas. Most definitely not a mountain, it is located on private land but is open to the public. There are no hiking trails leading to the "summit," but there is a picnic table, visitor registry, and steel sunflower sculpture.

The trail crosses the creek bed (dry in late winter) twice, at 1.03 and 1.73 miles. As you hike, keep an eye out for wildlife; the ranch supports a tremendous diversity of plants and animals. (I tracked a coyote for nearly 1 mile.) Pronghorn, swift fox, and mule and whitetail deer are also common on the ranch. While you may not see them, the ranch provides critical habitat for the lesser prairie chicken.

One animal you are certain not to see is bison, extirpated from western Kansas and much of the Great Plains in the late 1800s. The view at 1.54 miles overlooks the winding creek bed, dead timber, and an eroded hillside. According to the brochure available at the trailhead, this was once an ancient bison kill site. A human-made spearpoint was found in a bison skeleton in this area. Later research dated the spearpoint back 10,000 years. There is much more information about this area of the trail, so be sure to pick up the brochure at the trailhead.

Cross a fence at 2.04 miles. The trail has been heading east and will continue to do so more approximately the next 1 mile. The dry creeks the trail has crossed and follows connect with the Smoky Hill River, which lies just south of the trail. The trail begins to head northeast at 2.32 miles and passes more Niobrara Chalk breaks as it continues northeast.

At approximately the 3.5-mile point in the hike, the trail heads west on its return to the trailhead. You'll have three climbs as you hike west: two 50-foot hills to climb up and down, then a climb of nearly 100 feet back up to the trailhead and parking lot.

Miles and Directions

0.00 Start at the trailhead and keep right (south).

0.74 Keep right (east) for the long loop. (Bailout: Keep left to return to the trailhead via the short loop.)

1.03 Cross a dry creek bed, heading east.

1.10 Continue straight (south). Look for one of the small stone markers at the crest of the hill in front of you.

1.73 Cross a dry creek bed, heading southeast.

2.04 Come to a fence; continue east.

2.57 Turn right (east).

2.64 Turn left (north) at a stone marker.

2.75 Continue straight (northeast) at the stone marker.

2.84 Turn left (east) at a stone marker.

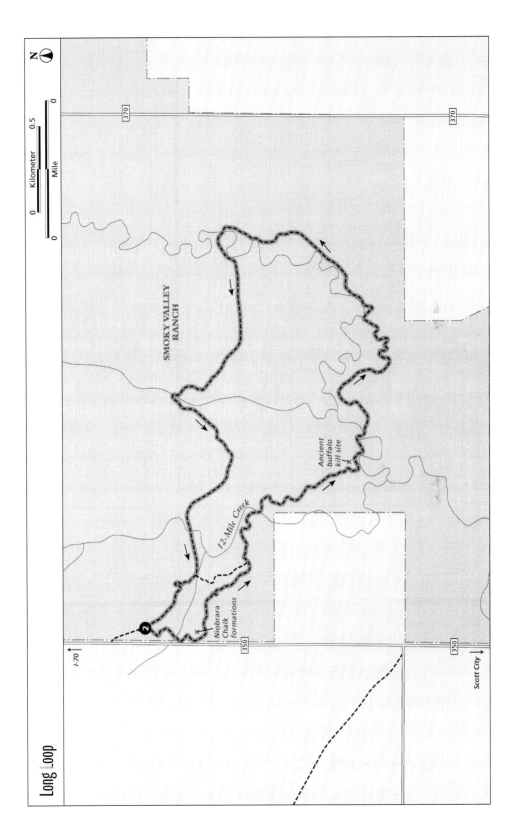

Long Loop

Chalk bluffs overlooking the Smoky Hill River.

2.94 Continue straight (northeast).

3.27 Cross a creek bed.

3.41 Turn left (west) at the stone marker.

3.57 Keep right (west) at the stone marker.

3.67 Continue straight (west) through an intersecting doubletrack that heads south toward the stock tank.

4.00 Come to a fence; continue straight (northwest).

4.48 Keep right (west) at the stone markers.

4.63 Continue northwest.

4.68 Continue straight (west/northwest) through a doubletrack that leads south of a stock tank.

4.95 Cross a creek bed.

5.14 Continue straight (north) at the junction with the short loop.

5.48 Arrive back at the trailhead.

3 Overlook and Life on the Rocks Trails

The newest state park in Kansas, Little Jerusalem Badlands State Park is home to one of the best hikes in the Sunflower State. While this nearly 3-mile out-and-back hike is easy, the stark beauty of the badlands makes any visitor question their previously held opinion of the natural beauty of Kansas. This hike follows gentle grades to three viewpoints overlooking fantastic formations of Niobrara Chalk. Take a seat on one of the benches at the overlooks and enjoy painted skies as the sun sets over the High Plains.

Start: West end of the parking area
Elevation gain: 2,758 feet (trailhead) to 2,774 feet
Distance: 2.92 miles out and back
Difficulty: Easy due to level terrain and well-maintained trail
Hiking time: 1–2 hours
Seasons/schedule: Open daily year-round, sunrise to sunset
Fees and permits: A daily vehicle permit or annual state park vehicle permit is necessary to enter the park; there is a self-pay station in the parking area.
Trail contact: Little Jerusalem Badlands State Park (there is no office at the park); (620) 872-2061
Dog-friendly: Yes, on leash
Trail surface: Crushed rock and natural surface

Land status: Little Jerusalem Badlands State Park (Kansas Department of Wildlife & Parks)
Nearest town: Oakley, 28 miles to the north; Scott City, 27 miles to the south
Maps: USGS Elkader SW, KS; trail map available on the park's website
Other trail users: None
Special considerations: The park is remote and far from services; plan and pack accordingly. No potable water is available at the park. Collecting anything (including rocks, fossils, flowers, and plants) is not allowed. Visitors are not allowed off-trail unless accompanied by park staff on a guided tour.
Amenities: Vault toilets
Maximum grade: 5%
Cell service: Adequate coverage at the trailhead and on the trail

Finding the trailhead: From Oakley, drive approximately 22 miles south on US 83 to Gold Road. Turn west onto Gold Road and drive 3.5 miles to CR 400. Turn north on CR 400 and drive 1 mile to the entrance for Little Jerusalem Badlands State Park.

From Scott City, drive approximately 21 miles north on US 83 to Gold Road. Turn west onto Gold Road and drive 3.5 miles to CR 400. Turn north onto CR 400 and drive 1 mile to the entrance for Little Jerusalem Badlands State Park. GPS: N38°48.166' / W100°55.771'

Trail conditions: The trails are impeccably well maintained and easy to follow. There is no shade on the trails. Watch your footing for trail hazards, including rough terrain and rattlesnakes. Avoid trail shoulders, as they are soft and may be unstable. Despite the park's remote location, the trails receive moderate traffic.

The Hike

Little Jerusalem Badlands State Park is the newest state park in Kansas, established by the legislature in 2018. The Nature Conservancy owns the 330 acres that compose

Overlook.

the park and partners with the Kansas Department of Wildlife & Parks to manage visitor access. The park is adjacent to the 17,290-acre Smoky Valley Ranch, also owned by The Nature Conservancy.

The dramatic spires and cliffs are composed of Niobrara Chalk; the park is the largest expanse of exposed Niobrara Chalk formation in Kansas. Niobrara Chalk is composed of sedimentary deposits from the vast interior sea that covered central North America nearly 150 million years ago. The unique geological formations were shaped by erosion—rock climbing on the formations and walking off-trail is strictly prohibited to protect the badlands.

Two trails are accessed from the parking lot. The Overlook Trail is a 0.5-mile out-and-back trail leading to a viewpoint overlooking the badlands. Life on the Rocks Trail heads west along the rim of the eroded Niobrara Chalk badlands. This hike combines the two trails for a nearly 3-mile hike through scenery that shatters the stereotype of a flat and unaesthetic Kansas landscape.

The hike on the Overlook Trail to the viewpoint leaves from the northwestern corner of the parking area. It heads north but then shortly bends northwest to descend almost 50 feet to the overlook. The grade is gentle along the crushed-rock path. There is a bench, two interpretive panels, and guardrails to prevent visitors descending into the badlands.

Once you return to the trailhead, access the Life on the Rocks Trail via the trailhead on the west end of the parking area. The trail heads due west and soon comes

Crushed rock trail surface through mixed-grass prairie.

Overlook and Life on the Rocks Trails

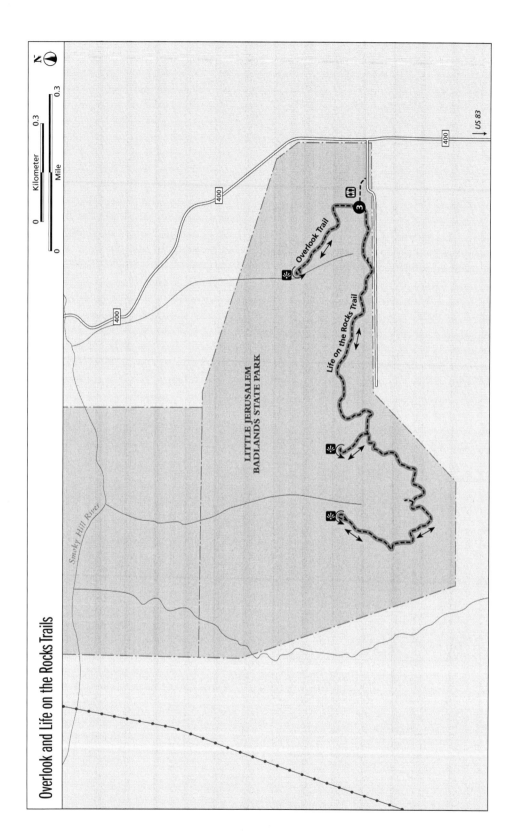

MONUMENT ROCKS AND CASTLE ROCK

Monument Rocks is one of the most iconic natural landmarks in Kansas. The Niobrara Chalk formation was the Sunflower State's first national natural landmark and is located east of Elkader. There are no official trails, and climbing the rocks is prohibited. Castle Rock is located 15 miles south and 4 miles east of Quinter Collyer. It was voted one of the Eight Wonders of Kansas. Like Monument Rocks, there are no hiking trails and climbing is prohibited. The roads to both sites are impassable in inclement weather and there are no nearby services, so check the weather forecast and road conditions before you visit.

right up to the rim of the eroded Niobrara Chalk. The first overlook is approximately 0.5 mile from the trailhead over gentle grades along the crushed-rock path. Several interpretive panels along the way describe the flora and fauna found in the region.

After the first overlook, continue west for 1 mile until reaching a short spur trail that leads to another viewpoint, this one without panels or a bench. From here, the Life on the Rocks Trail heads northwest then north until it reaches the final overlook at 1.73 miles. If you arrive before sunset, time your hike to witness the wonderful spectacle of the badlands turning a brilliant gold as the sun sets.

Miles and Directions

0.00 Start at the Overlook Trailhead and head north through the gate.

0.23 Reach the lookout; return to the trailhead.

0.45 Arrive back at the Overlook Trailhead and head to the Life on the Rocks Trailhead.

0.47 Start at the Life on the Rocks Trailhead and head west.

1.12 First overlook.

1.20 Turn right (west) to continue on the Life on the Rocks Trail toward the final overlook.

1.40 Footbridge.

1.73 Overlook.

2.10 Spur trail north to rim.

2.16 Footbridge.

2.37 Continue straight (east) past the spur trail to the overlook.

2.92 Arrive back at the Life on the Rocks Trailhead.

4 Lake Scott Loop

Nestled among picturesque hills, Historic Lake Scott State Park lies next to a lake created by a dam in the 1930s. Craggy bluffs and wooded canyons cut into the western Kansas prairie, creating an oasis around the lakeshore. This isn't a leisurely lakeside stroll, however, as the trail climbs up the steep bluffs to a stunning viewpoint. The hike also passes near several historical sites, including the El Cuartelejo pueblo ruins and the Steele Homestead.

Start: Trailhead to the north of the park office
Elevation gain: 2,854 feet (trailhead) to 2,949 feet
Distance: 6.12-mile loop
Difficulty: Moderate due to distance and steep climb up to a viewpoint
Hiking time: About 3 hours
Seasons/schedule: Open year-round
Fees and permits: A daily vehicle permit or annual state park vehicle permit is necessary to enter the park; there is a self-pay station at the park office.
Trail contact: Historic Lake Scott State Park, 101 West Scott Lake Dr., Scott City 67871; (620) 872-2061; ksoutdoors.com/State-Parks/Locations/Historic-Lake-Scott

Dog-friendly: Yes, on leash
Trail surface: Grass and dirt
Land status: Historic Lake Scott State Park (Kansas Department of Wildlife & Parks)
Nearest town: Scott City, 13 miles to the south
Maps: USGS Lake Scott, KS; map available online at the park's website
Other trail users: Mountain bikers and equestrians
Special considerations: Public hunting is allowed in the wildlife area west of the park.
Amenities: Restrooms, water, modern and primitive campsites, park office
Maximum grade: 21%
Cell service: Reliable coverage at the park office; adequate coverage on the trails

Finding the trailhead: From Scott City, head north on US 83 for nearly 10 miles. Turn left (northwest) onto KS 95 and continue for 3 miles. Turn left (northwest) onto West Scott Lake Drive to enter the state park. The park office is near the park entrance, and the trailhead is just north of the park office. GPS: N38°39.939' / W100°55.169'

Trail conditions: The trails have waymarks at important junctions and are well-maintained and well-trodden. Wear long pants to prevent ticks. The trails receive moderate traffic.

The Hike

As you approach Lake Scott State Park from the east, KS 95 drops from the flat High Plains landscape into a deep valley surrounded by rugged, wooded cliffs. Exotic names such as Horsethief Canyon, Devil's Backbone, and Suicide Bluffs describe the unique features of the area. Springs are found throughout the valley, which was settled by Taos Indians in the 1600s after they moved from the southwest. Herbert Steele moved to Scott County in 1888 and homesteaded with his wife, Eliza. The dam was created in 1930, and the state park is now a popular recreation spot in the western Kansas High Plains.

The trailhead is north of the park office.

BATTLE CANYON

South of Historic Lake Scott State Park is the location of the Battle of Punished Woman's Fork. On September 27, 1878, the Northern Cheyenne fought their last battle with the US Army in this canyon, now named Battle Canyon. The site became a national historic site in 2013, named Punished Woman's Fork National Historic Site. There is a monument overlooking the canyon and a 1.5-mile loop trail leading through the site. The trail can be hard to follow due to the amount of cattle paths through the area.

The Lake Scott Loop hike begins north of the park office near two hitching posts. The loop trail around the lake is over 6 miles, but a shorter alternative trail, Big Springs Nature Trail, loops around a small pond near the park office trailhead. Continue on the loop trail heading north. The trail passes through a meadow with eroded bluffs to the west. The trail intersects a doubletrack leading to a scout campsite after 0.5 mile; after 0.75 mile, you'll reach the base of a steep hillside.

If you are interested in history, head off-trail to the east of the park road to visit the Steele Homestead and El Cuartelejo pueblo, the northernmost pueblo in the United States. Herbert and Eliza Steele lived on their homestead in the late 1880s, first in a dugout and then in a four-room house of sandstone that now serves as a museum. Refer to the park map and signage to locate the two sites, which are both on the west side of the lake.

Continuing the hike, leave the trail and follow the narrow footpath up the hillside toward the structure on top of the hill. The stone hut at the 0.8-mile mark offers a great perspective of the sunken oasis in the western Kansas prairie. The Steele Monument, a short walk northeast from the stone shelter, commemorates the Steele homesteaders and is a nice spot for a rest after the steep climb.

Once rested, head back toward the stone shelter and continue southwest briefly until the trail bends to head north and descend via a ravine. The trail continues north, winding its way along the base of the bluffs until reaching the park road and running parallel to it at the 1.6-mile mark. The trail parallels the park road for the next mile, crossing Horsethief Canyon at 2 miles, until reaching Suicide Bluffs at the 2.5-mile mark. Descend the bluffs and reach the road. Follow the road briefly, then take the doubletrack near a vault toilet. The trail heads east around the north shore of the lake, passing the dam and Bull Canyon South Campground.

At the 4-mile mark, the trail heads south along the east shore of Lake Scott. The trail roughly parallels the park road for the final 2 miles to the park office, so if you're tired you can follow the road back to the office. The trail itself is not difficult, but the road offers a simple alternative to complete the loop. Reach Lakeside Campground after 0.5 mile, with a church campsite across the road. The hike continues south, passing the Elm Grove campground and later reaching the park office.

A stone hut overlooks Lake Scott and requires a steep climb up a hill.

Miles and Directions

0.00 Start at the trailhead just to the north of the park office. There are two hitching posts.

0.17 Reach a clearing and continue north, taking the left fork. The right fork heads northeast down to the park road.

0.45 Continue north, crossing a doubletrack road that heads west to a gate and east to the park road.

0.74 Leave the trail and follow a narrow footpath, heading northwest up the hillside toward the structure on top of the hill.

0.80 Stone hut atop the hill.

0.84 Steele Monument.

0.90 Turn right (north) to descend Horsethief Canyon back toward the main trail.

0.98 Turn left (west) to reconnect with the main trail. The trail bends north shortly after you rejoin the main trail.

1.09 Bench on a stone platform.

1.92 Continue straight (north).

2.01 Keep left as you cross Horsethief Canyon, then turn right to enter a wooded area, heading northwest.

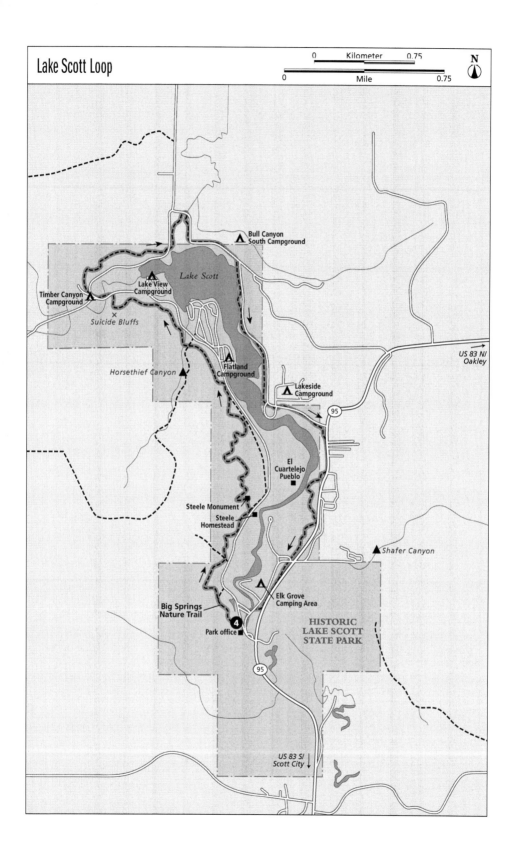

Lake Scott Loop

Bull Canyon
South Campground

Lake Scott

Lake View
Campground

Timber Canyon
Campground

× Suicide Bluffs

Horsethief Canyon

Flatland
Campground

Lakeside
Campground

US 83 N/
Oakley

95

El
Cuartelejo
Pueblo

Steele Monument

Steele
Homestead

Shafer Canyon

Big Springs
Nature Trail

Elk Grove
Camping Area

4

Park office

HISTORIC
LAKE SCOTT
STATE PARK

95

US 83 S/
Scott City

Lake Scott.

2.09 Keep left (north) at a fork.

2.52 Turn right (north) to descend Suicide Bluffs.

2.61 Turn left (west) onto the park road.

2.68 Leave the park road, heading northwest on a trail near a vault toilet.

2.72 Turn right (north).

2.94 Enter the disc golf course.

3.29 Turn left (northeast) onto the park road.

3.51 Turn right (east) onto a dirt road.

3.53 Turn right (south).

3.67 Spillway area; turn left (east) and follow the road or walk atop the levee.

3.92 Turn right (south) at a trail marker.

4.11 Continue south, passing campsites on the lakeshore.

4.66 Continue straight (south).

5.70 Continue straight (south).

5.99 Turn left (south) onto the paved park road.

6.12 Arrive back at the park office.

5 Agave Ridge Nature Trail

The Agave Ridge Nature Trail is a splendid trail that takes hikers through mixed-grass prairie to sweeping vistas of cedar-lined bluffs that give Cedar Bluff State Park its name. The trail is easy to follow, and the few hill climbs should not pose a challenge to most people with decent physical fitness.

Start: Trailhead in the Page Creek Area near White Tail Campground
Elevation gain: 2,151 feet (trailhead) to 2,244 feet
Distance: 4.81-mile lollipop
Difficulty: Moderate
Hiking time: 2–3 hours
Seasons/schedule: Open daily year-round; fall and spring best for hiking
Fees and permits: A daily vehicle permit or annual state park vehicle permit is necessary to enter the park.
Trail contact: Cedar Bluff State Park, 32001 Hwy. 147, Ellis 67637; (785) 726-3212; ksoutdoors.com/State-Parks/Locations/Cedar-Bluff
Dog-friendly: Yes, on leash

Trail surface: Grass and dirt with stones and rocks
Land status: Cedar Bluff State Park (Kansas Department of Wildlife & Parks)
Nearest town: WaKeeney, 30 miles to the north
Maps: USGS Cedar Bluff, KS; park map available online (does not list Agave Ridge Nature Trail)
Other trail users: Mountain bikers
Special considerations: Avoid hiking during midday in July and August.
Amenities: Restrooms nearby on a side road east of the trailhead; campsites near the trailhead and a water pump at a dump station on the road leading to the trailhead
Maximum grade: 9%
Cell service: Reliable coverage at the trailhead and on the trails.

Finding the trailhead: From I-70, take exit 127 and head south on US 283 for 18 miles. Turn east onto CR 474 and continue for 7 miles. Turn sharply left (northwest) onto 320 Avenue for 1.6 miles, then turn left (west) before reaching Pronghorn Campground. Continue west for 1.3 miles to the trailhead on the west side of the road. GPS: N38°46.628' / W99°47.221'

Trail conditions: The well-maintained trail is easy to follow. The asphalt section is rough, so anyone using a wheelchair or pushing a stroller will have difficulties. There is little shade along the trail and no water. The trail receives light to moderate traffic.

The Hike

Agave is the family name for the Great Plains yucca, which is prevalent on the Agave Ridge Nature Trail. The trail is in the Page Creek Area of Cedar Bluff State Park, which gets its name from the cedar-lined bluffs that can be seen from the western section of the nature trail. The trailhead is located near White Tail Campground. The first section of the hike follows an asphalt path, which is part of an easy 1-mile nature trail with interpretive displays about the local flora and fauna. The 4.81-mile hike and bike trail offers visitors a beautiful trek through mixed-grass prairie, with sweeping views of Cedar Bluff Reservoir at various points.

A bench overlooks Cedar Bluff Reservoir on the highest section of the trail.

The first three-tenths of the hike follows the narrow asphalt path with a grove of cottonwoods and red cedars to the right of the trail as you hike south. After passing an interpretive sign about wildlife, the trail passes a bench at 0.12 mile. The trees thin out at 0.27 mile and your first view of Boy Scout Cove and Cedar Bluff Reservoir come into view. An interpretive panel about animal tracks marks the point where you leave the asphalt path and continue south on a mowed path through open prairie. Look for the brown trail marker if the path is faint, but it is wide and hard to miss.

Yucca is prevalent to the east of the trail, with a few cedars, as it heads south across the undulating grassland. Look to your right as the southern end of Boy Scout Cove is taken over by reeds, shrubs, and cottonwoods. The trail crosses a firebreak at 0.54 mile and continues south, with rock outcroppings on the hillside ahead.

The outcroppings come into closer view at 0.75 mile as the trail descends and the view opens up to the east of the rocky hillsides. This wooded section is an excellent spot to view wildlife. Cross a wooden footbridge at 0.82 mile, then keep right at the fork at 0.85 mile to head north along the western side of Boy Scout Cove.

The trail begins to climb at 1.0 mile out of the bottomland into upland prairie, largely treeless with only the occasional red cedar. The climb rewards you with expansive views of the surrounding prairie, Boy Scout Cove to the east, and Cedar

Cedar-lined bluffs give the state park its name.

Bluff Reservoir to the north. Enjoy the view at 1.17 miles before the trail snakes down the hill into another lower-lying area.

The firebreak crosses the trail again at 1.28 miles; the trail then passes a brown trail sign that marks 1 mile since the trail left the asphalt path. At approximately 1.90 miles, the trail heads west as it approaches the southern shore of Cedar Bluff Reservoir.

Reaching a fork at 2.71 miles, keep right to shortly reach a viewpoint overlooking the reservoir. Return to the fork and head south. The view is great at that viewpoint, but the bench at 2.95 provides even better views of the reservoir and a deep canyon with rock outcroppings and large boulders to the west. Enjoy the views as you continue south through open prairie; this is the highest section of the hike. As the trail heads east at 3.62 miles, note the covered stock tank 30 yards off the trail to the west. Keeping right at 3.97 miles, you are now on the trail leading back to the asphalt path. Cross the firebreak one last time at 4.27 miles; continue straight once you reach the asphalt path or turn right, which will also lead back to the trailhead.

Agave Ridge Nature Trail

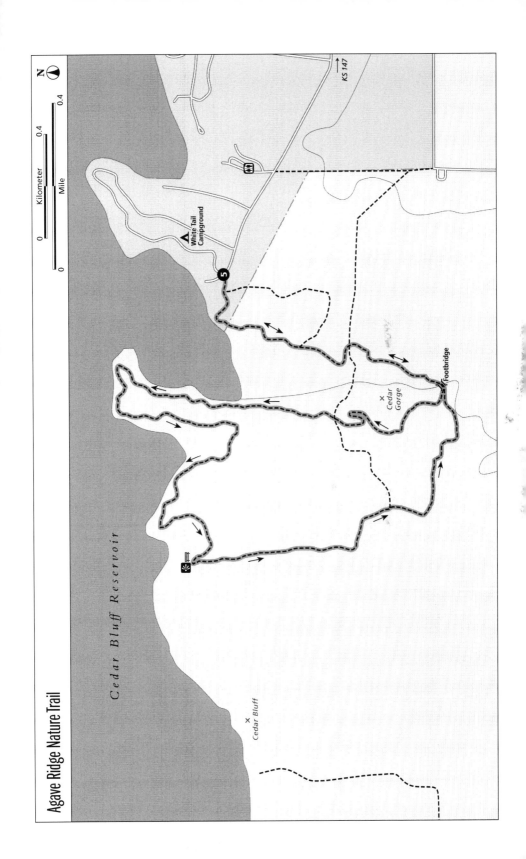

Cedar Bluff Reservoir

White Tail Campground

Cedar Gorge

Footbridge

Cedar Bluff

KS 147

N

Kilometer
0   0.4

Mile
0   0.4

The trailhead is located opposite White Tail Campground.

Miles and Directions

0.00 Start at the trailhead and head west.

0.03 Keep right (west).

0.36 Keep right (south) at the animal tracks sign to follow a mowed path marked with a brown trail marker.

0.54 Continue straight (south).

0.82 Cross a footbridge, heading west.

0.85 Turn right (north).

1.28 Continue straight (north).

2.71 Reach a fork and turn left (south) to continue on the trail. The right fork leads to a viewpoint overlooking the reservoir.

2.95 At a bench, the trail turns to head south.

3.54 Continue straight (south).

3.97 Continue straight (east).

4.27 Continue straight (north).

4.45 Keep left (north) to follow the asphalt trail to the trailhead.

4.81 Arrive back at the trailhead.

6 Prairie Fire Trail

The newer trail of two managed by the US Army Corps of Engineers at Wilson Lake, Prairie Fire Trail takes hikers to the south shore of the lake through an area rich with history. A fatal tornado in 1993 destroyed a campground, while wind and rising water overtook another, notorious campground. The trail can be accessed from one of two trailheads and should be included in any trip to Wilson Lake.

Start: West Trailhead
Elevation gain: 207 feet
Distance: 2.55-mile loop
Difficulty: Easy
Hiking time: 1–2 hours
Seasons/schedule: Open daily year-round; best in fall and spring at dawn or dusk
Fees and permits: None
Trail contact: Wilson Project Office, US Army Corps of Engineers, 4860 Outlet Blvd., Sylvan Grove 67481; (785) 658-2551; www.nwk .army.mil/Locations/District-Lakes/Wilson -Lake/; email: wilson.lake@usace.army.mil
Dog-friendly: Yes, on leash
Trail surface: Grass and dirt
Land status: Wilson Lake (US Army Corps of Engineers)

Nearest town: Russell, 23 miles to the west
Maps: USGS Dorrance NE, KS; Wilson Lake maps and brochures available online
Other trail users: None
Special considerations: Prairie Fire Trail is scheduled for a prescribed burn if conditions allow in either March or April. The trail will be closed the morning of the burn. However, there will not be much advanced warning since the burn depends on atmospheric conditions.
Amenities: None; restrooms and water at nearby campgrounds
Maximum grade: 8%
Cell service: Reliable coverage at the trailhead and on the trail

Finding the trailhead: Take exit 199 off I-70, heading north on 200th Boulevard/Dorrance Lucas Road for 5.5 miles. Turn right (north) onto an unnamed road to reach the trailhead. GPS: N38°56.051' / W98°35.221'

   Trail conditions: The trail is well maintained and easy to follow. There is no drinking water or shade along the trail. The trail receives light foot traffic.

The Hike

The Prairie Fire Trail was created in 2011 by the US Army Corps of Engineers in the Minooka Park area of Wilson Lake. The self-guided trail includes breathtaking views of Wilson Lake and several interpretive panels that explain the devastating 1993 tornado, a ghost campground, and other interesting facts about the area. There are two trailheads, West and East, each with a large wooden archway. The Corps has done a terrific job developing and maintaining the trail, and a visit to Wilson Lake should not be undertaken without a stop at Minooka Park to hike the Prairie Fire Trail.

   Beginning at the West Trailhead, head north along the wide mowed path as it cuts through a beautiful prairie dominated by little bluestem. Shortly after the trailhead,

Wilson Lake from the North Trail.

West Trailhead at Minooka Park.

reach a fork—the South Trail is to the right; the North Trail is to the left. Take the left fork and continue north as red cedar takes over the prairie.

The soil turns noticeably red at 0.41 mile, marked by a large boulder on the left side of the trail. Ahead you will pass an interesting section of the trail populated with dark red rocks. An interpretive panel describes the Dakota Sandstone in this area, which was formed 150 million years ago when a large inland sea covered Kansas and much of the Great Plains. The rock formations are fragile, so please don't disturb them by climbing.

At 0.54 mile, the trail bends around red cedars and begins to descend into a gully. Look north to see Wilson Lake. Continue along the trail as it approaches the south shore of the lake. Picturesque views of the lake and rock outcroppings farther east along the south shore come into view at 0.75 mile. The panel at 1.01 miles explains the rubbish and remnants of structures found in this area, which was known as Alcohol Point Campground due to the unsavory activities of campers. The campground was overtaken by wind and water, with the new campsite moved to a better location with stricter regulations.

Alongside most of the trail you will see evidence of red cedar management, which is described by the panel at 1.4 miles. Continue west as you approach the junction of North and South Trails before taking in the view of Wilson Lake at 1.61 miles. The

Prairie Fire Trail

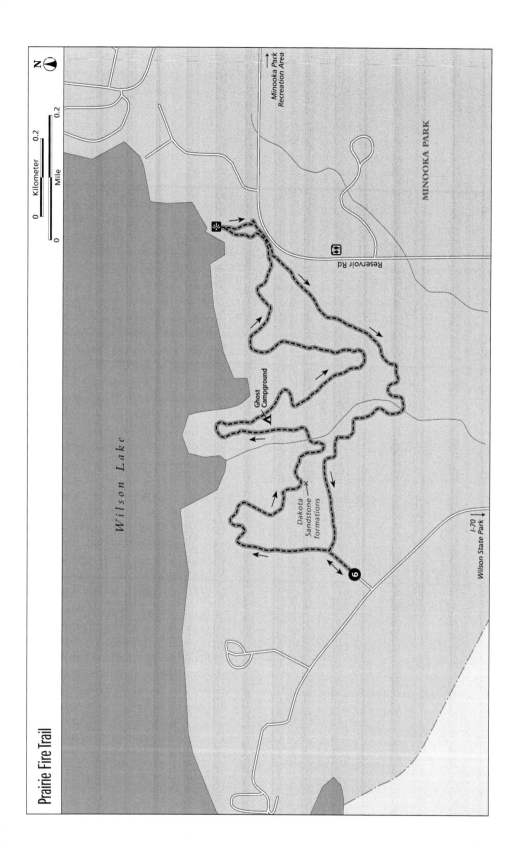

N

Kilometer
0   0.2

0   0.2
Mile

Wilson Lake

Minooka Park
Recreation Area

MINOOKA PARK

Reservoir Rd

Ghost
Campground

Dakota
Sandstone
formations

6

I-70
Wilson State Park

The North Trail reaches Wilson Lake, while the South Trail cuts across mixed-grass prairie.

aforementioned junction also leads to the East Trailhead. Take the trail for South Trail, which heads west back toward the West Trailhead through open prairie. If you need to use a restroom, there is a campground with a shower house and restroom to the south of the park road, which runs parallel to this section of the South Trail.

The final interpretive panel describes the devastating tornado in 1993 that left a path of destruction in Minooka Park, claiming the life of one person. Enjoy the view ahead of the prairie hills to the west before reaching the trailhead.

Miles and Directions

0.00 Start at the West Trailhead.

0.07 Keep left (north) at the fork onto North Trail.

0.47 Rock panel.

0.84 Ghost campground panel.

1.40 Cedar Cemetery panel.

1.59 Buffalo panel.

1.61 Wilson Lake viewpoint.

1.67 Turn right (southwest) onto South Trail.

2.05 Tornado panel.

2.47 Turn left (south).

2.55 Arrive back at the trailhead.

7 Rocktown Trail

Catch a breezy, sunny day on the Rocktown Trail at Wilson Lake and you will be rewarded with an unforgettable experience that will have you planning your return trip to hike one of the best trails in the state of Kansas. Beautiful mixed-grass prairie, sandy beaches in tranquil coves, and impressive rock formations that resemble a city skyline are awaiting you on the Rocktown Trail. The short distance, easy navigation, and minimal elevation gain make this a wonderful trail for hikers of any age or experience.

Start: Parking lot access area on the east side of Rocktown
Elevation gain: 233 feet
Distance: 2.66-mile lollipop
Difficulty: Easy
Hiking time: 1-2 hours
Seasons/schedule: Open daily year-round; best in fall and spring at dawn or dusk
Fees and permits: None
Trail contact: Wilson Project Office, US Army Corps of Engineers, 4860 Outlet Blvd., Sylvan Grove 67481; (785) 658-2551; www.nwk.army.mil/Locations/District-Lakes/Wilson-Lake/; email: wilson.lake@usace.army.mil
Dog-friendly: Yes, on leash
Trail surface: Grass, dirt, and sand

Land status: Lucas Park (US Army Corps of Engineers)
Nearest town: Lucas, 9 miles to the north
Maps: USGS Dorrance NE, KS; brochures for a self-guided hike available at the trail entrance; Wilson Lake maps and brochures available online
Other trail users: None
Special considerations: An early start, especially in summer, is best to avoid heat and boat traffic at the rock formations.
Amenities: Restroom and water nearby along the road to the trailhead
Maximum grade: 11%
Cell service: Reliable coverage at the trailhead and on the trail

Finding the trailhead: Take exit 206 off I-70 and head north on KS 232 for 9 miles. Turn left (west) onto 203 Street/Land Lane. After 1.3 miles, turn left (south) onto 203 Street and continue for 0.7 mile. Turn right (southwest) and continue for 1 mile to the Rocktown Trailhead. GPS: N38°56.981' / W98°32.030'

Trail conditions: The trail is in excellent condition and easy to navigate. There are some sandy sections near the rock formations. There is no shade or drinking water. The trail receives light to moderate foot traffic.

The Hike

The Rocktown Trail was designated a Natural and Scientific Area by the Kansas Biological Survey in 1986 for its rock formations. The sandy substrate and Dakota Sandstone and limestone rock formations are unique in this area of Kansas. The trail gets its name from several sandstone pillars that rise out of Wilson Lake, resembling a city skyline. You can hike this trail any time of the year, although the lack of shade would make a midday hike in the summer uncomfortable and potentially dangerous.

The sandstone pillars resemble a city skyline, giving the Rocktown Trail its name.

Fall and winter are the best times to hike the trail, as the little bluestem turns a beautiful shade of copper red.

The trailhead is marked by a beautiful stone sign with stylized Native American petroglyphs. The first 0.25 mile is the "stick" of the lollipop and descends almost 100 feet to reach the loop. Keep left (west) at 0.26 mile to follow the loop in a clockwise direction. The trail heads west toward Wilson Lake through a low-lying area with gentle hills covered in little bluestem and yucca rising on both sides. Look behind on occasion to take in the views of the pristine prairie.

At 0.9 mile, the trail begins to bend northwest and then north. An arm of Wilson Lake ahead that stretches east comes into view, then at 0.95 mile we get our first glimpse of Rocktown to the east. If you hike the trail in summer, try to go early to avoid boat traffic that congregates around the rock, obstructing your photo opportunities.

The trail is sandy in some sections as it passes two beautiful beaches at 1.05 miles. There are multiple places to step off the trail and take pictures or soak in the sun and views, but one in particular is at 1.22 miles, where a rocky platform is the perfect place to sit and enjoy the landscape. The Dakota Sandstone and limestone pillars rise more than 30 feet out of the water. The sandstone was deposited 80 million years ago during the formation of the Cretaceous Seaway and is a great source of fossils from

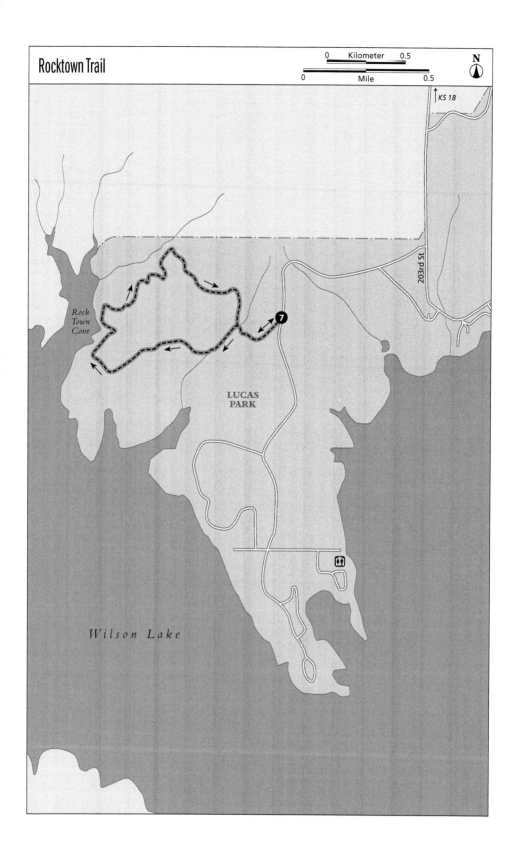

Rocktown Trail

0   Kilometer   0.5
0   Mile   0.5

N

↑ KS 18

203rd St

Rock
Town
Cove

7

LUCAS
PARK

Wilson Lake

The trail crosses mixed-grass prairie to reach the rock formations.

that epoch. It is illegal to remove fossils from the area, and vandalism or destruction of the rock formations is a federal offense.

Once you decide to continue the hike, the trail ascends the hillside at 1.3 miles as it heads east. For more than 0.5 mile, the trail traverses the highest section of the hike, passing through open prairie with views to the south of Wilson Lake; to the north the trail hugs the rim of a rocky bluff. The rock outcroppings are covered in colorful moss and lichen, and on a sunny day you may get lucky and spot a collared or Texas long-horned lizard.

Reach the end of the loop at 2.39 miles and turn left (southeast). Enjoy the final 0.25-mile hike back to the trailhead, with one final ascent to get your heart pumping.

Miles and Directions

0.00 Start at the Rocktown Trailhead.

0.26 Turn left (west).

1.30 Rock formations.

2.39 Turn left (southeast).

2.66 Arrive back at the trailhead.

8 Buffalo Tracks, Horsethief Canyon, and Red Rock Canyon Loop

The trails at Kanopolis State Park, the first state park in Kansas, offer challenges for the most seasoned of hikers. Dakota Sandstone bluffs, numerous water crossings, and more than 30 miles of trails allow hikers to create their own adventure. The 1.5-mile Buffalo Tracks Trail follows Bison Creek and is appropriate for most hikers, while the trails into Horsethief Canyon involve deep water crossings, rugged terrain, and a scramble out of the canyon. Red Rock Canyon introduces hikers to a rare landscape in the Sunflower State. This is perhaps the best hike in Kansas.

Start: Buffalo Tracks Trailhead
Elevation gain: 1,476 feet (trailhead) to 1,614 feet; 696 feet total elevation gain
Distance: 7.57-mile loop
Difficulty: Difficult due to distance and rugged terrain
Hiking time: 3–4 hours
Seasons/schedule: Open daily year-round; best in spring or fall for milder temperatures, spring for wildflowers, fall for colors
Fees and permits: A daily vehicle permit or annual state park vehicle permit is necessary to enter the park.
Trail contact: Kanopolis State Park; 200 Horsethief Rd., Marquette 67464; (785) 546-2565; ksoutdoors.com/State-Parks/Locations/Kanopolis
Dog-friendly: Yes, on leash
Trail surface: Dirt and grass; some rocky sections

Land status: Kanopolis State Park (Kansas Department of Wildlife & Parks)
Nearest town: Ellsworth, 24 miles to the northwest; Salina, 30 miles to the northeast
Maps: USGS Carneiro, KS, and USGS Venango, KS; trail map available at the visitor center and on the park's website
Other trail users: Mountain bikers, equestrians; some trails open only to hikers
Special considerations: There are several water crossings, some of which may be challenging or even impassable at times. Yield to equestrians on multiuse trails; mountain bikers must yield to both equestrians and hikers.
Amenities: Vault toilet at the Horsethief Canyon Trailhead (south of Buffalo Tracks Trailhead)
Maximum grade: 14%
Cell service: Average service at the trailhead; weak to no coverage in canyons and under tree cover; average coverage in open prairie

Finding the trailhead: From Ellsworth, head east on KS 140; from Salina, head west on KS 140. Turn south onto KS 141 and continue for 8 miles. Turn west onto Venango Road and continue 0.2 mile. Continue straight onto Horsethief Road for 2.1 miles, then turn right (east) to stay on Horsethief Road for 0.6 mile. Turn left (west) and continue for 0.5 mile. Turn right (north); the trailhead will be on the right after 0.3 mile. GPS: N38°40.310' / W97°59.974'

   Trail conditions: The trails are well maintained and marked; with a map and GPS device, navigation should be seamless. The water crossings can be challenging, even impassable, with high water. Turn around if you are not sure of crossings. Be aware of snakes. The trail receives moderate traffic.

Buffalo Tracks Canyon.

The Hike

Kanopolis State Park was the first, and thus is the oldest, state park in Kansas. While the creation of the reservoir in 1948 filled many of the ravines and canyons, there are still many to explore with more than 30 miles of multiuse trails throughout the park. Horsethief Canyon offers steep bluffs, several caves, and multiple water crossings. The trails in the Horsethief area and directly west, namely Prairie Trails and Red Rock Canyon, are not for novice hikers. The terrain is rugged, shade is sparse, and there is one water crossing in particular that is deep and dangerous—turn around if you are unable to safely manage a water crossing. It's best to hike Kanopolis with a partner or group, but if you do hike solo, make sure someone knows your route and expected time of return.

Buffalo Tracks Trailhead is a large, shady parking area with picnic tables and toilets. Several trails begin at the trailhead; take the hiker-only trail that is in the middle and climbs a sandy hill. Soon you will reach Sentinel Rock, which marks the beginning of Horsethief Canyon. The trail will follow Bison Creek upstream, and there could be sections with standing water and mud, especially in spring. The trail is narrow in places, with sandstone outcroppings on your right. After more than 0.5 mile, keep right at the sign for Cave 12 to explore the southeastern section of the canyon.

Follow the trail markers for 14; once you reach trail marker 14 itself, you will have to climb the steep canyon wall in front of you, which requires a short scramble. Once atop the wall, head north along the rim of the canyon. At the hike's 1-mile mark, you will have to descend to cross Bison Creek and then turn west to follow the creek downstream. Pass a cave on the hillside on your right at 1.3 miles—there is a hiker-only trail leading to the cave—and continue west until you reach a fork at 1.64 miles.

Here you have the option of returning to the trailhead; the described hike continues west shortly before turning north to explore two more canyons in the Horsethief area. There are water crossings at the northern end of each canyon, but they are made easier with footbridges. There is another water crossing at 3.4 miles, where you head west to reach the gate to enter the Kanopolis Wildlife Area. **Bailout option:** Turn around and follow the trails you just hiked, or turn south to return to the trailhead.

CORONADO HEIGHTS CASTLE

Francisco Vásquez de Coronado searched far and wide for the fabled "Seven Cities of Cibola." The Spanish conquistador set out from Mexico for the mythical cities of gold, wandering north through Mexico into present-day Arizona, New Mexico, Texas, Oklahoma, and eventually Kansas. The unending prairie broke him, and according to legend he gave up his quest near one of the sandstone bluffs south of Salina, now called Coronado Heights. A professor found chain mail on the hillside in 1915, giving credence to the legend. Today, a stone shelter resembling a castle adorns the hilltop, and unmarked trails allow visitors to explore the park.

There are several caves in the sandstone formations of Buffalo Tracks Canyon.

The hike into the wildlife area is worth the effort, as Red Rock Canyon is aptly named and a sight to see. You will cross through two more gates, 1A and 1B. Before the latter gate you have the option of following the trails that extend north into more wildlife areas. Instead, continue south to reach Red Rock Creek at 5 miles, which requires a serious water crossing. Complete the Red Rock Canyon loop and head east to return to the gated entrance to the Kanopolis Wildlife Area. If you want to avoid the major water crossing, retrace your hike through the two northern canyons; otherwise head south on the Prairie Trail. The water crossing at 6.84 is deep and wide—use extreme caution if you attempt to cross here. Your best option is to go off-trail to search for the best and safest place to cross. Once you cross, it's less than 1 mile back to the trailhead.

After leaving Kanopolis, or perhaps before you hike its trails, stop at nearby Mushroom Rock State Park. The eponymous rock formations are a delight to contemplate. While not a hiking destination, children will love the short footpaths leading to and around the rocks. Despite its size—Mushroom Rock is the smallest state park in Kansas—it has been dubbed one of the wonders of the Sunflower State. Like much of the rock formations in the state, the rocks at Mushroom are the result of the sediments from the ancient sea that once covered much of central North America.

Buffalo Tracks, Horsethief Canyon, and Red Rock Canyon Loop

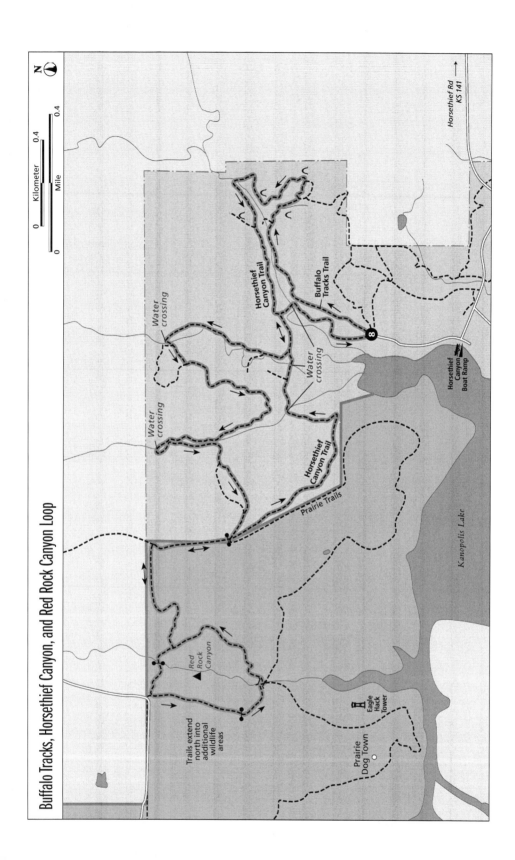

Miles and Directions

0.00 Start at the Buffalo Tracks Trailhead.

0.26 Keep left (north).

0.52 Keep right (east), following the rocky trail.

0.59 Reach a fork; keep right (southeast), following sign for 12.

0.62 Water crossing.

0.71 Keep right (east), following the trail sign for 14.

0.76 Reach trail marker 14; climb up the steep, rocky trail.

1.15 Water crossing at a fence.

1.32 Continue straight (west) on the multiuse trail. (Side trip: Turn right/north to follow the hiker-only trail to the cave.) (Bailout: Turn left/south to return to the trailhead via Buffalo Tracks Trail.)

1.64 Reach a fork; keep right (east). (Bailout: Turn left/south to return to the trailhead.)

1.76 At the fork, keep right (northwest).

2.20 Water crossing.

2.33 Turn left (south).

2.70 Keep right (northwest).

3.11 Reach a fence and turn left (west).

3.37 Water crossing.

3.71 Pass through the gate to enter the Kanopolis Wildlife Area; turn right (north). (Bailout: Don't enter the wildlife area; instead turn left (south) to follow Horsethief Canyon Trail back to the trailhead.

4.38 Turn right (northwest).

4.43 Gate 1A.

4.57 Turn left (south). (Option: Continue straight/west on the Prairie Trail.)

4.70 Pass through Gate 1B; continue south.

5.00 Water crossing through Red Rock Creek.

5.04 Turn left (northeast) after crossing the creek.

5.45 Turn right (east).

6.11 Gate 1; after closing the gate, turn right (south) to follow the leg of Horsethief Canyon Trail running parallel with the barbed-wire fence.

6.84 Water crossing.

6.97 Water crossing; if you don't want to cross here, look for a spot south if it's dry.

7.02 Keep right (east) at the fork.

7.14 Turn right (south).

7.19 Water crossing; turn right (south).

7.57 Arrive back at the trailhead.

9 Marty Bender Nature Trail

The Marty Bender Nature Area offers visitors a rewarding combination of outdoor recreation, wildlife observation, experiential learning, and an introduction to experimental research being conducted throughout the nature area. Located on the outskirts of Salina, the nearly 3-mile lollipop trail takes hikers through tallgrass prairie and riparian woodland, with excellent views atop the bluff overlooking the Smoky Hill River. The trail has some elevation gain but is relatively easy, with benches, tree swings, and a picnic table located along the trail, making it a great hike for families.

Start: Trailhead on the corner of South Holmes Road and East Schilling Road
Elevation gain: 1,348 feet (trailhead and highest point); 187 feet total elevation gain
Distance: 2.99-mile lollipop
Difficulty: Easy
Hiking time: 1–2 hours
Seasons/schedule: Open daily year-round; best in spring
Fees and permits: None
Trail contact: The Land Institute, 2440 E Water Well Rd., Salina 67401; (785) 823-5376; landinstitute.org

Dog-friendly: Yes, on leash
Trail surface: Grass and dirt
Land status: Marty Bender Nature Area (managed by The Land Institute)
Nearest town: Salina, 7 miles to the northwest
Maps: USGS Salina, KS; trail map available at landinstitute.org/visit-us/
Other trail users: None
Special considerations: The trail through the prairie may be faint after haying.
Amenities: None
Maximum grade: 7%
Cell service: Weak to average

Finding the trailhead: From Salina, head south on South Ohio Street. At the intersection with Magnolia Road, turn east and continue for 2 miles. Turn south onto South Holmes Road. After 1 mile, the parking area and trailhead will be on the northwest corner of South Holmes Road and East Schilling Road/East Brad Way. GPS: N38°47.029' / W97°33.475'

Trail conditions: The well-marked trails are in excellent condition. The only shade is the section running parallel to the Smoky Hill River. Poison ivy is present in the woodland section; stay on the designated path. The trail receives heavy foot traffic.

The Hike

Officially opened to the public in 2019 at the Prairie Festival, the Marty Bender Nature Area is located 1 mile north of the main campus of The Land Institute. The 206-acre nature area consists of prairie and woodland along the Smoky Hill River and is named for a former energy scientist and naturalist at the institute. Local volunteers created the nearly 3-mile trail through the nature area, using Osage orange wood for the signage and benches located along the trail. The Marty Bender Nature Area is not only open to low-impact outdoor recreation and wildlife observation but

Sandberg Overlook above the Smoky Hill River.

The Marty Bender Nature Area is 7 miles southeast of Salina.

is also a place for experiential learning and experimental research. There are several research plots and art installations scattered throughout the property.

The trailhead is located in the southeastern corner of the nature area. Due to its proximity to Salina, the trail is very popular and parking is limited. The kiosk has information about the trail guidelines and upcoming events. The trail heads west beginning at the kiosk for 0.33 mile, passing through a large patch of bundleflower until reaching an open-gated fence. The trail becomes a loop at the gate, so hikers can choose to hike the loop in either direction. The recommended direction is clockwise, which takes you west toward the Smoky Hill River. Before continuing, check out the book share box or take a rest on one of the two benches.

At the 0.5-mile point of the hike, keep left (south) at the fork; the right fork is a shortcut that avoids the descent to the wooded bluff overlooking the river. The Ash Overlook at 0.56 mile overlooks the wooded bank of the Smoky Hill River. After passing the overlook, the trail descends steeply into the woods then bends on itself to head north, following the river. The Sandberg Overlook at 0.87 mile has an excellent view of the river.

The trail meanders through the woods until the spur trail at 1.06 miles that leads to Bull Frog Bottoms. It's a short out-and-back trail to a bench, so decide if you want

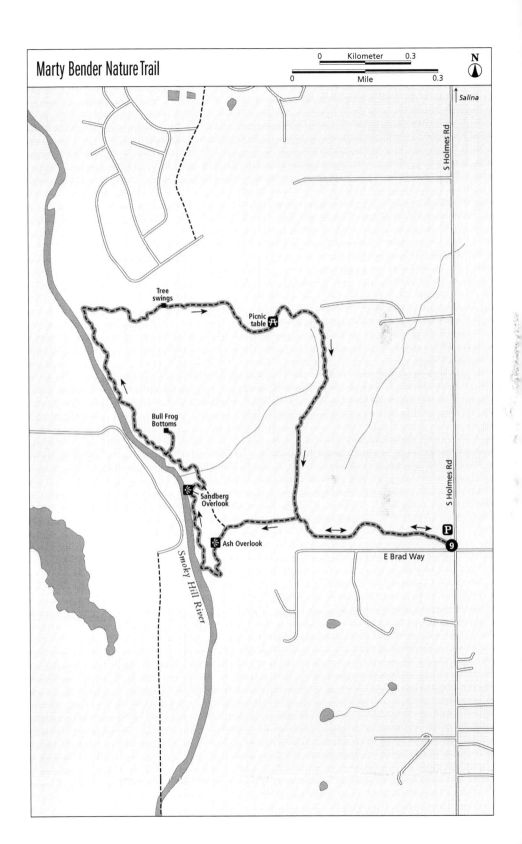

Marty Bender Nature Trail

Kilometer
0   0.3

Mile
0   0.3

N

Salina

S Holmes Rd

Tree swings

Picnic table

Bull Frog Bottoms

Sandberg Overlook

Ash Overlook

S Holmes Rd

Smoky Hill River

E Brad Way

P

9

to make the side trip or continue heading northwest alongside the river, with the Goelz Triangle Intercrop Experiment plot on your right. After 0.5 mile, reach the northern boundary of the nature area and head east with oak woodland to the north.

The tree swings at 1.81 miles are a fun place to stop for a rest on the swings hanging from the large tree. The next place for a rest stop is at 2.04 miles, where there is a picnic table in the middle of the prairie. Nearby, continuing east on the trail, you'll come to an experimental plot researching plant disease. At 2.21 miles, the trail begins to head south alongside a barbed-wire fence to the east and a rugged, wooded ravine to the west. This would be a good area to spot birds and other wildlife seeking cover in the ravine. Pass an art exhibit at 2.44 miles and then a Silphium education plot before completing the loop at the gate. The trailhead is another 0.33 mile east through the open prairie.

Miles and Directions

0.00 Start at the trailhead and head west.

0.35 Gate; keep left (west) at the fork at the benches and book share.

0.51 At the fork, keep left (south).

0.56 Ash Overlook.

0.87 Sandberg Overlook.

0.92 Turn sharply left (north).

1.06 Right (northeast) to Bull Frog Bottoms, a short out-and-back spur trail.

1.13 Bull Frog Bottoms.

1.58 Reach the northern boundary of the nature area; turn right (east), indicated by an arrow near a bench.

1.71 Turn left (east) at the wooden arrow.

1.81 Tree swings.

2.04 Picnic area; keep left (northeast).

2.21 Continue straight (south).

2.63 Turn left (east) and pass through the gate.

2.99 Arrive back at the trailhead.

Honorable Mentions

A Steve Mathes Nature Trail

The short distance, level grade, and informative interpretive panels make the Steve Mathes Nature Trail a wonderful family-friendly hike. The reservoir offers fishing and swimming opportunities, while the prairie dog town will be popular with children. If you come in spring, you are likely to see migrating sandhill cranes flying overhead as they head north.

Start: Trailhead at the parking area south of the prairie dog town
Elevation gain: 2,379 feet (trailhead) to 2,382 feet
Distance: 1.36-mile loop
Difficulty: Easy
Hiking time: 0.5–1 hour
Seasons/schedule: Open daily year-round; best in spring or fall to view migrating birds and the nearby prairie dog town

Fees and permits: A daily vehicle permit or annual state park vehicle permit is necessary to enter the park.
Trail contact: Prairie Dog State Park, 13037 Hwy. 261, Norton 67654; (785) 877-2953; ksoutdoors.com/State-Parks/Locations/Prairie-Dog
Dog-friendly: Yes, on leash
Trail surface: Paved and dirt

The first 0.25 mile of the Steve Mathes Nature Trail is ADA-accessible.

Land status: Prairie Dog State Park (Kansas Department of Wildlife & Parks)
Nearest town: Norton, 6 miles to the northeast
Maps: USGS Norton, KS; park map available on the park's website
Other trail users: None
Special considerations: No water is available in winter.
Amenities: Restrooms at the visitor center
Maximum grade: 4%
Cell service: Reliable

Finding the trailhead: From Norton, head west on US 36 for 4 miles. Turn south onto KS 261 and continue for 1.3 miles. After passing the park office and over the railroad, turn east after the prairie dog town. The trailhead is on the south side of the road. GPS: N39°48.504' / W99°57.690'

Trail conditions: The trail is easy to follow. After precipitation, the dirt section of the trail will be muddy. There are trees along the trail, but most of the trail is exposed to the sun. The trail receives light traffic.

B Coyote Trail

The Coyote Trail takes hikers along a 3-mile trail through rolling prairie in the picturesque Chalk Hills. Two loop options allow for a short hike or the full 3-mile loop. Interpretive signs along both loops describe the local flora and fauna. Waterfowl and shorebirds are common wildlife sightings, and there are more trails beyond the official Coyote Trail to continue exploring the prairie.

Start: Old Marina/Coyote Shelter
Elevation gain: 1,893 to 1,941 feet; 160 feet total elevation gain
Distance: 2.9-mile loop
Difficulty: Easy
Hiking time: 1.5–2 hours
Seasons/schedule: Open year-round, dawn to dusk
Fees and permits: Daily vehicle permit or annual state park vehicle permit required
Trail contact: Webster State Park, 1140 10 Rd., Stockton 67669; (785) 425-6775; ksoutdoors.com/State-Parks/Locations/Webster
Dog-friendly: Yes, on leash
Trail surface: Mowed grass
Land status: Webster State Park (Kansas Department of Wildlife & Parks)
Nearest town: Stockton, 12 miles to the east
Maps: USGS Webster Dam, KS; trail map available on the park website
Other trail users: None
Special considerations: There is no shade on the trail.
Amenities: Vault toilet
Maximum grade: 9%
Cell service: Adequate

Finding the trailhead: From Stockton, head west on US 24 for 10 miles. Turn south onto 9 Road, and after 1.4 miles turn west at Old Marina Campground. The trailhead is at the end of the road on the north side. GPS: N39°24.076' / W99°27.437'

Trail conditions: Some sections of the trail are well marked, particularly the two loops described on the park's website. There are more trails beyond the two recommended loops, but trail markings may not be as frequent. There is no shade along the trail. The trail receives light traffic.

ⓒ Smoky Hills Audubon Sanctuary

Located 6 miles from Salina near the interchange of I-35 and I-70, the Smoky Hills Audubon Sanctuary offers 2.5 miles of family-friendly trails through grasslands and woodlands and around a small fishing pond. As this is an Audubon sanctuary, bird-watching is an excellent activity while hiking the trails.

Start: 2500 W Stimmel Rd., Salina
Elevation gain: Variable depending on route
Distance: 2.5 miles of trails
Difficulty: Easy
Hiking time: 1-2 hours
Seasons/schedule: Open year-round, dawn to dusk
Fees and permits: None
Trail contact: Smoky Hills Audubon Society, 2700 W Stimmel Rd., Salina 67401; smokyhillsaudubon.com
Dog-friendly: Dogs not allowed
Trail surface: Natural

Land status: Smoky Hills Audubon Sanctuary (Smoky Hills Audubon Society)
Nearest town: Salina, 6 miles to the southeast
Maps: USGS Salina SW, KS; trail maps available at the trailhead kiosk
Other trail users: None
Special considerations: There is a secure wheelchair-accessible, protected photo blind.
Amenities: Portable toilet
Maximum grade: Variable, depending on route; trails mostly level, with few inclines
Cell service: Adequate

Smoky Hills Audubon Sanctuary near Salina.

Finding the trailhead: From I-70, take exit 249 south onto North Halstead Road. At the first intersection, turn east onto West Stimmel Road. GPS: N38°52.258' / W97°39.302'

Trail conditions: Trails are mowed and natural surface; they can be muddy after rain. The trails are easy to follow and, due to the sanctuary's size, it is difficult to get lost. Trails receive moderate traffic.

D Green Recreational Trail

The Green Recreational Trail includes almost 2 miles of trails on 117 acres alongside the Ninnescah River. The land is leased to the Kansas Department of Wildlife & Parks, which receives help from the Kansas Outdoor AmeriCorps Action Team as well as volunteers. The grove of trees provides both shade and wonderful wildlife viewing opportunities.

There are a variety of trails along the Ninnescah River.

Start: Green Property Trail parking south of the Pratt Waste Water Treatment Plant
Elevation gain: Variable, depending on the route
Distance: Over 1.5 miles of trails
Difficulty: Easy
Hiking time: About 1 hour
Seasons/schedule: Open year-round, dawn to dusk
Fees and permits: None
Trail contact: Kansas Department of Wildlife & Parks, 702 Country Club Rd., Pratt 67124; (620) 672-5911; ksoutdoors.com/State-Parks/Locations/Green-Recreational-Trail

Dog-friendly: Yes, on leash
Trail surface: Natural
Land status: Private property leased to Kansas Department of Wildlife & Parks
Nearest town: Pratt
Maps: USGS Pratt, KS
Other trail users: Mountain bikers
Special considerations: None
Amenities: None
Maximum grade: Variable, depending on the route; trails are flat, with few inclines
Cell service: Adequate but may be limited under tree cover

Finding the trailhead: From US 400, head south on Country Club Road. After 0.4 mile, turn east onto Green Street. The parking area and trailhead are at the end of the road. GPS: N37°38.261' / W98°43.022'

Trail conditions: There is a trail distance sign near the trailhead, but the trails themselves are not marked. Several trails intersect each other as they snake through the riparian woods along the South Fork of the Ninnescah River. The trails receive moderate traffic.

Arkansas-Wellington-McPherson Lowlands

The Arkansas River (pronounced Ar-Kansas, not Ar-kansaw like the state) flows across Kansas from the Colorado border to Wichita, where it turns south to leave the state and enter Oklahoma. The river's relatively flat floodplain is composed of sand and gravel deposited by the river, which begins in the Colorado Rockies and is fed by rain and snowmelt. Due to declining groundwater levels, much of the Arkansas River in western Kansas runs dry for most of the year. There are a few significant wildlife habitats located along the Arkansas River, notably Cheyenne Bottoms and Quivira National Wildlife Refuge. Both areas are hot spots for migratory birds, in particular shorebirds and waterfowl. The former has several short hiking trails that are excellent during the migratory season for bird-watching. Cheyenne Bottoms lacks hiking trails, but simply driving through the refuge will delight bird enthusiasts. The woodland trails along the Arkansas River at the Chaplin Nature Center are another bird-watcher's paradise; the center is run by the Wichita Audubon Society. In some places south of the river, wind and water have deposited large amounts of sand. The resulting sand dunes were stabilized by prairie grasses, creating a unique ecosystem in the state. Sand Hills State Park has miles of hiking trails around, and on top of, sand dunes just outside Hutchinson. The Wellington-McPherson Lowlands are dissected by the Arkansas River. The landscape is very similar to the Arkansas River Lowlands, with rich soils for farming and areas of low-lying wetlands. Chisholm Creek Park, located on the eastern side of Wichita, is one of the top family hiking destinations in the state.

Chisholm Creek Park.

10 Migrant's Mile Nature Trail

The prairies and wetlands of Quivira National Wildlife Refuge provide habitat for a variety of waterfowl, shorebirds, and other bird species. Migrant's Mile offers refuge visitors an easy 1.15-mile loop—or a shorter ADA-accessible loop—through prairie, wetland, and woodland. Visit in spring or fall to witness migrating geese, cranes, and other waterfowl; the trail is named for these migrating birds. An interpretive trail guide, available at the trailhead, is a great way for adults and children alike to learn about the natural history of the wildlife refuge.

Start: Trail "Start" sign south of the parking area located on South Sterling Road next to Park Smith Lake

Elevation gain: 1,794 feet (trailhead) to 1,802 feet

Distance: 1.15-mile loop

Difficulty: Easy

Hiking time: 0.5–1 hour

Seasons/schedule: Open daily, 1.5 hours before sunrise to 1.5 hours after sunset; best in spring for geese and crane migration

Fees and permits: None

Trail contact: Quivira National Wildlife Refuge, 1434 NE 80th St., Stafford 67578; (620) 410-4011; www.fws.gov/refuge/quivira

Dog-friendly: Yes, on leash

Trail surface: Paved on short loop to footbridge; dirt and grass after the footbridge

Land status: Quivira National Wildlife Refuge (US Fish & Wildlife Service)

Nearest town: Sterling, 20 miles to the east; Great Bend, 30 miles to the northwest

Maps: USGS Alden NW, KS; interactive map available online; refuge maps available at kiosks throughout the refuge; interpretive trail guide available at the trailhead

Other trail users: None

Special considerations: The inner loop is paved and ADA accessible. There is one species of venomous snake found on the refuge, the massasauga rattlesnake.

Amenities: None at the trailhead; however, there are vault toilets just to the north, as well as near the visitor center at the southern end of the refuge. There is a photo blind near the trailhead.

Maximum grade: 1%

Cell service: Reliable at the trailhead and on the trail

Finding the trailhead: From Sterling, head south on KS 14 for 3 miles. Turn west onto 101st Street/Avenue Y and continue for 1.5 miles. Turn south onto North Peace Road, and after 0.5 mile turn west onto 95th Avenue/Northeast 140 Street and continue for 14 miles. Turn south on South Sterling Road and reach the trailhead after 1 mile.

From Great Bend, head south on US 281 for 14.5 miles. Turn east onto Northeast 140th Street and continue for 14 miles, then turn south onto South Sterling Road. Reach the trailhead after 1 mile. GPS: N38°8.636' / W98°29.500'

Trail conditions: The inner loop is paved and easy to navigate. The trail past the footbridge follows a footpath, faint in places, through grass; look for the next interpretive trail sign ahead to find the route. Ticks are abundant in the taller grasses during warmer months. The trail receives moderate traffic.

Migrant's Mile passes through woodlands in addition to prairie and wetlands.

A boardwalk crosses a marsh and can be used to hike a shorter loop.

The Hike

Quivira National Wildlife Refuge lies in the Central Flyway, and as a result is a major stopover point for migratory waterfowl, shorebirds, and other bird species. The rare inland salt marsh and sand prairie provide habitat for these migrating birds. At peak migration, approximately 750,000 geese are present at the refuge, mainly Canada, snow, and white-fronted geese. Enormous flocks of ducks join the geese, creating a cacophony of quacks and honks at the refuge.

Located only 45 minutes west of Hutchinson, and 90 minutes northwest of Wichita, Quivira NWR has a variety of activities for families to make an enjoyable day trip. While bird-watching is an obvious top attraction, fishing is also popular and is permitted throughout the refuge. A 15-mile Auto Tour Route allows visitors to see the refuge at their own pace; the 5-mile section called Wildlife Drive gets you up close to the Big Salt Marsh to see wildlife.

Hiking is another attraction at the refuge, and the trails at Quivira are family-friendly; some are also dog-friendly. Two trails near the headquarters—the Headquarters Trail (0.20 mile out and back) and Little Salt Marsh Trail (0.58 mile out and back)—are ideal for children. Migrant's Mile Nature Trail, located north of Big Salt

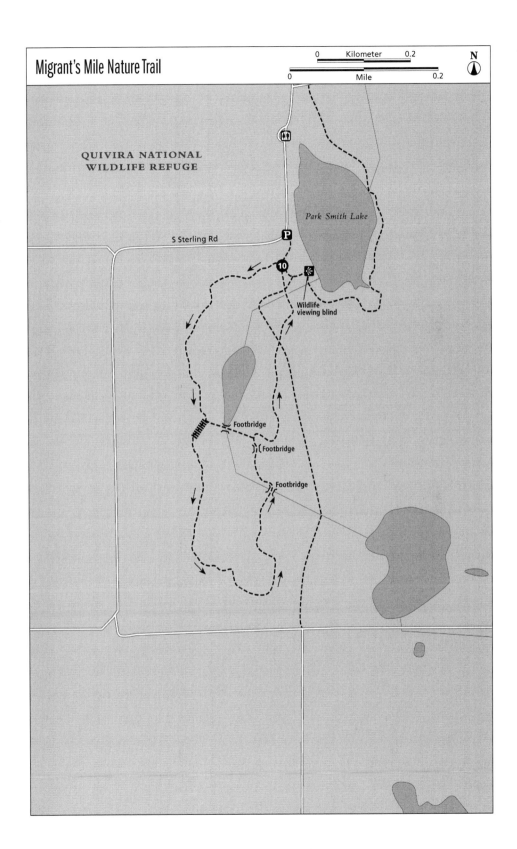

Migrant's Mile Nature Trail

0   Kilometer   0.2
0   Mile   0.2

N

QUIVIRA NATIONAL
WILDLIFE REFUGE

Park Smith Lake

S Sterling Rd

P

10

Wildlife
viewing blind

Footbridge

Footbridge

Footbridge

Marsh on South Sterling Road, is also great for families and allows hikers to connect with nature on a longer trail.

Migrant's Mile Nature Trail begins just south of the parking area next to Park Smith Lake. There is a photo blind nearby overlooking the lake. The trail offers hikers two options: an ADA-accessible inner loop that totals about 0.67 mile or a longer loop of just over 1 mile. A helpful interpretive trail guide, available at the trailhead, provides natural history information every 0.1 mile along the trail.

The guided interpretive trail follows a counterclockwise loop, so keep right (south) at the trailhead to follow it. The trail to the boardwalk is paved, so people with mobility issues will be able to enjoy the inner loop. Once you reach the boardwalk, turn left (east) to cross the marsh over the boardwalk if you wish to complete the shorter inner loop. To hike the full loop, keep right (north) at the boardwalk to follow a narrow footpath through grass. The path here can be faint in places, so look for the interpretive trail signs to follow the loop. At about 0.5 mile, the trail bends east and enters a wooded area. After 0.6 mile, the trail begins to slowly bend north to head back toward the boardwalk at 0.9 mile. Keep right (north) at the boardwalk to follow the trail for the remaining 0.3 mile to the trailhead. If you haven't visited the photo blind, head over with binoculars to do some bird-watching.

Miles and Directions

0.00 Start at the trail "Start" sign and keep right (south).

0.32 Reach the boardwalk; keep right (south). (Option: Keep left and cross the boardwalk to hike the inner loop—0.7-mile total.)

0.78 Footbridge.

0.87 Boardwalk; turn right (east).

1.10 Footbridge.

1.15 Arrive back at the trailhead.

11 Sand Hills Loop

Just north of Hutchinson, Sand Hills State Park is a popular hiking and horseback riding destination. Fourteen miles of trails meander underneath and sometimes over sand dunes that are stabilized by prairie grass. The trails also cross through grasslands, woodlands, and wetlands, making the park the perfect spot for bird-watching or a wildflower walk. The trail system allows hikers to enjoy any length of hike they desire; this hike leads up to an overlook on top of a dune, then follows the Prairie Trail to the park's northern boundary, where it returns to the trailhead via the sandy and aptly named Rolling Hills Trail.

Start: Large parking area on 56th Avenue opposite the park office, self-pay station, and campground
Elevation gain: 1,530 feet (trailhead) to 1,560 feet
Distance: 4.49-mile loop
Difficulty: Moderate due to sandy terrain
Hiking time: About 2 hours
Seasons/schedule: Open daily, year-round
Fees and permits: State park vehicle permits required for entrance or use
Trail contact: Sand Hills State Park, 4207 E 56th, Hutchinson 67502; (316) 542-3664; ksoutdoors.com/State-Parks/Locations/Sand-Hills
Dog-friendly: Yes, on leash
Trail surface: Grass, dirt, and sand
Land status: Sand Hills State Park (Kansas Department of Wildlife & Parks)

Nearest town: Hutchinson, 7 miles to the southwest
Maps: USGS Hutchinson SE, KS; park map available on the park's website
Other trail users: Equestrians
Special considerations: During rainy times of the year expect some muddy sections on the trails. Please be aware that the trails will be closed when controlled burns are taking place. The Department of Wildlife and Parks performs the controlled burns during March and April. Before the burn, signs will be posted at the park entrances notifying the public.
Amenities: Modern restroom and water at the campground; trails have four areas with vault toilets
Maximum grade: 4%
Cell service: Adequate coverage at the trail-head and on the trails

Finding the trailhead: From Hutchinson, head north on KS 61. Take the East 56th Avenue exit and head east for 1 mile. The trailhead is on the north side of 56th Avenue. GPS: N38°6.965' / W97°51.357'

Trail conditions: There are multiple intersecting trails; take a park map with you, or take a picture of the trail map at the trailhead. The trails are well maintained but not waymarked. Rolling Hills Trail traverses sandy terrain. The trails receive moderate traffic.

The Hike

Sand Hills State Park gets its name from the deposits of sand carried by streams that created the Arkansas River Valley. The sand was picked up by southwesterly winds and deposited into dunes, later stabilized by prairie grasses. The park is the best place in

View from a sand dune overlooking the state park.

Kansas to experience this type of ecosystem, and the 14 miles of multiuse trails are popular with hikers and equestrians.

Begin at the information kiosk in the parking area on 56th Avenue opposite Sand Hills Campground. Head northwest, taking the trail on the left that crosses a short boardwalk. The trail soon passes by vault toilets; keep left (northwest) at the fork at 0.12 mile. Shortly after the fork, take a right (north) to climb to the top of a sand dune and reach the Dune Trail Overlook.

At just over 1,600 feet, this is the highest point on the hike. The overlook affords you great views of the state park. Look to the north to see the trails cutting through the tallgrass prairie. After taking in the views, descend the north side of the dune via a set of stairs. Once you reach the bottom of the dune, turn left to head northwest then north along Dune Trail, crossing a firebreak at 0.33 mile.

There are numerous spur trails, including some that do not appear on the park map, like the one at 0.49 mile. You can take this unmarked trail to connect with Prairie Trail or continue straight at 0.49 mile. Both trails join Prairie Trail at 0.6 mile.

Continue north on the Prairie Trail for 0.25 mile, then turn right (east) at 0.84 mile. The trail heads east through open prairie until it passes through a wooded area at around the 1-mile mark of the hike. The aptly named Cottonwood Trail takes

Deer are a common sight in the park.

hikers through this wooded section of the park before it heads north at 1.4 miles. The grove of cottonwoods is on your left as you head north, with open tallgrass prairie to the east.

Cottonwood Trail reaches the park's northern boundary at 1.61 miles, where it heads east, running parallel to 69th Avenue for just over 0.5 mile. At the parking lot at 2.13 miles, head south on Rolling Hills Trail. The first section of this trail is grassy, but it eventually becomes sandy, making the last 2 miles of the hike slow going and tiresome. The landscape, however, is enchanting as the trail traverses rolling grass-stabilized sand dunes, some of which have footpaths leading to the top of the dunes.

Bluestem Spur Trail, at 2.42 miles, offers a more direct route back to the trailhead. If you continue on Rolling Hills Trail, however, the junction at 2.53 miles gives access to Pond Trail. If the pond is dry or the water level is low, it's recommended to continue on Rolling Hills Trail. If there is water, Pond Trail is worth the side trip—two wildlife observation blinds allow visitors a close-up peek at nature in action. Ducks, geese, songbirds, deer, muskrats, and many other creatures are frequently seen from these blinds.

From the junction with Pond Trail, Rolling Hills Trail continues in a southwestern direction for 2 miles until reaching the trailhead. As noted previously, this section is sandy but offers a tranquil hike meandering through the dunes that give the park its name.

Sand Hills Loop

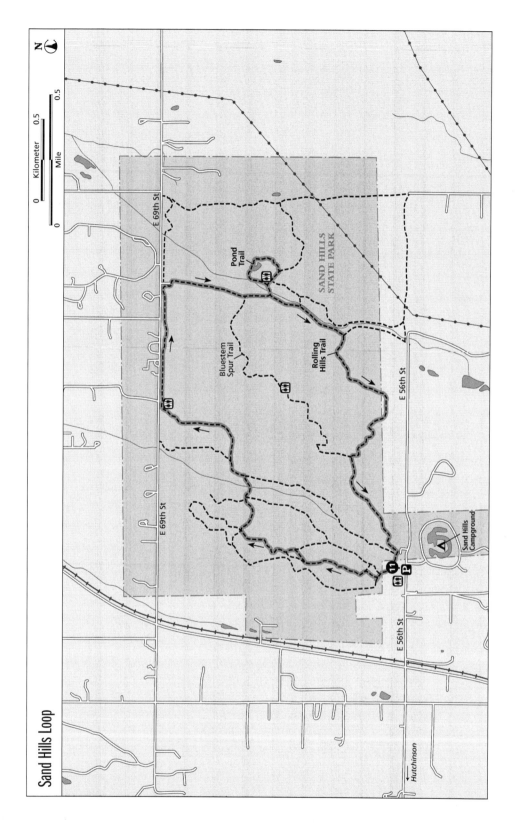

Hutchinson

E 56th St
E 69th St

SAND HILLS STATE PARK

Pond Trail

Bluestem Spur Trail

Rolling Hills Trail

Sand Hills Campground

Kilometer
Mile
0   0.5
0   0.5

N

Miles and Directions

0.00 Start at the large parking area and take the boardwalk, heading northwest.

0.12 Reach a fork; keep left (northwest).

0.14 Turn right (north) to climb the dune.

0.23 Turn left (north) at a bench at a junction.

0.33 Continue north through a firebreak.

0.49 Keep right (north), then keep right (northeast) at the next fork.

0.56 Turn left (north).

0.60 Turn right (north).

0.84 Turn right (east).

0.99 Keep right (east), then keep left (east).

1.08 Turn left (north). (Bailout: Turn right/south to return to the trailhead.)

1.18 Continue straight (east).

1.61 Turn right (east) at the park's northern boundary.

2.13 Turn right (south) onto Rolling Hills Trail.

2.42 Continue straight (south). (Bailout: Turn right/southwest onto Bluestem Spur Trail to return to the trailhead.)

2.54 Keep left (east).

2.58 Turn left (north) onto Pond Trail.

2.63 Picnic table.

2.75 Keep right (south).

2.81 Picnic table.

2.82 Turn right (southwest).

2.88 Turn right (northwest).

2.93 At the vault toilets, continue straight (west); cross the bridges, then keep left (west).

2.99 Turn right (south).

3.12 Continue straight (south).

3.34 Turn right (west).

4.05 Continue straight (west) at the junction with Bluestem Spur Trail.

4.34 Continue straight (southwest) through a firebreak.

4.49 Arrive back at the trailhead.

12 West Side Trail

Located in windy central Kansas, Cheney State Park contains one of the best sailing lakes in the country. The lake is a popular recreation destination not only for Wichita residents but for all Kansans. The West Side Trail takes hikers and mountain bikers through wooded areas, along a creek, and through open grasslands on the west side of Cheney Reservoir, totaling over 5 miles one way. This easy and peaceful hike begins at the Lakeshore Drive Day-Use Area and heads north to a viewpoint on the lakeshore.

Start: Lakeshore Trailhead
Elevation gain: 1,426 feet to 1,447 feet; 66 feet total elevation gain
Distance: 3.77 miles out and back
Difficulty: Easy due to level terrain and easy route finding
Hiking time: 1.5–2 hours
Seasons/schedule: Open daily year-round
Fees and permits: State park vehicle permits required for entrance or use
Trail contact: Cheney State Park, 16000 NE 50th St., Cheney 67025; (316) 542-3664; ksoutdoors.com/State-Parks/Locations/Cheney
Dog-friendly: Yes, on leash
Trail surface: Natural (grass and dirt)

Land status: Cheney State Park (Kansas Department of Wildlife & Parks)
Nearest town: Cheney, 10 miles to the south
Maps: USGS Cheney, KS, and USGS Haven SE, KS; park map (no trails listed) available at ksoutdoors.com
Other trail users: Mountain bikers
Special considerations: There is no shelter on the trail, so check the forecast before you leave the trailhead.
Amenities: Toilets near the trailhead; potable water available at the park's campgrounds
Maximum grade: 2%
Cell service: Adequate to above average reception at the trailhead and along the trail

Finding the trailhead: From the interchange of US 54/400 and KS 251, head north on KS 251 for 3.4 miles. Turn left (west) onto West 21st Street N/Northeast 50th Street. After 1 mile, West 21st Street N becomes Northeast 50th Street; continue for 1.5 miles. At Cheney Lake Road, turn right (north) to reach the west entrance permit station. Take the next two left turns to continue northwest on Cheney Lake Road. After 1.2 miles, reach a small parking area with vault toilets at the trailhead. GPS: N37°44.649' / W97°50.836'

Trail conditions: The grass trail is wide and level but may get muddy after recent rain. The trail receives average traffic, but the state park is very popular. Major junctions are marked with directional signs, while some unmarked side trails intersect West Side Trail. High winds can create tree hazards.

The Hike

Cheney Reservoir was completed in 1964, the result of a study to provide clean water to Wichita. Since its construction, the lake has become a popular outdoor recreation spot for Kansas's most populous city. Camping, fishing, hiking, and boating, in particular, are popular at Cheney State Park. The park is divided into two areas on the

Lakeshore Trailhead.

south end of the lake. The Ninnescah Sailing Center is located on the west side of Cheney Reservoir, one of the premier sailing destinations in the Midwest. The best hiking trail is also on the west side of the lake, and you'll likely hear boaters as you hike along the lakeshore.

The West Side Trail totals more than 5 miles from near the park entrance to the northern end of the trail. This hike begins at the Lakeshore Trailhead and traverses the least-developed section of the trail. After leaving the trailhead, the trail passes through a disc golf course as it heads north through open prairie. The trail bends to the west through a wooded section and reaches a junction at just over the 0.5-mile mark of the hike. Continue north, following the sign for Cedar Loop, through the woods. You'll pass a handful of primitive campsites on your right, located between the trail and the lakeshore, that would make great spots to pitch a tent and hang a hammock for a relaxing weekend.

Beginning around the 1.25-mile mark, keep an eye on the side of the trail. There are many eastern red cedar trees that have been uprooted or knocked over, likely the result of the strong winds that make Cheney Reservoir a premier sailing destination. There are several side trails through this section that you can explore, but continue on the West Side Trail to reach the Cedar Loop after 1.6 miles. Several footpaths lead to

Cedar Loop and Prairie Loop.

the lakeshore, but the easiest access is at the viewpoint at 1.76 miles. If you brought a beach towel and snacks, this is an excellent spot to take a break before heading back to the trailhead. The hike back follows the same trail; however, at 3.19 miles continue straight to hike the other half of the Prairie Loop through the disc golf course. If you're lucky, the final stretch of your hike will be accompanied by meadowlark song as you walk through a peaceful prairie to the trailhead.

If you are looking for additional hiking at Cheney State Park, you can hike the full length of the West Side Trail, including the Forest Loop. Additional trailheads are located near the Smarsh Creek Campground and Geifer Creek Day-Use Area, east of the park entrance. The total distance of the trail, out and back, is over 10 miles, so be sure to bring a backpack with sufficient water, snacks, and other supplies. Two additional trails at Cheney State Park are great options for families with children. The Geifer Creek Nature Trail and Spring Creek Wildlife Observation Trail are also located on the west side of Cheney Reservoir. Part of the Spring Creek Trail is elevated over a wetland and stream. This 0.75-mile hike is an excellent option to observe wildlife and nature.

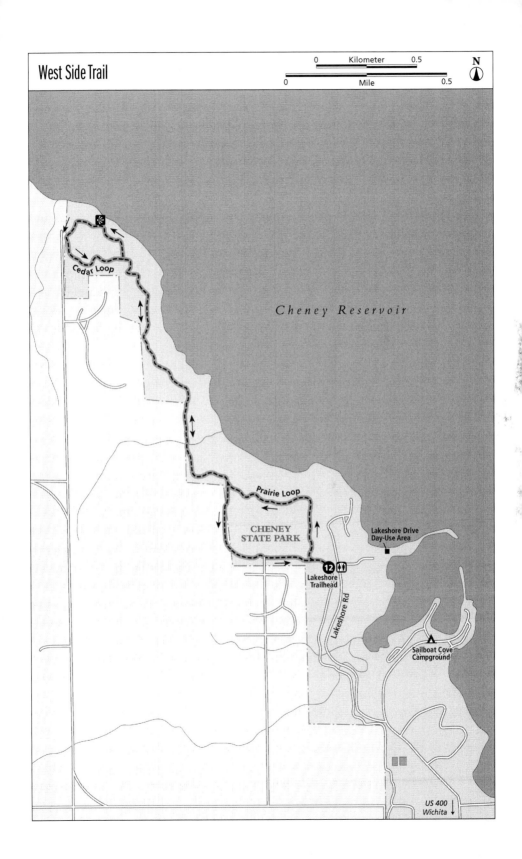

West Side Trail

Cedar Loop

Cheney Reservoir

Prairie Loop

CHENEY
STATE PARK

Lakeshore Drive
Day-Use Area

12 Lakeshore
Trailhead

Lakeshore Rd

Sailboat Cove
Campground

US 400
Wichita

0   Kilometer   0.5

0   Mile   0.5

N

Miles and Directions

0.00 Start at the trail sign near the toilets and head south.

0.08 Turn right (north).

0.22 Keep right (north).

0.58 Turn right (north) to follow the sign to Cedar Loop. (Bailout: Turn left/south to return to the trailhead via Prairie Loop.)

1.05 Continue straight (north).

1.32 Keep right then left at consecutive forks to continue northeast.

1.35 Continue straight (north).

1.48 Reach a junction and turn left (west).

1.52 Turn right (northeast) to continue on the main trail.

1.60 Reach the Cedar Loop; keep right (north) at the fork to follow the loop counterclockwise.

1.73 Short spur trail on your right leads to the lakeshore.

1.76 Viewpoint.

1.86 Keep left (south). (Option: Keep right/north for another access trail to the lakeshore.)

2.19 Complete the Cedar Loop; keep right (southeast) to follow West Side Trail.

2.27 Turn left (east).

2.43 Continue straight (southeast).

2.45 Keep right then immediately turn left to continue southeast.

3.19 Reach the Prairie Loop junction; continue straight (south).

3.39 Continue straight (east).

3.67 Turn left then right to continue east.

3.77 Arrive back at the trailhead.

13 Chisholm Creek Trail

Chisholm Creek Park packs all of the major habitats in Kansas in its 282 acres on the northeastern edge of Wichita. More than 2 miles of trails wind through native and restored prairie, wetlands, and woodlands. Despite its urban location, the park provides habitat for a variety of wildlife—bird-watching is a particular delight, with a mix of grassland and woodland species. The accessibility of the trails and the Great Plains Nature Center make this one of the best family hikes in Kansas.

Start: Great Plains Nature Center
Elevation gain: 33 feet total elevation gain
Distance: 1.79-mile loop
Difficulty: Easy
Hiking time: About 1 hour
Seasons/schedule: Open daily, dawn to dusk
Fees and permits: None
Trail contact: Great Plains Nature Center, 6232 E 29th St. N, Wichita 67220; (316) 683-5499; gpnc.org/chisholm-creek-park/
Dog-friendly: Pets not allowed on the trails at Chisholm Creek Park; dogs allowed on the bicycle path around the outside of the park
Trail surface: Pavement and boardwalks

Land status: Chisholm Creek Park (Wichita Parks & Recreation)
Nearest town: Wichita
Maps: USGS Wichita East, KS; trail map available on the park's website and at a kiosk outside the Great Plains Nature Center
Other trail users: None
Special considerations: Please respect the flora and fauna you are visiting while in the park by leaving nothing but footprints and taking nothing but photos.
Amenities: Toilets near the northwest corner of the parking lot; water and restrooms in the nature center (during open hours)
Maximum grade: Flat for the entire loop
Cell service: Clear in the entire park

Finding the trailhead: From KS 96, take the south exit for either North Woodlawn Boulevard or North Oliver Street. From Woodlawn Boulevard, turn west onto East 29th Street North; from Oliver Street, turn east onto East 29th Street. The parking lot at the Great Plains Nature Center is located near the corner of East 29th Street and North Woodlawn Boulevard. GPS: N37°44.375' / W97°15.857'

Trail conditions: The trail is accessible to wheelchairs, strollers, and people with mobility difficulties. There are sections with rougher pavement on the northern half of the loop. The loop crosses several wooden footbridges and boardwalks. Hiking boots or athletic shoes are sufficient.

The Hike

The Great Plains Nature Center is a collaborative effort by the US Fish & Wildlife Service, Kansas Department of Wildlife & Parks, City of Wichita Parks & Recreation, and the nonprofit Friends of the Great Plains Nature Center. They share the joint mission to provide environmental education and outdoor recreation to the public. Both the nature center, which provides a variety of programs and activities, and the trails at Chisholm Creek Park are free to the public. Chisholm Creek Park has been

Osage orange hedgerow.

Boardwalk over a wetland area.

designated a Wichita Wildlife Area, which belies its location just south of KS 96. There's an excellent chance that you will see white-tailed deer, wild turkey, ducks, and both grassland and woodland birds.

After visiting the Great Plains Nature Center to learn about Kansas's ecosystems, head north over the footbridge toward the small covered kiosk that includes a map of the trail system. Continue north on Quail Trail through a grove of trees, then keep right at the next junction onto Heron Trail. Reach a boardwalk over a wetland then, after passing through another grove of trees, cross the footbridge, heading north to follow Bluestem Trail. The boardwalk is an excellent place for bird-watching.

Bluestem Trail skirts the southern end of a prairie for almost 0.5 mile. You can see the bicycle path across the prairie on the northern border of the park, with KS 96 on the other side of the fence. A couple of mowed trails through the prairie connect Bluestem Trail with the bicycle path. When you reach the next junction at 0.67 mile, turn right (north) onto Cottonwood Trail. If you want to hike a shorter loop, turn left to cross Chisholm Creek via another footbridge.

Bluestem Trail continues west along the edge of the prairie to the north and wooded Chisholm Creek to the south. Shortly after the previous junction, you will reach a boardwalk with an area that is excellent for bird-watching. The Cottonwood

Chisholm Creek Trail

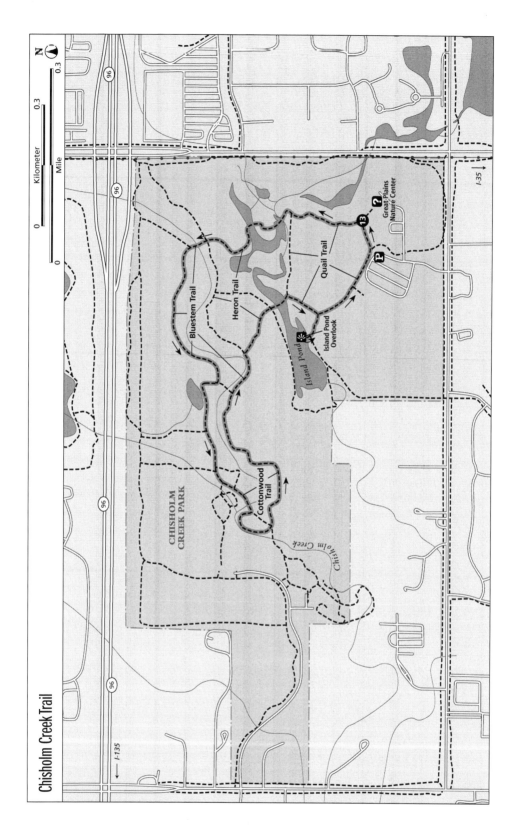

Trail continues southwest into the woods, then crosses Chisholm Creek and heads east. The trail again follows the edge of prairie and woodland, with the former to the south now and the woods on your left to the north. Look for wildflowers in the prairie and perhaps foraging deer if you are hiking at dawn or dusk.

Turn right (southeast) after 1.38 miles onto Heron Trail, which will lead you to Island Pond. After crossing the footbridge, keep right (southwest) and then right again at the next junction to reach the Island Pond Overlook. Enjoy the serene view before turning around and heading southeast on Quail Trail to return to the nature center.

If you are looking for more hiking within the Wichita city limits, Pawnee Prairie Park has several miles of trails through woodland. A park map is available and some of the junctions are marked; however, these trails are best to wander without a plan, as the numerous intersecting footpaths become confusing if you follow the trail map. If you are looking for an easy, gentle hike, the Prairie Sunset Trail is a 15-mile rail trail between Garden Plain, Goddard, and Wichita in southwest Sedgwick County.

Miles and Directions

0.00 Start at the Great Plains Nature Center and head north over the footbridge on Quail Trail.

0.05 Covered kiosk with a trail map.

0.17 Turn right (east) onto Heron Trail.

0.39 Continue straight (northwest) onto Bluestem Trail.

0.67 Turn right (north) onto Cottonwood Trail. (Bailout: Turn left/south to hike a shorter loop.)

0.76 Continue straight (west) onto the boardwalk.

0.87 Continue straight (southwest).

1.01 Continue straight (east).

1.29 Continue straight (southeast) onto Bluestem Trail.

1.38 Turn right (southeast) onto Heron Trail.

1.49 Turn right (southwest) onto Quail Trail.

1.55 Turn right (northwest) toward Island Pond Overlook.

1.60 Island Pond Overlook; turn around and continue straight (southeast) at the junction to return to the nature center.

1.79 Arrive back at the nature center.

14 River Trail, Bluff Trail, and Lost Prairie Trail Loop

The Wichita Audubon Society maintains more than 4 miles of trails at the Chaplin Nature Center. Located along the Arkansas River, the trails traverse prairie and riparian woodland, offering birding enthusiasts a variety of habitats to spot the 225 species of birds that have been recorded at the nature center. The 0.25-mile sandbar along the Arkansas River allows hikers to cool their feet in summer, while the bottomland timber provides plenty of shade. A giant-size wooden chair in the forest will entice young hikers to climb it for a fun photograph.

Start: West side of the Chaplin Nature Center
Elevation gain: 1,073 feet to 1,145 feet; 102 feet total elevation gain
Distance: 2.30-mile loop
Difficulty: Easy due to level terrain
Hiking time: 1–2 hours
Seasons/schedule: Trails open year-round, dawn to dusk. The visitor center is open year-round on Sat, 9 a.m.–5 p.m., and Sun, 1–5 p.m.; closed Mon and holidays. Check the park's website for seasonal weekday hours.
Fees and permits: None
Trail contact: Chaplin Nature Center, 27814 27th Drive, Arkansas City 67005; (620) 442-4133; wichitaaudubon.org/cnc/; email: CNC@wichitaaudubon.org

Dog-friendly: No
Trail surface: Natural (dirt, grass, and sand)
Land status: Chaplin Nature Center (Wichita Audubon Society)
Nearest town: Arkansas City, 6 miles to the southeast
Maps: USGS Arkansas City, KS; trail map available on the park's website
Other trail users: None
Special considerations: Stay on designated trails. No collecting of anything is allowed.
Amenities: Visitor center with restrooms
Maximum grade: 7%; Lost Prairie Trail has five short but steep climbs.
Cell service: Adequate, although service may be limited under tree cover

Finding the trailhead: From Arkansas City, head west on US 166 for 2 miles. Turn right (north) onto 31st Road. After 2 miles, 31st Road turns slightly left (west) and becomes 140th/272nd Road. Take the next right (north) onto 27th Drive to reach Chaplin Nature Center.

From I-35, take exit 4 and head east on US 166. Turn north onto 21st Road and continue for 2 miles. Turn right (east) onto 140th/272nd Road, then left (north) onto 27th Drive to reach Chaplin Nature Center. GPS: N37°5.302' / W97°6.026'

Trail conditions: The mowed trails are well maintained and easy to follow. Take precautions to avoid ticks. Sandbar Trail disappears once it reaches the river, so walk along the forest edge to continue on River Trail. The trails receive moderate foot traffic.

The Hike

The Chaplin Nature Center, located northwest of Arkansas City, is owned by the Wichita Audubon Society. The park features bottomland timber and prairies, upland prairies, a spring-fed creek, and the Arkansas River. More than 4 miles of hiker-only trails are perfect for birders, families, and anyone looking for a quiet forest walk. Some

River Trail provides access to the Arkansas River.

225 species of birds have been recorded at the park. Bald eagles can be seen in winter, and pileated woodpeckers have been found in the timber.

Begin the hike at the southwestern corner of the nature center, going around the building to its north side and turning right onto Bluff Trail. Another option is to continue straight at the junction, go down the stairs, and then take the next right onto the other half of the Bluff Trail loop; this section will take you along Spring Creek. For the described hike, head southeast on the dirt and wood chip footpath through the woods. Be aware of poison ivy along the trail. Several interpretive signs along the trail describe the flora and fauna found around the nature center.

At the 0.16-mile mark, there is a spur trail that shortly rejoins Bluff Trail. The trail continues and crosses a footbridge across a drainage and then enters a glade, a small island of prairie in the woodlands. The trail has been beneath the shaded canopy until this clearing and shortly passes through another clearing. As the trail descends toward the Arkansas River, take care—there are some rocks and tree roots on the trail that could be hazardous. Descend the stairs to reach the junction of Bluff and River Trails. If you prefer a shorter hike, keep left to stay on Bluff Trail and return to the nature center. However, if you want to hike to the Arkansas River, turn right onto River Trail.

You will cross a bridge at the 0.5-mile point of the hike. The bench on the other side of the bridge is a nice spot to take a rest and listen for the barred owls described by the nearby interpretive sign. Continue north on River Trail until you reach the junction with Sandbar Trail. Both trails provide access to the river, although Sandbar Trail is more direct. Keep right at the fork to follow Sandbar Trail, which is true to its name—the trail becomes sandier as you approach the river.

Once you reach the river, Sandbar Trail disappears. Continue north until you see an opening in the woods where you can rejoin River Trail. There is a picnic table near the junction of Sandbar and River Trails. Wading in the river is popular in summer. No campfires or camping is allowed, and please pack out any trash you create.

River Trail heads west through the forest for 0.25 mile until it reaches an interesting location. At a bench at 1.19 miles, the trail turns right (north) toward a large prairie. However, if you look south you will see a giant-size wooden chair in the middle of the forest. This is a fun side trip, especially with children, to stop for a photo opportunity on, or atop, the chair. After, head north on River Trail until you reach the prairie at the 1.23-mile mark.

River Trail cuts through the southwestern corner of the prairie. However, if you'd like to extend this hike, you can follow a maintenance road along the edge of the prairie. This mowed path will loop back and reconnect with River Trail at the edge of the forest at 1.37 miles.

River Trail ends at the edge of the forest, becoming a maintenance road that leads to the naturalist's residence. Continue briefly and then turn north onto Spring Creek Trail. This trail runs parallel to Spring Creek for almost 0.25 mile before crossing the

Interesting finds await in the riparian forest.

creek via a small footbridge. Continue southeast, following the trail on the west side of Spring Creek until it reaches Kingfisher Wetland.

To return to the nature center, continue straight on Spring Creek Trail, passing Kingfisher Wetland, to rejoin the maintenance road leading to the naturalist's residence. To continue hiking, turn right (southwest) onto Lost Prairie Trail. This trail climbs through the hardwood forest for 0.5 mile until it reaches the upland prairie that lies south of the naturalist's residence and nature center. After a mostly flat and easy hike, this final section climbing through the forest will get you sweating as you return to the parking lot.

Miles and Directions

0.00 Start at the nature center.

0.04 Turn right (southeast) onto Bluff Trail.

0.16 Keep left (east) on Bluff Trail.

0.22 Turn left (east).

0.37 After descending the stairs, turn right (southeast) onto River Trail. (Bailout: Keep left/north to return to the nature center on Bluff Trail.)

River Trail, Bluff Trail, and Lost Prairie Trail Loop

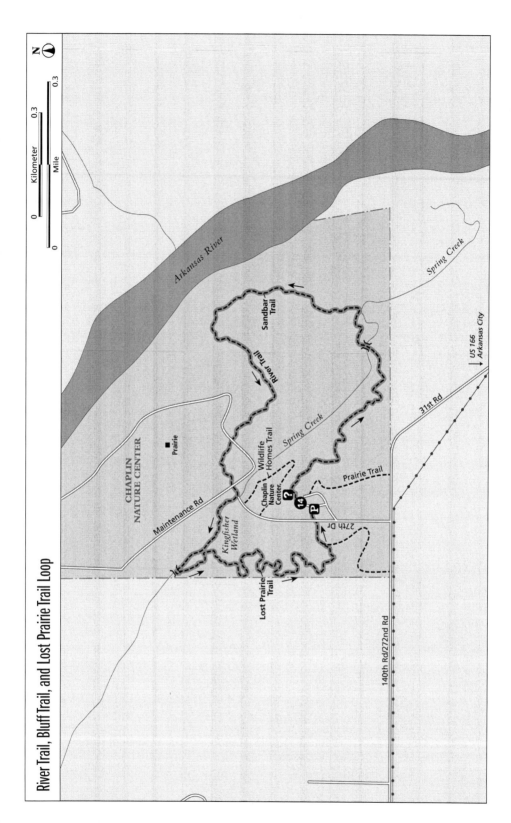

Spring Creek runs through the Chaplin Nature Center.

0.48 Bridge.

0.63 At the fork, keep right (north) to follow Sandbar Trail.

0.82 Arkansas River.

0.90 At the trail marker and picnic table, turn right (north).

0.94 Turn left (southwest).

1.19 At a bench, turn right (north) to continue on River Trail.

1.23 Continue straight (northwest) at the junction with a maintenance road.

1.34 Continue straight (west).

1.37 Turn right (north) onto Spring Creek Trail.

1.57 Cross the footbridge over Spring Creek.

1.69 At the northern end of Kingfisher Wetland, turn right (southwest) onto Lost Prairie Trail. (Option: Continue straight/southeast on Spring Creek Trail.)

2.20 Turn right (north) onto Prairie Trail.

2.26 Cross the road and continue straight (east) toward the parking lot.

2.30 Arrive at the parking lot.

Honorable Mentions

E George Stumps Nature Trail

The nearly 0.5-mile George Stumps Nature Trail is an ADA-accessible trail with excellent interpretive signage. The paved trail weaves through a windbreak, and the trees provide habitat for a number of bird species. Learn about wetland ecosystems in the adjacent Kansas Wetlands Education Center, then take a driving tour of nearby Cheyenne Bottoms, a critical stopping point on the Central Flyway for migratory birds.

George Stumps Nature Trail.

Start: Next to the shelter in the parking lot at the Kansas Wetlands Education Center
Elevation gain: 3 feet total elevation gain
Distance: 0.43 mile
Difficulty: Easy
Hiking time: Less than 1 hour
Seasons/schedule: Open year-round
Fees and permits: None
Trail contact: Kansas Wetlands Education Center, 592 NE KS 156, Great Bend 67530; (620) 566-1455; wetlandscenter.fhsu.edu/index.html
Dog-friendly: Yes

Trail surface: Paved
Land status: Managed by Kansas Wetlands Education Center
Nearest town: Great Bend, 9 miles to the southwest
Maps: USGS Ellinwood NW, KS
Other trail users: None
Special considerations: There are no restrooms if the education center is closed.
Amenities: Restrooms and water inside the education center (when open)
Maximum grade: 0%
Cell service: Adequate

Finding the trailhead: From Great Bend, head west on US 56. After 2.3 miles, turn northeast onto KS 156. Continue northwest for 6.5 miles to the Kansas Wetlands Education Center. GPS: N38°26.419' / W98°37.753'

Trail conditions: The trail is accessible to wheelchairs and strollers. There are several benches along the trail, as well as interpretive signage. The trail receives light traffic.

F Woodard Nature Trail

The Dillon Nature Center is a 100-acre urban sanctuary located in northeast Hutchinson. The 3 miles of trails have been designated as National Recreation Trails. The woodland trails lead to two ponds, while a prairie trail offers the option to extend your hike. Educational programming and a fun playscape make Dillon Nature Center a family-friendly experience.

Start: North end of the parking lot
Elevation gain: Variable, but most of the trails are fairly level.
Distance: 3 total miles of trails
Difficulty: Easy
Hiking time: Variable; 1.5–2 hours if you hike all 3 miles
Seasons/schedule: Open year-round, dawn to dusk
Fees and permits: None
Trail contact: Dillon Nature Center, 3002 E 30th Ave., Hutchinson 67502; (620) 663-7411; hutchrec.com/dillon-nature-center/
Dog-friendly: Yes, on leash
Trail surface: Natural and paved

Land status: Managed by the Dillon Nature Center
Nearest town: Hutchinson
Maps: USGS Hutchinson, KS; trail map available online
Other trail users: None
Special considerations: Collection of mushrooms, wildflowers, butterflies, or any other items is prohibited.
Amenities: Water and restrooms (when the nature center is open)
Maximum grade: Most of the trails are fairly level and easy to walk.
Cell service: Reliable

Finding the trailhead: The Dillon Nature Center is located in northeastern Hutchinson on East 30th Avenue, directly east of KS 61. The trailheads can be accessed from the parking lot. GPS: N38°5.333' / W97°52.556'

Trail conditions: The trails are well marked with signs and arrows. Due to heavy use and excellent maintenance, the trails are easy to navigate and in great condition.

Woodard Nature Trail at the Dillon Nature Center.

Flint Hills

The Flint Hills contain the largest remnant of tallgrass prairie, an ecosystem that once stretched across much of North America. The region escaped the plow because of the cherty and thin topsoil and the large presence of flint; both made the Flint Hills more suited for grazing than growing row crops. Less than 5 percent of the original tallgrass prairie remains in North America, and most of it lies in the Flint Hills. If you like prairie hikes with never-ending views of the horizon, dramatic sunsets, colorful wildflowers, and 6-foot-tall prairie grass, the Flint Hills is your perfect destination. The region was historically known as the Blue-stem Hills for the big bluestem that can grow over 6 feet tall in late summer and early autumn. Numerous conservation organizations are working to preserve this large remnant of tallgrass prairie. The Nature Conservancy partnered with the National Parks Service to create Tallgrass Prairie National Preserve. While cattle dominate the horizon in the Flint Hills, the region once was roamed by hundreds of thousands of bison. Hikers can mingle with bison on trails at the preserve. Managed by The Nature Conservancy for fifty years, the Flint Hills Tallgrass Prairie Preserve was opened to the public in 2023. Konza Prairie is a popular 8,600-acre preserve just south of Manhattan, with more than 6 miles of trails, and there are wonderful short hikes, excellent for families and wildflower enthusiasts, at Allegawaho Memorial Heritage Park and Mount Mitchell Heritage Prairie Park.

Konza Prairie.

15 Eagle Pass and Canyon Trails

Set below the dam at Tuttle Creek State Park, Eagle Pass Trail crosses a narrow peninsula with wonderful views of River Pond and Willow Lake, both excellent fishing and birding spots—bald eagles can be spotted at various times of the year. Canyon Trail takes hikers up the "Little Grand Canyon," created by the 1993 floodwater releases from the overflow spillway.

Start: Rocky Ford Campground

Elevation gain: 1,017 feet to 1,056 feet; 52 feet total elevation gain

Distance: 2.73 miles out and back

Difficulty: Easy; Canyon Trail is rougher than Eagle Pass.

Hiking time: 1–2 hours

Seasons/schedule: Open year-round

Fees and permits: Daily vehicle permit or annual state park vehicle permit required

Trail contact: Tuttle Creek State Park, 5800 River Pond Rd., Manhattan 66502; (785) 539-7941; ksoutdoors.com/State-Parks/Locations/Tuttle-Creek

Dog-friendly: Yes, on leash

Trail surface: Natural and paved surfaces

Land status: Tuttle Creek State Park (Kansas Department of Wildlife & Parks)

Nearest town: Manhattan, 7 miles to the south

Maps: USGS Manhattan, KS, and USGS Tuttle Creek Dam, KS; park map available on the website

Other trail users: Mountain bikers

Special considerations: A short section follows a main park road, so walk with caution along the side of the road.

Amenities: Water, restrooms, and camping available near the trailhead in the Rocky Ford Campground; no trail information at the trailhead

Maximum grade: 4%; while generally flat, the steepest section is on Canyon Trail, which gains about 50 feet over 0.5 mile.

Cell service: Weak service at the trailhead; adequate reception in open areas

Finding the trailhead: From Manhattan, head north on US 24/Tuttle Creek Boulevard. After 4 miles, turn right and then immediately left on River Pond Road. Continue on River Pond Road for 1.8 miles until it becomes Beach Drive. Continue on Beach Drive for 1.3 miles to Rocky Ford Campground. Keep right onto Island Loop; the trailhead is shortly after turning onto Island Loop. GPS: N39°14.800' / W96°34.927'

Trail conditions: Besides the trailhead sign, Eagle Pass is not waymarked, but the trail is easy to follow. Take caution on the park road. Canyon Trail is also not signposted; it is more difficult to navigate, as sections can be overgrown. Canyon Trail traverses loose rock and slippery natural surfaces; Eagle Pass is relatively level and wide. While not paved, strollers and wheelchairs may be able to navigate Eagle Pass Trail under dry conditions. Ticks, spiderwebs, and insects can be nuisances.

The Hike

Tuttle Creek Lake is the second-largest reservoir in Kansas. Covering 12,000 acres, with more than 100 miles of wooded shoreline, the state park is a popular outdoor recreation destination just north of Manhattan. The lake impounds the Big Blue

Canyon Trail.

River in the northernmost reaches of the Flint Hills. The dam was created by the US Army Corps of Engineers to control regular flooding of the Big Blue watershed. Tuttle Creek State Park was born as a result, with five units totaling 1,200 acres.

The Rocky Ford unit lies just south of the reservoir. This area is perfect for those looking for a more intimate lake experience. Eagle Pass Trail begins at the Rocky Ford Campground and crosses a narrow peninsula that divides River Pond and Willow Lake. Canyon Trail is slightly more difficult, as it traverses a section with geologically significant rock formations that were exposed during the 1993 flood.

Eagle Pass Trail begins near the entrance to the Rocky Ford Campground. The trail is a wide dirt path; however, do not be surprised by overgrowth in summer. Shortly after the trailhead, the trail passes a beautiful spot on the shore of River Pond on your left. There is a makeshift fire ring made of rocks, a footpath leading to the shore, and an excellent view of River Pond. The trail bends to the east away from River Pond as it continues through the woods and spiderwebs. At one point the trail passes between two towering cottonwoods.

After nearly 0.5 mile, both River Pond and Willow Lake become visible as the trail traverses the narrowest section of the peninsula and approaches the spillway channel. Look to your left at the narrow, rocky jetty for herons fishing in the shallow

Eagle Pass Trailhead.

water; you'll likely see human anglers as well. This section would be the best place to spot the raptors that give name to this trail.

Continue northeast on Eagle Pass as the trail passes two floating platforms on Willow Lake before reaching the northern trailhead and the park road. If you are out for a short hike, turn around and head south back to the Rocky Ford Campground. However, the rock formations along Canyon Trail are worth continuing the hike.

You need to follow the park road shortly to reach the trailhead for Canyon Trail, which is on the western side of the spillway channel. Canyon Trail is rougher than Eagle Pass Trail; strollers and wheelchairs may be able to handle the latter, but the former will prove too rugged. Canyon Trail will likely be overgrown in several sections during the summer, making navigation more difficult, but the contrast in scenery from Eagle Pass is worth the extra effort.

"Little Grand Canyon" was created as a result of the 1993 flood. The spillway gates were opened for three weeks to release floodwaters. Once the gates were closed and the water dissipated, 300-million-year-old rock formations were exposed. The exposed rock layers are rarely seen outside of road cuts, and the combination of five formations in one location makes the Little Grand Canyon geologically significant.

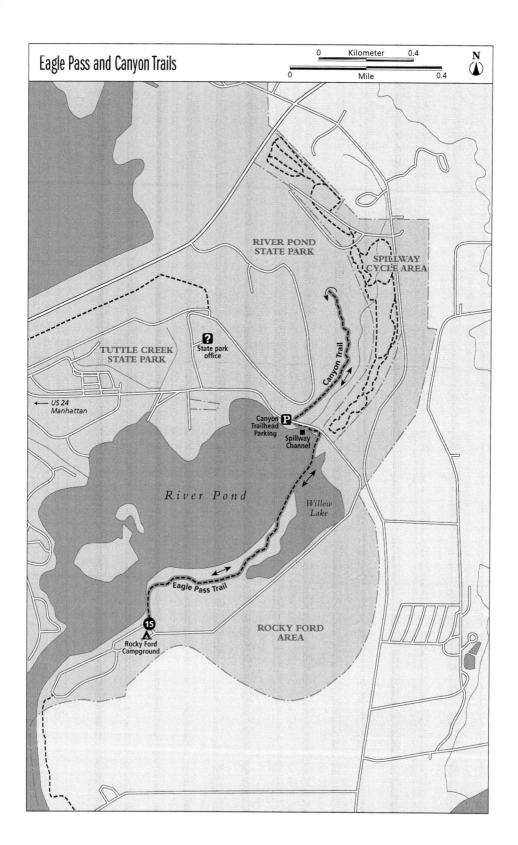

Eagle Pass and Canyon Trails

0 Kilometer 0.4

0 Mile 0.4

N

RIVER POND
STATE PARK

SPILLWAY
CYCLE AREA

TUTTLE CREEK
STATE PARK

State park
office

Canyon Trail

← US 24
Manhattan

Canyon
Trailhead
Parking

Spillway
Channel

River Pond

*Willow
Lake*

Eagle Pass Trail

ROCKY FORD
AREA

15

Rocky Ford
Campground

Tuttle Creek River Pond from Eagle Pass Trail.

Follow the narrow footpath northeast and then northwest up into the canyon. At times the footpath disappears, but the objective is to continue north. Before the trail reaches 1.5 miles (from the Eagle Pass Trailhead), it disappears in a rocky ravine choked with brush, requiring hikers to turn around and return to the Rocky Ford Campground.

Miles and Directions

0.00 Start at the Eagle Pass Trailhead.

0.68 Continue straight (northeast) onto the paved path.

0.76 Bench.

0.82 Turn left (northwest) onto the park road.

0.90 Turn right (north) into the Canyon Trailhead parking area.

1.36 Turn around and return to the Canyon Trailhead.

1.80 Turn left (southeast) onto the park road.

1.89 Turn right (southwest) onto Eagle Pass Trail.

2.73 Arrive back at the trailhead.

16 Godwin Hill Loop

Three connected loops at Konza Prairie allow hikers to explore bottomland timber, Kings Creek, and exquisite tallgrass prairie. A jewel in the Flint Hills, the prairie explodes with the bright colors of wildflowers in spring and summer and the verdant green of the prairie. Come in fall and winter as well, when the bluestem turns copper and gold. A visit to Konza Prairie is a delight to the senses and will win over any skeptic of the prairie.

Start: Trailhead kiosk on Konza Prairie Lane
Elevation gain: 1,057 feet (lowest) to 1,368 feet (highest); 479 feet total elevation gain
Distance: 6.42-mile loop
Difficulty: Moderate
Hiking time: About 3 hours
Seasons/schedule: Open daily, year-round, 6 a.m.–9 p.m.
Fees and permits: Suggested donation of $2 per person
Trail contact: Division of Biology, Kansas State University, 116 Ackert Hall, Manhattan 66506; (785) 587-0441; keep.konza.k-state.edu/visit/index.html
Dog-friendly: No
Trail surface: Crushed rock and natural (grass and packed earth)

Land status: Konza Prairie Biological Station (Kansas State University and The Nature Conservancy)
Nearest town: Manhattan, 8 miles to the north
Maps: USGS Swede Creek, KS; trail map available on the website
Other trail users: None
Special considerations: Collection or removal of flowers, rocks, feathers, or other materials from the conservation area is prohibited. Trails are closed when the bridge is out or during prescribed burns (usually in April).
Amenities: Porta-potty at the trailhead and a second one near the Hokanson Homestead area; no other restroom facilities
Maximum grade: 17%; the trail climbs about 250 feet over the first mile of the hike.
Cell service: Adequate to above average at the trailhead and along the trail

Finding the trailhead: From Manhattan, take KS 177 over the Kansas River. Immediately past the river turn right (west) onto McDowell Creek Road (this road skirts the river and goes under the "KS" hill). Proceed 6 miles until you see the sign for Konza Prairie on your left.

From I-70, take exit 307 and turn north. Proceed 4.5 miles east on McDowell Creek Road; the entrance to Konza Prairie will be on your right. GPS: N39°6.405' / W96°36.538'

Trail conditions: The trails are in excellent condition and superbly waymarked. There are trail markers at major junctions. The trails are not accessible to wheelchairs or strollers. Trail surfaces may be muddy after recent rains. The only serious climb is at the beginning of the hike; the rest of the route is level or descending.

The Hike

Konza Prairie Biological Station, jointly owned by Kansas State University and The Nature Conservancy, is an outdoor laboratory dedicated to scientific research,

Suspension bridge over Kings Creek.

conservation, education, and outdoor recreation. Named for the Kaw, or Kanza, who were stewards of the land for thousands of years, Konza Prairie is emblematic of the Flint Hills, the largest remaining tract of tallgrass prairie in the United States. Long-term research has taken place at Konza Prairie since 1980 and continues to this day. Be respectful of research projects while hiking at this pristine and beautiful slice of remnant prairie.

There are three loop options at Konza Prairie, making hiking the trails convenient for anyone. The 2.6-mile Nature Trail loop climbs up a hill to an excellent viewpoint, down a drainage to the Hokanson Homestead, and back to the trailhead. Kings Creek Loop adds 2 miles to the Nature Trail, and the Godwin Hill Loop adds another 1.5 miles to explore the breadth of Konza Prairie. This hike follows Godwin Hill but offers opportunities to cut the hike short at the junctions for the Nature Trail and Kings Creek loops.

The trail is a wide, crushed rock path at the trailhead. It crosses two footbridges not far from the trailhead, the second a bouncy rope footbridge (only three people can cross at a time). The rope footbridge crosses a creek with steep banks and is likely to be the site of scientific research, so please stay on the trail. After the footbridge, there is a wooden stand to take a photograph and send it to Kansas State researchers.

Godwin Hill Loop.

After 0.3 mile, you reach a junction where the Nature Trail loop begins. Continue straight (east) to follow the loop clockwise. The trail climbs 200 feet over nearly 0.5 mile to reach an outstanding viewpoint overlooking Konza Prairie and the Kings Creek watershed. The trail heads northeast along the top of the ridge, reaching the junction of Nature Trail and Kings Creek Loops at 1.34 miles. There are three large boulders to rest on at the junction. If you want to complete the shorter Nature Trail loop, turn right (south) and go downhill toward the Hokanson Homestead. Otherwise, continue east onto Kings Creek Loop.

Kings Creek Loop continues east along the ridgetop for nearly 1 mile. Take in the views all around, with the Kansas River and the city of Manhattan visible to the north. Bobwhites, dickcissels, and meadowlarks provide the soundtrack as you hike along the ridge. The junction of Kings Creek and Godwin Hill Loops is at the 2.23-mile mark. Turn south if you want to hike the shorter 4.6-mile Kings Creek Loop. Godwin Hill Loop continues east for more than 0.5 mile until it reaches a gravel road at 2.91 miles.

Turn south onto the gravel road, which runs parallel to a barbed-wire fence. You will follow this gravel road for 0.4 mile until you reach a well-marked turn at 3.28 miles. There is information about the nearby ecological monitoring station, and it is

Godwin Hill Loop

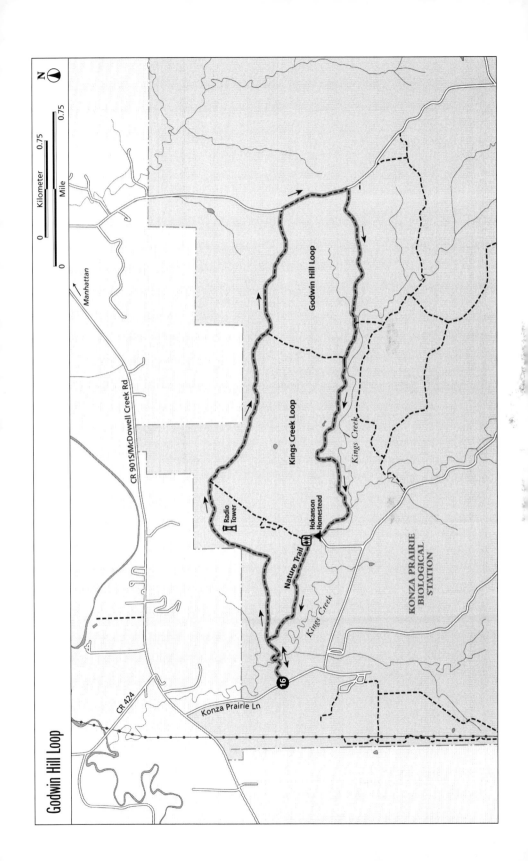

worth taking a break to read about it. Continue south along the ridge until the trail turns west and begins to head downhill toward Kings Creek.

As you reach Kings Creek at the 4-mile mark, you will welcome the shade of trees lining the creek, as there hasn't been any shade since the trailhead. You'll cross a couple of streams, likely dry in summer, as Godwin Hill Loop continues west toward the junctions with Kings Creek and Nature Trail Loops. The creek runs right along the trail at the 5.3-mile mark, also where part of the hillside has eroded on your right, exposing the limestone layers that are characteristic of the Flint Hills.

Turn right (north) at 5.39 miles and pass several buildings that were part of the Hokanson Homestead, then continue straight at the junction at 5.48 miles. Back on Nature Trail Loop, it's 0.5 mile back to the beginning of Nature Trail Loop, where you cross the two footbridges to return to the trailhead.

Miles and Directions

0.00 Start at the trailhead.

0.09 Footbridge.

0.15 Rope footbridge (only three persons at a time).

0.32 Reach a junction and continue straight (east).

0.75 Viewpoint.

1.34 Continue straight (east) onto Kings Creek Loop.

2.23 Continue straight (east) onto Godwin Hill Loop. (Bailout: Turn right/south to continue on Kings Creek Loop.)

2.91 Turn right (south) onto a gravel road to continue on Godwin Hill Loop.

3.28 Turn right (west) to continue on Godwin Hill Loop.

4.21 Continue straight (west).

5.39 Turn right (north) and pass the Hokanson Homestead.

5.48 Continue straight (west) following the sign for the parking area.

6.07 Turn left (west).

6.21 Rope footbridge.

6.27 Footbridge.

6.42 Arrive back at the trailhead.

17 Scenic Overlook Loop

The Tallgrass Prairie National Preserve protects nearly 11,000 acres of grasslands. A herd of bison roam Windmill Pasture and West Traps Pasture, which are open to hikers. The scenic overlook provides unbroken vistas of unplowed, treeless prairie. Bring plenty of water, sunscreen, and proper clothing, as there is no shade on almost the entire trail. A field guide can help identify 300 species of wildflowers and 70 grasses. If you brought your canine companion, three nature trails are pet-friendly. Bottomland Trail is wheelchair accessible when dry.

Start: Tallgrass Prairie National Preserve Visitor Center

Elevation gain: 1,222 feet to 1,495 feet; 417 feet total elevation gain

Distance: 7.23-mile loop

Difficulty: Moderate

Hiking time: 3–3.5 hours

Seasons/schedule: Open daily, year-round

Fees and permits: None

Trail contact: Tallgrass Prairie National Preserve, 2480B KS Hwy. 177, Strong City 66869; (620) 273-8494; www.nps.gov/tapr/index.htm

Dog-friendly: Leashed pets are allowed on the Southwind Nature Trail section of this hike; pets are not allowed on any other trail described in this hike.

Trail surface: Gravel road and natural surface (dirt and grass)

Land status: Tallgrass Prairie National Preserve (National Parks Service)

Nearest town: Strong City, 3 miles to the south

Maps: USGS Strong City, KS; trail map available at the visitor center and online

Other trail users: Foot traffic only on hiking trails

Special considerations: The presence of bison in Windmill and West Traps Pastures may require off-trail hiking if bison are on or near the trails. Always give sufficient distance, at least 100 yards, to bison. If unsure, turn around or wait until the bison move away. Never approach bison under any circumstances.

Amenities: Restrooms and water available at the visitor center; ample parking at the visitor center; park maps available outside the visitor center if it is closed

Maximum grade: 9%; the trail climbs 100 feet over the first 0.5 mile from the visitor center to Windmill Pasture. The other significant climb is from the entrance to Big Pasture to the scenic overlook, climbing 100 feet over 0.6 mile.

Cell service: Coverage at the visitor center and parking lot; reception may be spotty in the open pastures but is generally adequate throughout the entire hike.

Finding the trailhead: Tallgrass Prairie National Preserve is located 3 miles north of Strong City on KS 177. The trailhead for this hike is on the west side of the visitor center. GPS: N38°25.934' / W96°33.511'

Trail conditions: The trails are not accessible to wheelchairs or strollers. Heavy rains may cause surfaces to become muddy and rutted. The trails are well maintained but are not waymarked; please take a physical and/or digital copy of the trails map. The trails receive moderate to heavy foot traffic. This is a natural area; watch for snakes, poison ivy, and wild animals.

Stream crossing on Davis Trail.

The Hike

For thousands of years, the tallgrass prairie ecosystem of North America provided habitat for hundreds of species of plants, notably big bluestem and a dizzying array of wildflowers. Herds of countless bison roamed the prairie, followed by indigenous peoples who used fire to manage the land. In less than one hundred years after the first arrival of Europeans, the prairie became almost unrecognizable to its original stewards. The bison disappeared, hunted to near extinction, and the prairie was plowed under. Some remnants remained untouched, however, thanks to the difficulty of dominating its land.

The Flint Hills of Kansas are one of those untouched remnants of the once vast tallgrass prairie, saved by the rocky substrate that lay beneath the big bluestem. It took decades for the National Park Service to recognize the ecological value of grasslands, instead preferring mountainous aesthetics. The prairie, however, not only offers ecological value but also simple beauty and incredible biodiversity.

Tallgrass Prairie National Preserve is a joint public-private partnership that protects nearly 11,000 acres of grasslands. Bison were introduced in 2009 from Wind Cave National Park in South Dakota. Bison are essential to the prairie ecosystem, as is fire. About one-third of the preserve is burned every year to manage the tallgrass prairie ecosystem. As you hike the trails, be mindful in pastures where bison are present. Prescribed burns are typically done in spring, so check the preserve's website or call ahead before making plans to visit.

The amount of trails allows visitors a plethora of options. A classic day hike traverses Windmill Pasture to reach the scenic overlook with sweeping views of the prairie. Beginning on the west side of the visitor center, head northwest on a gravel doubletrack that is used by small bus tours. A strenuous 0.5-mile climb brings you to Windmill Pasture. As you head west, then northwest, you will likely encounter bison. Keep a safe distance of at least 100 yards, stopping or turning around if necessary—don't risk a dangerous encounter just to complete a hike.

The trail bends to the northwest at 1.4 miles, where you can also turn south onto Ranch Legacy Trail if you want to hike Crusher Hill Loop. Otherwise, continue on the path northwest and soon pass Windmill Pasture Hill on your left. There are few trees—only in the distance in draws and drainages—so drink plenty of water as you continue north. After more than 2.5 miles of hiking, you will reach the entrance to Big Pasture.

If you want to explore the far northern reaches of the preserve, keep left at 3.15 miles to follow Prairie Fire Loop. We will continue east, climbing to the highest point on the hike, the scenic overlook at 1,495 feet. The views are incredible atop the overlook (there is no marker or benches). After taking in the views, continue east to follow Prairie Fire Loop, which becomes a mowed grass path. This section can get muddy and accumulate standing water after heavy rain.

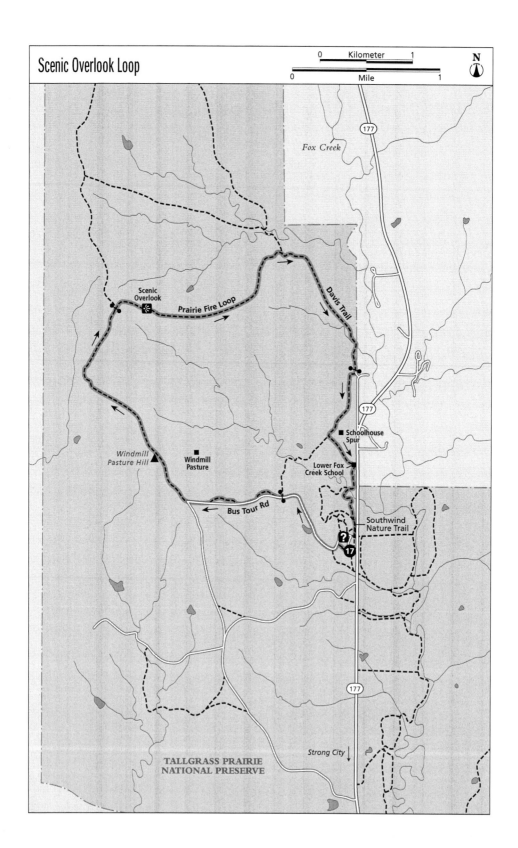

Scenic Overlook Loop

0   Kilometer   1

0   Mile   1

N

Fox Creek

177

Scenic
Overlook

Prairie Fire Loop

Davis Trail

177

Schoolhouse
Spur

*Windmill
Pasture Hill*

Windmill
Pasture

Lower Fox
Creek School

Bus Tour Rd

Southwind
Nature Trail

?

17

177

Strong City

**TALLGRASS PRAIRIE
NATIONAL PRESERVE**

At 4.3 miles, the trail bends northeast and begins to descend toward the junction with Davis Trail, which is reached at 4.64 miles. Keep right to head east and then south on Davis Trail. The landscape changes, with the wooded Fox Creek on your left. The trees provide a bit of shade in places, a welcome relief if you're hiking on a sunny day. Manage the water crossing at 5.5 miles, then continue south toward the corrals. You'll enter West Traps Pasture, where bison may be present, and continue south to reach the junction with Schoolhouse Spur at 6.26 miles. Take the spur southeast toward Lower Fox Creek School, then follow Southwind Nature Trail to the Ranch Complex and visitor center parking lot.

There are over 40 total miles of trails to explore at the preserve, from the backcountry trails that probe deep into the protected prairie as described above, to nature trails where pets are allowed on leash, such as Southwind Nature Trail. The Bottomland Trail is wheelchair accessible, while all 40 miles of trails are accessible to visitors with visual impairments using a handheld Trekker Breeze+.

Miles and Directions

0.00 Start from the visitor center and head northwest through the field toward an open gate.

0.07 Turn left (southwest) onto the gravel road.

0.13 Continue on the gravel road.

0.68 Enter Windmill Pasture via the hiking gate.

1.40 Continue straight (northwest) on Scenic Overlook Trail. (Option: Turn left/south to access Ranch Legacy Trail and Crusher Hill Loop.)

2.67 Use the gate to enter Big Pasture and head north on the gravel road.

3.15 Keep right (northeast) on Scenic Overlook Trail. (Option: Keep left/north to follow Prairie Fire Loop.)

3.39 Scenic overlook.

3.43 Keep right (east) to follow Prairie Fire Loop.

4.64 Reach a junction and keep right (east) onto Davis Trail.

5.54 Water crossing.

5.78 Use the hiking gate to enter West Traps Pasture and continue south.

6.26 Turn left (southeast) onto Schoolhouse Spur.

6.50 Gate.

6.54 Lower Fox Creek School; head south through the parking lot to the Southwind Nature Trail entrance.

6.76 Water crossing.

6.78 Keep left (south).

7.08 At the kiosk, continue straight (south) and pass through the gate; continue south along the highway, passing the Ranch Complex on your right.

7.23 Arrive at the visitor center parking lot.

18 Bluestem Trail

As of summer 2023, Flint Hills Tallgrass Prairie Preserve is the newest addition to publicly accessible lands in the Flint Hills of Kansas. The Nature Conservancy has owned the land for fifty years, but it was finally opened to the public with wonderful trails, albeit with work yet needed. Bluestem Trail is a nearly 3-mile journey across the prairie that includes a water crossing over the wooded South Fork of the Cottonwood River. For the more adventurous, tackle Prairie Chicken Trail, which (as of July 2023) required off-trail navigation as the trail disappeared near the stream.

Start: Trailhead opposite the parking area on Northeast 150th Street
Elevation gain: 1,440 feet to 1,539 feet; 164 feet total elevation gain
Distance: 2.9-mile loop
Difficulty: Moderate due to lack of shade and remote location
Hiking time: 1.5–2 hours
Seasons/schedule: Open during daylight hours only
Fees and permits: None
Trail contact: 16999 NE 150th St., Cassoday 66842; (785) 233-4400; nature.org/en-us/get-involved/how-to-help/places-we-protect/flint-hills-tallgrass-prairie-preserve/; email: kansas@tnc.org
Dog-friendly: Yes, on leash
Trail surface: Natural prairie grass path
Land status: Flint Hills Tallgrass Prairie Preserve (The Nature Conservancy)

Nearest town: Cassoday, 6.5 miles to the west (country store only; gas station located 5.5 miles north of Cassoday on I-35)
Maps: USGS Matfield Green SE, KS; trail map available online
Other trail users: Pedestrian traffic only, except for wheelchairs
Special considerations: There is no water at the trailhead; the only shade is along the creek. No camping, hunting, trapping, fishing, or fires. Take nothing but pictures. Fossil hunting and collecting of any kind—including rocks, flowers, and plants, even if found lying on the ground—is not allowed.
Amenities: Portable toilet, no water
Maximum grade: From flat to 15%, with a few short, steep hills
Cell service: Weak due to the preserve's remote location

Finding the trailhead: From Cassoday, head east on Northeast 150th Street/1st Street Road/Sunbarger Street, passing Fox Lake to the south. After 6.3 miles, turn right (south) into the parking area. The trailhead is opposite the parking area on the north side of Northeast 150th Street. GPS: N38°2.582' / W96°31.375'

Trail conditions: Natural prairie grass path, approximately 5 feet wide; slope ranges from flat to 15 percent, with a few short, steep hills; 4 stream crossings, which may be slick; trail markers at major junctions. Prairie Chicken Trail disappears near the stream near the northern boundary.

The Hike

The Nature Conservancy managed the land on the Flint Hills Tallgrass Prairie Preserve for fifty years before opening it to the public in summer 2023. The land that

Vista Overlook.

Bluestem Trailhead.

makes up the preserve was purchased in 1972 and 1973, and The Nature Conservancy named it the Flint Hills Tallgrass Prairie Preserve. However, that name will not last, as the organization is seeking to deepen its ties with the indigenous communities that were the original stewards of these lands. For more than 13,000 years, indigenous peoples have lived on, hunted on, managed, and cultivated these lands. The Nature Conservancy is taking the time necessary to deepen their understanding of the land's history and the people that depended on it.

In the meantime, the Flint Hills Tallgrass Prairie Preserve offers several options for hikers to explore the tallgrass prairie ecosystem. The preserve is remote, but The Nature Conservancy has done an excellent job of providing amenities at the trailhead to facilitate outdoor recreation and an appreciation of this overlooked ecosystem. When the author visited in late July 2023, soon after the preserve opened to the public, there was a portable toilet and multiple interpretive panels explaining the history and future of the preserve, as well as the natural and cultural history. The trailhead is clearly marked opposite the parking area, and the major junctions of the trails are marked. There are no physical maps available at the parking area or trailhead, but there is a panel at the trailhead where you can snap a picture if you haven't already downloaded the map on the preserve's website.

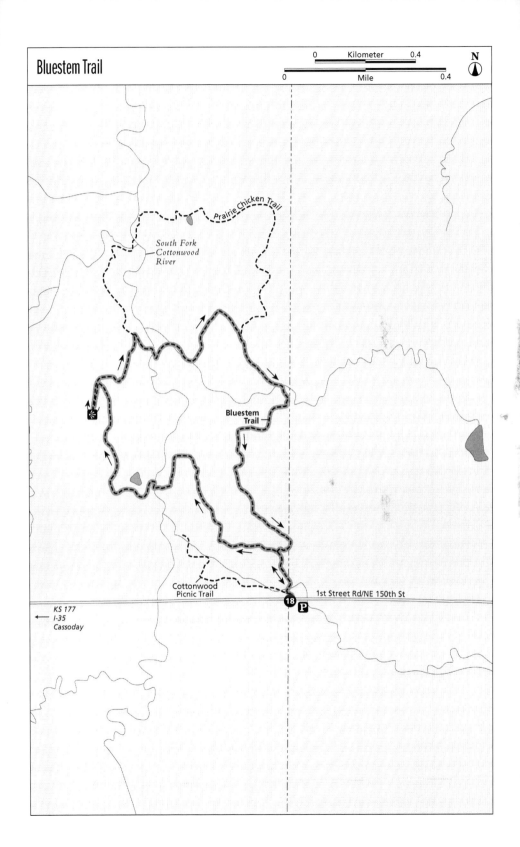

Bluestem Trail

0 Kilometer 0.4

0 Mile 0.4

N

Prairie Chicken Trail

South Fork Cottonwood River

Bluestem Trail

Cottonwood Picnic Trail

18 P 1st Street Rd/NE 150th St

KS 177
I-35
Cassoday

The majority of the trails were in excellent condition when the author visited, with the exception of the far northern section of Prairie Chicken Trail near the stream. The trail here disappeared on both sides. However, with a copy of the map and a GPX track, in addition to savvy trail finding and navigation, adventurous hikers can complete the 4.5-mile loop of Bluestem and Prairie Chicken Trails. The entirety of Bluestem Trail was navigable and well maintained, but the stream crossings at the 1.5-mile mark did require navigation skills. Cottonwood Picnic Trail is a short out-and-back trail that leads to a picnic area beneath the shade of cottonwoods on the appropriately named South Fork of the Cottonwood River.

If you are looking to experience the solitude and vast vistas of the Flint Hills, without the trail traffic that Tallgrass Prairie National Preserve attracts, then the trails at the Flint Hills Tallgrass Prairie Preserve are an excellent choice. Just 7 miles from I-35, you don't have to venture far to experience one of the last truly wild places in Kansas.

Miles and Directions

0.00 Start from the trailhead and head north.

0.14 Keep left (west) at the fork.

0.69 Stream crossing.

1.15 Reach a junction; turn left (south) onto Vista Overlook Trail.

1.21 Vista Overlook; turn around and continue north onto Bluestem Trail.

1.48 Turn right (east) to stay on Bluestem Trail.

1.54 Stream crossing.

1.60 Stream crossing.

1.88 Stone bench.

1.97 At the junction of Bluestem and Prairie Chicken Trails, keep right (southeast) on Bluestem Trail.

2.25 Bench.

2.78 Turn left (south) toward the trailhead.

2.88 Arrive back at the trailhead.

19 Pioneer Nature Trail

The Pioneer Nature Trail is a 1.17-mile loop with an option for a shorter loop through tallgrass prairie and woodland just south of Council Grove Lake. The hike is an excellent option for those traveling the Flint Hills National Scenic Byway, which begins in nearby Council Grove. The area is not only ecologically but also culturally important—many sites on and around the trail are related to Native American history, the Santa Fe Trail, and pioneer settlement.

Start: Trailhead just west of the US Army Corps of Engineers Lake Office
Elevation gain: 1,253 to 1,322 feet; 92 feet total elevation gain
Distance: 1.17-mile loop
Difficulty: Easy
Hiking time: About 1 hour
Seasons/schedule: Open daily year-round, dawn to dusk
Fees and permits: Day-use fee or annual pass required
Trail contact: Council Grove Project Office, US Army Corps of Engineers, 945 Lake Rd., Council Grove 66846; (620) 767-5195; www.swt .usace.army.mil/Locations/Tulsa-District -Lakes/Kansas/Council-Grove-Lake/

Dog-friendly: Yes, on leash
Trail surface: Mowed grass and natural surface
Land status: Council Grove Lake (US Army Corps of Engineers)
Nearest town: Council Grove, 1.5 miles to the southeast
Maps: USGS Council Grove Lake, KS
Other trail users: None
Special considerations: The shorter loop passes through a wooded area, offering more shade than the longer loop described in this chapter.
Amenities: Restrooms, camping, picnic area
Maximum grade: 7%; mostly level trail with only gentle ascents and descents
Cell service: Adequate to above average

Finding the trailhead: From Council Grove, head north on Lake Road. After 1 mile, turn left (south) onto Jerry Moran Roadway/Dam Road to reach the Council Grove Project Office parking lot and trailhead for the hike. GPS: N38°40.588' / W96°30.619'

Trail conditions: The trail is well maintained and easy to navigate. There are markers and signage at the trailhead, and the mowed paths are wide and regularly maintained. Ticks, chiggers, and mosquitoes can be problematic in summer. The trail receives light to moderate foot traffic.

The Hike

Council Grove gets its name from a meeting between the Osage tribe and US government agents in 1825. The area had long been attractive to both Native Americans and pioneers, as the reliable water source, grazing land for horses, and timber for fuel were valuable in the Great Plains. The area was an important waypoint for those on their way to Sante Fe.

The reservoir that attracts outdoor recreationists was created more than one hundred years after the council meeting between the Osage and US government agents. It was created for flood control, water resources, and outdoor recreation. There are

Stone trail marker on Pioneer Nature Trail.

Wildflowers blooming along the trail.

several campgrounds, boat ramps, and other outdoor recreation amenities around the lake. Unfortunately, there are not many hiking trails, which makes the Pioneer Nature Trail all the more attractive.

Ticks, chiggers, and mosquitos are nuisances in the summer months. Hikers who stay on the trail and out of the tall grass or woods will avoid these pesky insects and arachnids. If you want to step off the trail, insect repellent is highly recommended in addition to permethrin-treated clothing. Poison ivy is another hazard to be aware of

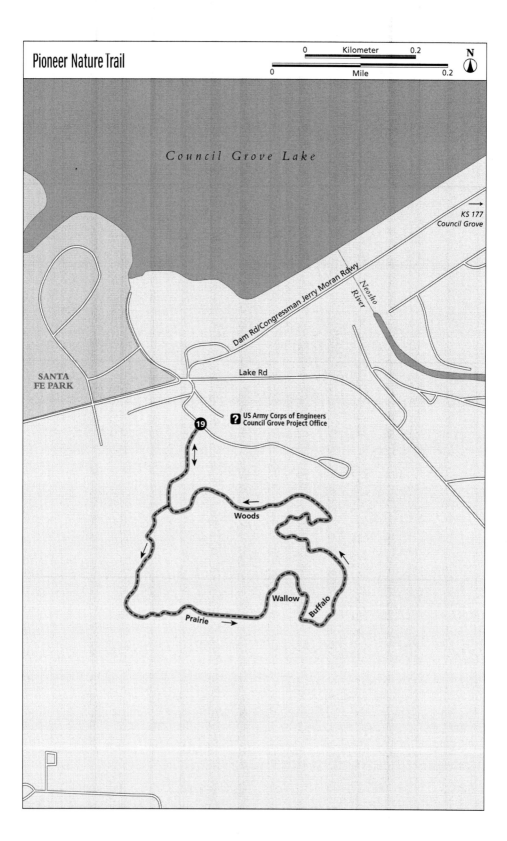

Pioneer Nature Trail

Council Grove Lake

KS 177
Council Grove

Dam Rd/Congressman Jerry Moran Rdwy

Neosho River

Lake Rd

SANTA
FE PARK

US Army Corps of Engineers
Council Grove Project Office

19

Woods

Wallow

Buffalo

Prairie

while hiking the Pioneer Nature Trail. Hikers who stay on the trail and out of the tall grass or woods are generally safe from poison ivy. If you want to step off the trail, having a keen eye on the plants and your surroundings will help prevent brushing up against poison ivy.

The trails consist of two loops. The first was created in 1981 and is approximately 0.75 mile long. The second loop, the Buffalo Wallow Loop, was created in 2006 and extends the trails further south, totaling 0.5 mile. Combine the trails for a leisurely yet rewarding 1.25-mile-long loop through Flint Hills tallgrass prairie and shady woodland.

There is excellent signage at the trailhead, and the stone markers make navigating the first stretch of the hike easy until reaching the wooded section. The trails are wide, mowed paths through the prairie and woods. There are no intersecting trails, so navigation is easy. The only decision you have to make is whether you complete the shorter loop through mainly woodland or extend the hike by following the Buffalo Wallow Loop through the southernmost section of the trail system.

The Buffalo Wallow Loop is worth the additional mileage, as there is a bench with an excellent view of the sunset; it's also a great place to sit and watch for grassland birds and pollinators. The trail gets its name from an old buffalo wallow that is on the southeastern part of the loop. In addition to the signage at the trailhead, there are a few interpretive panels along the trails that describe the tallgrass prairie ecosystem and the buffalo wallows.

Miles and Directions

0.00 Start at the trailhead.

0.10 Keep right (south) at the fork.

0.15 Keep right (south) onto Buffalo Wallow Loop.

0.28 Bench.

0.50 Bench.

0.74 Keep right (northeast). (Option: Turn left/northwest and cross the footbridge.)

0.77 Footbridge.

0.79 Culvert and bench.

0.82 Footbridge.

0.90 Footbridge and bench.

0.98 Footbridge.

1.05 Turn right (north).

1.17 Arrive back at the trailhead.

20 Kanza Heritage Trail

In 2002, the Kaw Nation dedicated Allegawaho Memorial Heritage Park as their return to the state of Kansas after their forced removal in 1873. The park is highlighted by the 35-foot limestone spire, the Monument to the Unknown Kanza Warrior. The Kanza Heritage Trail loops through beautiful prairie and peaceful woods, with thoughtful pause points located along the trail. The Little John Creek Valley Overlook provides sweeping views of the Flint Hills. A proposed visitor center will add interpretive information for visitors.

Start: South 525 Road, just north of Flint Hills Nature Trail
Elevation gain: 1,214 feet to 1,346 feet; 125 feet total elevation gain
Distance: 2.08-mile loop
Difficulty: Easy
Hiking time: 1–1.5 hours
Seasons/schedule: Open year-round
Fees and permits: None
Trail contact: Kaw Nation; (580) 269-2552; kawnation.gov; kawmission.org/places/kaw mission/reconnectionshistoriccouncilgrove22.htm
Dog-friendly: Yes
Trail surface: Mowed grass
Land status: Allegawaho Memorial Heritage Park (Kaw Nation)
Nearest town: Council Grove, 4 miles to the northwest

Maps: USGS Council Grove, KS; trail map available online
Other trail users: None
Special considerations: The Kaw Nation requests that no one approach the Kanza Monument. You can pick up a map and get more information about the tour of Allegawaho Memorial Heritage Park at the Kaw Mission State Historic Site (500 North Mission, Council Grove 66846; 620-307-2754).
Amenities: No amenities at the trailhead; toilet near Grandfather Oak on the northern end of the loop
Maximum grade: 8%; the steepest section, beginning at the 0.8-mile mark, climbs 60 feet in 0.1 mile.
Cell service: Adequate service at the trailhead and along the trail

Finding the trailhead: From Council Grove, head southeast on Dunlap Road. After 3.3 miles, turn east onto Four Mile Road/X Avenue for 0.4 mile, then turn north onto South 525 Road. Pass the Agency Building ruins and cross over the Flint Hills Nature Trail. The small parking area at the trailhead will be on the west side of the road. GPS: N38°37.646' / W96°25.904'

Trail conditions: The mowed grass trail is easy to follow. There are no trail markers, but with the online map and a GPX track, it is easy to navigate. The trail follows the edge of the prairie and woodland on the west half of the loop. As of May 2023, there were pink ribbons throughout the wooded section; do not follow these or any paths in the woods. The grass may be long and will be wet early in the morning. Ticks and biting insects will be a nuisance in the warmer months.

The Hike

Allegawaho Memorial Heritage Park is a 168-acre park that was established and dedicated on April 20, 2002 by the Kaw Nation. On the occasion, Kaw Nation park

Grandfather Oak.

Kaw Tribal Seal (front) and the Monument to the Unknown Kanza Warrior.

director Betty Durkee said, "This officially marks the return of the Kanzas to the state that bears their name." (The Kanza were forcibly removed from Kansas in 1873.)

As of summer 2023, the park consists of several features, most notably the Monument to the Unknown Kanza Warrior. The Kaw Nation requests that no one approach the monument. The 35-foot limestone tower was erected in 1925 by locals to commemorate the Kanza people as well as to honor an unknown warrior whose remains were found in an eroded streambed. The Kaw Nation plans to construct a visitor center and a replica of a bark lodge. There is a pavilion in the southwest section of the park on the edge of the woodland.

The hike begins 0.1 mile north of the Agency Building ruins; the Flint Hills Nature Trail runs directly south of the trailhead. Head east on the mowed path to shortly reach Pause Point #1. A large Kaw Tribal Seal is positioned with the Monument to the Unknown Kanza Warrior in the distance behind it. The text around the edge of the seal is a prayer that reads: "Wakanda—Bless all who walk here. May we know and respect all your creation and what you have taught our people. Wiblaha."

The trail bends to head north, with great views of the monument on your left and the Little John Creek Valley on your right to the east. The trail climbs gently through the prairie, bends to the west, then heads north again. The steep but short

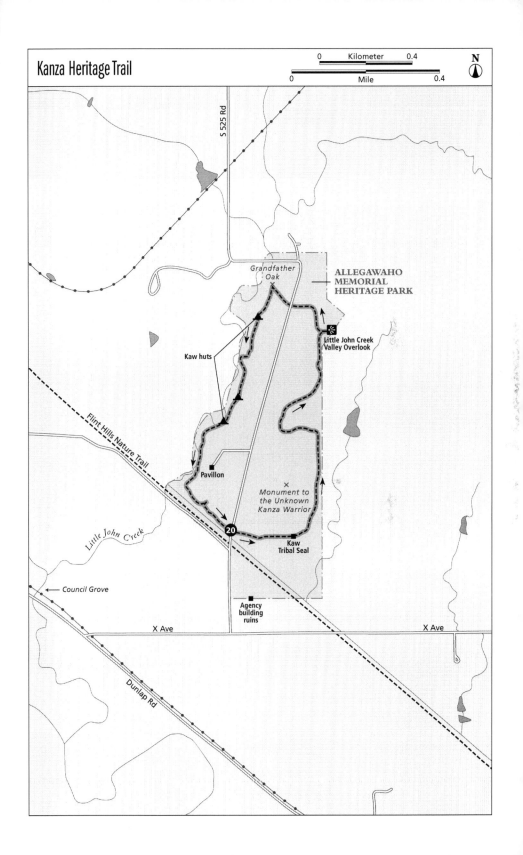

Kanza Heritage Trail

0   Kilometer   0.4

0   Mile   0.4

N

S 525 Rd

Grandfather
Oak

ALLEGAWAHO
MEMORIAL
HERITAGE PARK

Little John Creek
Valley Overlook

Kaw huts

Flint Hills Nature Trail

Pavillon

Monument to
the Unknown
Kanza Warrior

Little John Creek

20

Kaw
Tribal Seal

Council Grove

Agency
building
ruins

X Ave

X Ave

Dunlap Rd

climb reaches the Little John Creek Valley Overlook at the 1-mile mark of the hike. The trail then descends steeply toward South 525 Road; cross the road and continue heading west toward the trees.

Before you turn south to continue on the trail, find the Grandfather Oak, an immense bur oak that predates the Kanza settlement of this valley. The trail continues south along the edge of the prairie, with the woods on your right to the west. You will pass the ruins of three stone huts that were part of the 138 huts built by the US government for the Kanza people, who used them as horse stables instead of living quarters. You will also pass near the Little John Creek as the trail continues south into the woods. There is a picnic area at 1.8 miles; an overgrown trail leads to the pavilion that you can see through the trees to the east. Pause Point #2 marks the conclusion of the hike. Sixteen Kanza clan camp names are engraved in the outer rim of the circle.

After your hike, make a stop in Council Grove, which is 4 miles to the northwest of Allegawaho Memorial Heritage Park. Dubbed the "Main Street of the Flint Hills," the town has quaint shops and a handful of dining options. The Neosho Riverwalk is a 1-mile paved trail that begins on Main Street and links to the Flint Hills Nature Trail on the south side of town. The Flint Hills National Scenic Byway also passes through Council Grove. The 47-mile scenic drive offers wonderful vistas of the tall-grass prairie and is a delight to drive in spring and summer as the prairie turns a verdant green and explodes with wildflowers.

Miles and Directions

0.00 Start at the trailhead and head right (east).

0.20 Sovereign Nation of the Kaw marker.

0.90 Turn right (east).

1.00 Little John Creek Valley Overlook.

1.10 Cross South 525 Road and continue west.

1.20 Near Grandfather Oak and the toilets, turn left (south).

1.30 Wah Sko Mi A's hut.

1.60 Kick A Poo's hut.

1.80 Picnic area.

2.00 Pause Point #2 and earth lodge.

2.08 Arrive back at the trailhead.

21 Mount Mitchell Historical Trail

Hike at Mount Mitchell through tallgrass prairie brimming with wildflowers in spring and summer and 6-foot-tall bluestem in the fall. The song of dickcissels and meadowlarks will fill the air as you hike to the 1,223-foot summit that stands out from the surrounding Flint Hills tallgrass prairie. Natural history is not the only draw to Mount Mitchell; the park is steeped in cultural history as well.

Start: Parking area at the end of Mitchell Prairie Lane

Elevation gain: 1,080 feet to 1,223 feet; 157 feet total elevation gain

Distance: 1.8-mile loop

Difficulty: Easy but with gradual inclines

Hiking time: About 1 hour

Seasons/schedule: Open year-round, dawn to dusk. Spring and summer are excellent for wildflowers; in fall the big bluestem reaches up to 7 feet tall.

Fees and permits: None

Trail contact: Mount Mitchell Prairie Guards, PO Box 136, Wamego 66547; (785) 221-4061; mountmitchellprairie.org

Dog-friendly: Yes, on leash

Trail surface: Gravel and mowed grass

Land status: Mount Mitchell Heritage Prairie Park (Mount Mitchell Prairie Guards)

Nearest town: Wamego, 4.5 miles to the north

Maps: USGS Wamego, KS; trail map displayed on the trailhead kiosk

Other trail users: None

Special considerations: Removal of plants and animals from the park is strictly forbidden.

Amenities: None

Maximum grade: 9%; the trail climbs 100 feet from the trailhead to the top of Mount Mitchell over 0.3 mile.

Cell service: Adequate to above average

Finding the trailhead: From Wamego, head south on KS 99. After 4 miles, turn left (east) onto Mitchell Prairie Lane. Reach the parking lot and trailhead after 0.5 mile. GPS: N39°8.635' / W96°17.772'

Trail conditions: The trail is well maintained, wide, clean, and easy to follow. Ticks will be present roughly April through October, perhaps longer. There is no shade with the exception of a small grove of trees on the southern flank of Mount Mitchell. Storms can roll in quickly during the summer, and there is no shelter at the park. The trail receives moderate foot traffic.

The Hike

Mount Mitchell Heritage Prairie is managed by a group of local volunteers and supporters from around the country known as the Mount Mitchell Prairie Guards. The nonprofit's vision is "to create an outdoor place where Kansas youth can experience and learn about the tallgrass prairie, and at the same time develop a sense of place and pride in the region's rich history." School classes from the surrounding area visit the park every year to learn about the prairie and the park's unique natural and cultural history.

Mount Mitchell summit.

Limestone and shale can be seen on sections of the 2.5-mile trail system, evidence of the inland sea that covered the Great Plains millions of years ago. Quartzite boulders strewn about the prairie were deposited by glaciers hundreds of thousands of years ago. Mount Mitchell has a wealth of recent history as well. The hill is a sacred ancestral burial site for Native Americans. In the mid-1800s, a group of free-state abolitionists arrived with the aim to keep Kansas a slavery-free state. There are even old ruts and swales from a wagon route that was part of the Underground Railroad in the 1850s and 1860s.

The natural history of the park is excellent as well. A visit during any time of year will reward the hiker with a tapestry of colors, sights, and sounds. Spring and summer bring bright wildflowers that attract pollinators like monarch butterflies—the variety of milkweed species present has earned the park an official designation as a Monarch Butterfly Waystation. Verdant green grasses in summer attract grasshoppers and, yes, ticks. Come in fall to hike among 6-foot, or taller, big bluestem.

The hike is straightforward. Leave the parking area, heading north. The trail climbs to a picnic table underneath a shady tree then continues climbing to reach the summit of Mount Mitchell. Enjoy the views, and the limestone and shale outcroppings,

The historic Topeka–Fort Riley Road passed by Mount Mitchell.

before beginning your descent down the hill. If you are crunched for time, or just tired, keep right at the 0.7-mile mark to return to the trailhead. Otherwise, turn north to continue down the hill and head toward a bench and panel about the Topeka–Fort Riley Road. The trail then travels around the northwestern side of Mount Mitchell through a beautiful prairie filled with wildflowers. The trail winds along the southern flank of the hill as it heads east back toward the trailhead. Pass a grove of trees that provide the only shade on the hike before reaching the parking area.

After your hike, plan a stop at Pillsbury Crossing Wildlife Area. One of the most scenic spots in the northern Flint Hills, the area is west of Mount Mitchell. The highlight of the wildlife area is Deep Creek Waterfall. A limestone ledge on Deep Creek creates a 5-foot waterfall that is 60 feet across. There is a short hiking trail, but hikers can also hike alongside the creek to explore more of this picturesque area. While swimming is prohibited, kayaking is allowed. Alcohol is also prohibited; even so, the spot is a popular party hangout. Bird-watching is excellent here, making it a great place to enjoy the Flint Hills after hiking at Mount Mitchell.

Mount Mitchell Historical Trail

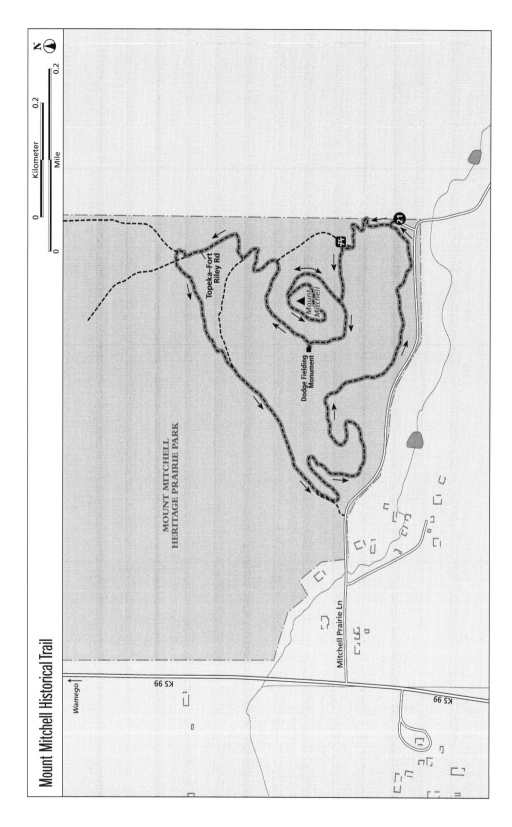

Painted lady on a compass plant.

Miles and Directions

0.00 Start at the trailhead and head north.

0.11 At the picnic tables, keep left (west).

0.18 Turn right (northeast) at the rock to reach the summit.

0.31 Mount Mitchell summit.

0.48 Keep right (west).

0.55 Continue straight (north).

0.66 Bench.

0.70 Turn left (north). (Bailout: Continue straight/east to return to the trailhead.)

0.77 Turn right (east).

0.88 Bench and panel about the Topeka–Fort Riley Road.

0.89 Continue straight (southwest).

1.03 Keep right (southwest).

1.23 Turn left (northeast).

1.34 Bench.

1.80 Arrive back at the trailhead.

22 Dove Roost Trail

Perhaps one of the most kid-friendly hikes in Kansas, Dove Roost Trail circles Dove Roost Pond, passing through native prairie and heavily wooded habitats. While the short distance and level terrain might discourage seasoned hikers, Dove Roost Trail is the perfect hiking trail for wildlife observation and disconnecting in nature. Eagle Point Observation Area, a rocky outcropping overlooking the John Redmond Reservoir, provides a great vantage point for spotting bald eagles in the winter.

Start: Trailhead at the parking area off 18th Road Northwest
Elevation gain: 1,061 feet to 1,084 feet; 26 feet total elevation gain
Distance: 0.73-mile loop
Difficulty: Easy due to short distance and level terrain
Hiking time: 0.5–1 hour
Seasons/schedule: Open daily, year-round; excellent any time of year but great in winter for bald eagle observation
Fees and permits: None
Trail contact: Flint Hills National Wildlife Refuge, 530 West Maple, Hartford 66854; (620) 392-5553; fws.gov/refuge/flint-hills

Dog-friendly: Yes, on leash
Trail surface: Crushed rock and natural surface
Land status: Flint Hills National Wildlife Refuge (US Fish & Wildlife Service)
Nearest town: Burlington, 14 miles to the southeast
Maps: USGS Ottumwa, KS; trail map displayed at the trailhead kiosk
Other trail users: None
Special considerations: None
Amenities: None
Maximum grade: No significant ascents on the hike
Cell service: Adequate to above average

Finding the trailhead: From Burlington, head north on US 75 for 5.5 miles. Turn west onto 17th Road Northwest and continue for 1.5 miles to Kafir Road. Continue north on Kafir Road for 2 miles, then turn west onto 19th Road Northwest. Continue west for 4 miles, then turn south onto Garner Road. After 1 mile, turn west onto 18th Road Northwest and continue until the turn south into the parking area. GPS: N38°17.311' / W95°50.536'

Trail conditions: The trail is excellently maintained and easy to follow. There is plenty of shade along most of the trail. The trail receives light foot traffic.

The Hike

The Flint Hills National Wildlife Refuge encompasses more than 18,000 acres, most of which occupies the Neosho River floodplain upstream of the John Redmond Reservoir. The dam was created in 1966 as a flood-control project. The prairies, wetlands, and bottomland forest that remain are managed as habitat for migratory birds and other wildlife. The refuge's location is ideal for bird-watching, as hundreds of thousands of waterfowl migrate through the area throughout the year. The Dove Roost Trail, located on the northern end of the reservoir, is an excellent birding trail that is also one of the most kid-friendly and accessible hikes in the state of Kansas.

Beaver Dam Bridge at Dove Roost Pond.

Dove Roost Trail leaves the parking area and heads southwest through a prairie. The map at the trailhead kiosk indicates there is an observation tower in the prairie, but as of May 2023, the observation tower was no longer there. The trail soon leaves the prairie for the woodland. The hiking is easy and pleasant, as the trail is wide and impeccably maintained. The easy terrain, short distance, and excellent trail encourage hikers to put away their maps and mobile phones, using in their place their senses to experience the wildlife refuge.

After 0.2 mile, the trail reaches Dove Roost Pond. A fishing access footpath heads north, leading to the boat ramp. Continue east along the trail atop the pond dam. The trail bends to head south, reaching a spur trail after 0.3 mile that leads to the Eagle Point Observation Area. There is no bench or other improvement; the observation area is simply a rocky outcropping overlooking the John Redmond Reservoir. The dead timber and tree snags to the south are prime habitat for bald eagles in winter, making the Dove Roost Trail a year-round destination. After checking out the observation point, continue north on the trail. You will cross a footbridge at the 0.5-mile mark then pass by an observation area in the forest. The Beaver Dam Bridge at the 0.65-mile mark is an idyllic spot and excellent photo opportunity before reaching the end of the hike at the parking area.

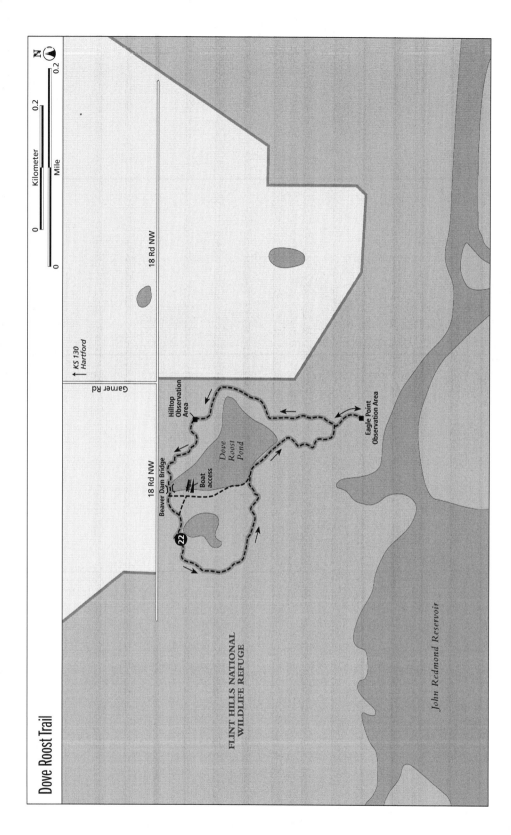

Dove Roost Trail

N

Kilometer
0   0.2
Mile
0   0.2

KS 130
Hartford

Garner Rd

18 Rd NW

18 Rd NW

Hilltop
Observation
Area

Beaver Dam Bridge

Boat
access

Dove
Roost
Pond

Eagle Point
Observation Area

22

FLINT HILLS NATIONAL
WILDLIFE REFUGE

John Redmond Reservoir

John Redmond Reservoir.

Additional hikes: If you are looking for more hiking after the Dove Roost Trail, consider the Townsite Trail, another hiking trail in the wildlife refuge. The trail can be accessed on the north side of the town of Hartford, which is 8 miles to the west of the Dove Roost Trail. Townsite Trail meanders through a wooded area along the Neosho River through an area that was once part of Hartford. The area was cut off from the rest of the town when the John Redmond Reservoir was built. The Dale Griener Nature Trail is another option in nearby Emporia. The trail runs through Campus Woods and includes interpretive panels about local flora and fauna. The 1.6-mile trail runs alongside the Neosho River through riparian forest.

Miles and Directions

0.00 Start at the southwest corner of the parking lot and head southwest past the trail panel.

0.18 Dove Roost Pond.

0.32 Reach a fork; keep right (southeast) to hike to Eagle Point Observation Area.

0.50 Footbridge.

0.65 Beaver Dam Bridge.

0.70 Turn right (west).

0.73 Arrive back at the parking lot

Honorable Mentions

G Flint Hills Trail

The Flint Hills Trail is a 118-mile rail trail that traverses the largest remaining intact tallgrass prairie in the United States. There are multiple access points along the length of the trail, allowing out-and-back day hikes of varying lengths. The section between Pressonville and Virginia Roads west of Osawatomie runs along the wooded bluffs of the Marais des Cygnes River.

Start: Variable

Elevation gain: Variable; mostly level, as trail follows an old railroad corridor.

Distance: 118-mile rail trail

Difficulty: Easy to moderate

Hiking time: Variable

Seasons/schedule: Open year-round

Fees and permits: None

Trail contact: Trent McCown, Manager, Kansas Prairie Spirit Rail Trail Park; (785) 448-2627; kanzatrails.org/flint-hills-trail; email: trent .mccown@ks.gov

Dog-friendly: Yes

Trail surface: Packed gravel

Land status: Rail trail park

Nearest town: Access points in Osawatomie, Rantoul, Ottawa, and Pomona

Maps: Trail map available online

Other trail users: Road and mountain bikers

Flint Hills Trail.

Special considerations: Check the website for trail conditions, closures, and detours. Several segments of the trail are unimproved or closed, but long-range plans call for it to be improved along its entire length.

Amenities: There are services in the towns along the trail. There are currently no restrooms or water fountains next to the trail, so plan accordingly.

Maximum grade: Variable; mostly level, with some inclines

Cell service: Variable; generally adequate at the access points

Finding the trailhead: Refer to the website for trailheads and access points.

Trail conditions: Some sections of the trail are still under construction. Where it is open, the trail is well maintained.

H Eagle Ridge Trail

Milford State Park, located on the edge of the Flint Hills, has an extensive trail system that explores the Sunflower State's largest lake. Eagle Ridge and Crystal Trails are the two most popular trails in the park. In total, Eagle Ridge Trail is just over 6 miles, but there are multiple checkpoints where you can shorten the hike.

Eagle Ridge Trail at Milford State Park.

Start: Trailhead opposite Eagle Ridge Campground
Elevation gain: 1,152 feet to 1,283 feet; 390 feet total elevation gain
Distance: 6.4-mile loop
Difficulty: Moderate
Hiking time: About 3 hours
Seasons/schedule: Open year-round, dawn to dusk
Fees and permits: Daily vehicle permit or annual state park vehicle permit required
Trail contact: Milford State Park, 3612 State Park Rd., Milford 66514; (785) 238-3014; ksoutdoors.com/State-Parks/Locations/Milford
Dog-friendly: Yes
Trail surface: Natural (mowed grass and dirt)

Land status: Milford State Park (Kansas Department of Wildlife & Parks)
Nearest town: Junction City, 8 miles to the southeast
Maps: USGS Milford Dam, KS; trail map available online
Other trail users: Equestrians and mountain bikers
Special considerations: Avoid the trails after recent rains to avoid trail degradation.
Amenities: Restrooms and water at nearby Eagle Ridge Campground
Maximum grade: 7%
Cell service: Reliable service at the trailhead; adequate service on most of the trail

Finding the trailhead: From Junction City, head northwest on US 77 Alternate/North Jackson Street. After 3.5 miles, turn north onto US 77. Continue north for 3.4 miles, then turn west onto KS 57. After 1.2 miles, turn northwest onto State Park Road then southwest onto South State Park Road. The trailhead is opposite Eagle Ridge Campground; there is additional parking on Eagle Ridge Shelter Road. GPS: N39°6.011' / W96°54.428'

Trail conditions: The trails are mowed grass. Due to equestrian use, the trails can be beat up and muddy after rain.

| Sea of Grass Trail

Oregon Trail Nature Park, owned by utility company Evergy but open to the public, straddles the Flint Hills and Glaciated Region. The grain silo with a mural is the landmark of the park, which explodes with wildflowers in spring and summer. Nearly 2 miles of trails take hikers through rolling prairie, with some steep inclines. The Sea of Grass Trail leads to the Jeffrey Energy Center Overlook with a view of the reservoir.

Start: Near the grain silo
Elevation gain: 977 feet to 1,158 feet; 187 feet total elevation gain
Distance: 1.28-mile loop
Difficulty: Easy
Hiking time: About 1 hour
Seasons/schedule: Open year-round, dawn to dusk
Fees and permits: None
Trail contact: Oregon Trail Nature Park, Oregon Trail Road, St. Marys 66536

Dog-friendly: Yes
Trail surface: Paved and natural
Land status: Oregon Trail Nature Park (owned/managed by Evergy)
Nearest town: St. Marys, 5 miles to the southeast
Maps: USGS Belvue, KS; trail map posted at the trailhead
Other trail users: Road or mountain bikers, depending on surface
Special considerations: None

Amenities: Restrooms

Cell service: Adequate

Maximum grade: 17%; the hike to the overlook is steep, climbing almost 200 feet over less than 0.5 mile

Finding the trailhead: From St. Marys, head northwest on US 24. After 4 miles, turn north onto Schoeman Road. After 0.6 mile, turn northwest onto Oregon Trail Road and continue 0.4 mile to the parking area. GPS: N39°13.758' / W96°9.169'

Trail conditions: Trails are well marked and maintained. There is little shade along the trail, and some sections are steep.

Oregon Trail Nature Park.

Glaciated Region

The Glaciated Region is in the northeast corner of the state, north of the Kansas River and east of the Big Blue River. The region is the most populated part of the Sunflower State, including the capital of Topeka, the college town of Lawrence, and the urban metropolitan area of Kansas City. The surface of the Glaciated Region is covered by glacial debris from several glaciers that extended into Kansas between 2.6 million and 11,700 years ago. Besides the large deposits of glacial drift, called loess, left behind by the retreating glaciers, you can also find pinkish Sioux Quartzite boulders littering some fields and hillsides in northeastern Kansas. Erosion and farming have erased much of the evidence of glaciation. There are numerous hiking trails throughout the region, from prairie hikes to wetland wonderlands to beautiful lake loops. Alcove Spring Historic Park hosted the infamous Donner Party on their ill-fated journey west on the Oregon-California Trail. The Baker University Wetlands is an oasis on the south side of Lawrence, with restored wetlands and wet meadows that provide habitat to almost 300 species of birds. The 27-mile Perry Lake Trail and 10-mile Wyandotte County Lake Loop allow hikers to put in long distances just a short drive from major metro areas. The Lawrence River Trail, Kaw River State Park, Shawnee Mission Park, and Olathe Prairie Center offer peaceful yet busy trails right in the heart of urban areas.

Iliff Commons.

23 Alcove Spring

One of the "8 Wonders of Kansas Geography," Alcove Spring Historic Park is also a notable historical site. Explorers such as John C. Frémont and Kit Carson passed through, while the infamous Donner Party spent five days here before fording the Big Blue River. Severe storms in 2021 and 2022 badly damaged the trails, but a group of dedicated volunteers has been working to turn Alcove Spring Historic Park into one of the premier trail destinations in northern Kansas.

Start: Historic Trails Trailhead next to the kiosk in the parking area

Elevation gain: 1,135 feet to 1,284 feet; 148 feet total elevation gain

Distance: 1.8-mile loop (nearly 5 miles of trails)

Difficulty: Easy (Other trails at the park are moderate due to trail conditions as of July 2023.)

Hiking time: About 1 hour

Seasons/schedule: Open year-round, dawn to dusk

Fees and permits: None

Trail contact: Alcove Spring Preservation Association, PO Box 98, Blue Rapids 66411; (785) 363-7991

Dog-friendly: Yes, on leash

Trail surface: Natural (packed dirt and mowed grass)

Land status: Alcove Spring Historic Park (Alcove Spring Historical Trust)

Nearest town: Blue Rapids, 5.5 miles to the south; Marysville, 8 miles to the north

Maps: USGS Blue Rapids KS, USGS Marysville KS; trail map displayed at the trailhead kiosk

Other trail users: Mountain bikers

Special considerations: There are no amenities, so pack accordingly. Many of the trails are undergoing substantial clearing after recent storms; be prepared to turn around or modify your hike. Due to numerous dead trees on the woodland trails, it is advised to avoid them during windy conditions.

Amenities: None

Maximum grade: 6%; the trail climbs 150 feet over the first mile of the hike (other trails in the park have steeper grades).

Cell service: Adequate; may be limited under tree cover

Finding the trailhead: From Marysville, head south on US 77 for 3.4 miles. Turn west onto Osage Road; at 0.7 mile, turn south onto East River Road. After 3.2 miles, arrive at the Alcove Spring parking area.

From Blue Rapids, head north on US 77. After 2.6 miles, turn west onto Sunflower Road and continue for 1 mile, then keep right onto 8th Road, heading northwest for 0.9 mile. Turn north onto East River Road, and after 1.1 miles turn east into the Alcove Spring parking area. GPS: N39°44.975' / W96°40.741'

Trail conditions: The trails at Alcove Spring Historic Park suffered from severe storms, including a tornado, in 2021 and 2022. A small but dedicated group of volunteers has been working tirelessly to clear trails, remove hazardous dead trees, and improve the general state of the trails. The author attempted to hike the trails twice in summer 2023 but encountered disappearing trails, trail blockages, and other conditions that impeded hiking the entirety of the park's trails. The park is steeped in history and is beautiful, so a visit is worth the effort. Just be prepared to modify your hike if conditions do not allow exploring all the trails.

The park's eponymous spring is a trickle in summer.

Stella's Meadow.

The Hike

Alcove Spring has seen its fair share of visitors over the years. The presence of water made it a popular and well-known stopover for emigrants on the Oregon-California Trail. Famous visitors include explorer John C. Frémont, frontiersman Kit Carson, and, in 1846, the ill-fated Donner Party. While the Donner Party camped here for five days, Sarah Keyes passed away. The Daughters of the American Revolution placed a stone marker near her supposed grave. Frémont supposedly left his initials carved in a limestone outcropping near the eponymous spring.

In 1993, the Alcove Spring Historical Trust bought the private property that makes up the 220-acre Alcove Spring Historic Park. The park is listed on the National Register of Historic Places and is one of the "8 Wonders of Kansas Geography." It garnered the latter recognition due to "its historical significance as a stop for Indians, fur traders, and emigrants on the Oregon Trail." The waterfall that gives the park its name is intermittent, supplied by wet spring weather. If you visit in summer, you will be lucky if there is a trickle.

In 2021 and 2022, the area was hit by severe storms. A tornado in 2021 did considerable damage in the county, and the strong winds from storms in both years did

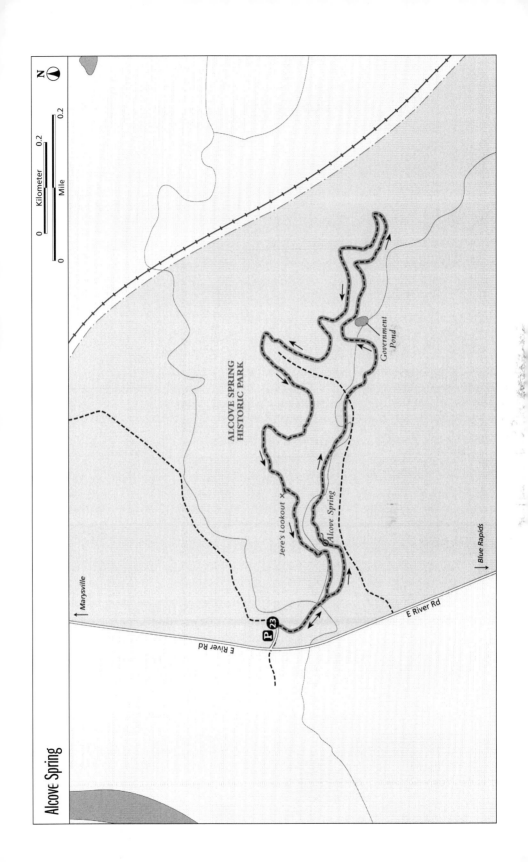

Alcove Spring

N

0   Kilometer   0.2

0   Mile   0.2

ALCOVE SPRING
HISTORIC PARK

Jere's Lookout ×

Alcove Spring

Government
Pond

← Marysville

P 23

E River Rd

E River Rd

Blue Rapids →

a number on the trees in the park. A small but determined group of volunteers has been working as time permits to clear the trails and remove hazardous dead trees. The described hike makes the best attempt to create a route that follows clean trails while taking in as many of the park's highlights as can be reasonably accessed. The trail to Alcove Spring is clear and easy to follow. Continuing east on Homestead Trail takes hikers deep into the park, while Fremont Trail gives hikers great views of the surrounding countryside, as does Jere's Lookout. For additional hiking, take Creek Trail to beautiful and serene Stella's Meadow, then on to Grace's Campground. If trail conditions allow, there are several more miles to explore in Alcove Spring Historic Park.

Additional hikes: In nearby Marysville, hikers looking for an easy stroll through northern Kansas farmland along the Blue River can hike the Blue River Rail Trail. The trail roughly follows the course of the river for almost 13 miles to the Nebraska border, where it connects with Chief Standing Bear in the Cornhusker State. For another hiking option in northeastern Kansas, Banner Creek Reservoir has 13 miles of trails, including 3 miles of ADA-accessible trails. The main hiking trail takes hikers around the entire reservoir, creating a 10-mile loop. There is a daily entrance fee to enter the park.

Miles and Directions

0.00 Start at the kiosk and head southeast toward Alcove Spring on Historic Trails.

0.03 Footbridge.

0.06 Continue straight (southeast) on Historic Trails.

0.07 Turn right (south) to stay on Historic Trails.

0.17 Alcove Spring; turn right (east) onto Homestead Trail.

0.37 Footbridge.

0.43 Continue straight (east).

0.52 Keep left (north).

0.82 Reach a junction; turn left (west) onto Fremont Trail then immediately left (south) onto the trail leading into the trees.

1.00 Keep left (west) on Kit Carson Trail.

1.40 Bench.

1.50 Turn left (southwest) onto Jere's Lookout Trail.

1.55 Jere's Lookout.

1.70 Turn left (west) onto Homestead Trail.

1.80 Arrive back at the trailhead. (Option: Head north from the parking area on Creek Trail to explore Stella's Meadow and Grace's Campground.)

24 Iliff Commons

The hiking trails at Iliff Commons wind through open prairie, offering views of Topeka and the Kaw River Valley. The woodland trails have an assortment of treasures that will delight children and adults alike, including an exquisitely built replica log cabin, a fun tree house, and the playful Wild Cat Hollow, with faces and animal figures hiding in the forest.

Start: A chipped driveway 50 feet east of the intersection on the south side of 31st Street
Elevation gain: 898 feet to 997 feet; 207 feet total elevation gain
Distance: 2.05-mile loop
Difficulty: Easy, with three steep but short inclines
Hiking time: 1–1.5 hours
Seasons/schedule: Open year-round, dawn to dusk
Fees and permits: None
Trail contact: Iliff Commons, 2329 NE 31st St., Topeka 66617; doctoriliff.com/commons.html
Dog-friendly: Dogs allowed off-leash once you get to the monument or starting line
Trail surface: Natural (grass and dirt)

Land status: Private property open to the public
Nearest town: Topeka
Maps: USGS Grantville, KS; map available on the website
Other trail users: Mountain bikers welcome on the peripheral service trails and woodland trails
Special considerations: The trails are located on private property but are open to the public. Please respect the property and leave no trace.
Amenities: None
Maximum grade: 13%; three steep yet short inclines, each 40–60 feet in elevation gain
Cell service: Above average on most of the trail; may be limited under tree cover

Finding the trailhead: From US 24 north of Topeka, take the KS 4 exit toward Valley Falls. Head north on KS 4 for 0.7 mile, then turn left (west) onto Northeast 31st Street. After 0.5 mile, turn left (south) to enter Iliff Commons. GPS: N39°6.050' / W95°36.227'

Trail conditions: The trail is well maintained. There is a trail map at a kiosk near the trailhead, but there are no markers on the trail itself. The park is small, so it is difficult to get lost. The trail receives heavy foot traffic due to its location in Topeka.

The Hike

The prairie and woodlands at Iliff Commons have never been developed thanks to the purchase of 80 acres by Dr. and Mrs. Iliff. The area is private property, but the several miles of trails are open to the public. Hiking, running, biking, and cross-country skiing are allowed on the trails from dawn to dusk.

From the trailhead kiosk, take the trail on the left, heading south. When you approach the tree and Iliff Commons monument, keep right (southwest) to follow the wide mowed path through the prairie. As you traverse Ad Astra Ridge, a pair of bison statues will come into view; head toward those. Continue southwest past the

Native prairie and woods at Iliff Commons.

statues at the 0.33-mile mark as the din of the interstate traffic becomes louder. When you reach Wilson Junction after 0.5 mile, you will have a decision to make. If you want a shorter loop through the prairie, turn right to follow the trail along the edge of the woods and prairie. We will continue south into the woods.

Mountain bikes are allowed on the woodland trails, so follow the mile directions to follow this hike, or just wander as you will. Be sure to visit Founders Cabin, built by Eagle Scout candidate Joshua Layne and volunteers. The cabin is a replica of the one where the city's founders signed an agreement to form the Topeka Town Association on December 5, 1854.

Continue through the woods, climbing the various ascents that have been named for Kansas high school track athletes. After you cross the footbridge at 1.45 miles, you will enter Wild Cat Hollow. This area is sure to be a delight to children, with figures attached to and hanging from trees. Try to find all the faces and animals hiding in the forest, but please don't remove any of the objects. The tree house after Wild Cat Hollow will entertain children and adults alike. Once you leave the forest and return to the prairie, head east toward the pond. You should see the tree and monument ahead, and the trailhead kiosk beyond.

Replica of Founders Cabin.

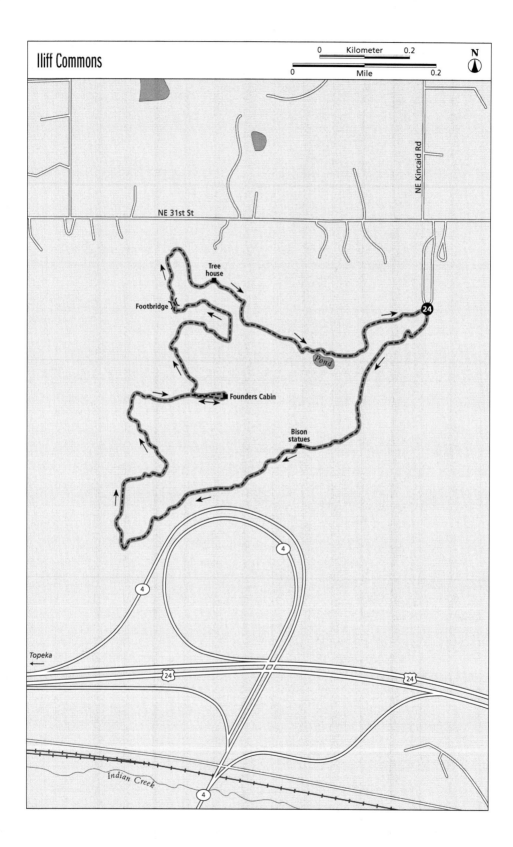

Additional hikes: Iliff Commons is on the northeastern edge of Topeka. There are a couple of other fine hiking trails on the opposite side of the city. Located on the western side of Topeka just north of I-70, the Kansas Historical Society's Nature Trail offers families a 2.5-mile trail system divided into four sections, making it easy to create shorter loops. Only foot traffic is allowed and dogs are welcome, so this is a very family-friendly hiking area. Numerous interpretive panels along the trail describe Kansas history and local flora and fauna. As of July 2023, the museum was closed, but trail brochures and trail activity guides were available on the website (www.kshs.org/p/nature-trail-introduction/11891).

If you want one of the best views of Topeka, head to Skyline Park on the southwestern edge of town. Trails lead up to Burnett's Mound, with panoramic views of Topeka and Shawnee County. Interpretive signs at the parking area tell the history of the Potawatomi people, and a prairie plant guide is available on the park's website (http://parks.snco.us/facilities/Facility/Details/254). The 4.5-mile trail system loops through wooded areas and restored prairie in the higher elevations. It is also popular with mountain bikers.

Miles and Directions

0.00 Start at the trailhead and go left, heading south.

0.05 Keep right (southwest).

0.19 Keep left (south) at Forbes Junction.

0.33 Continue straight (southwest) at the junction next to the bison statues.

0.57 Turn left (south) at Wilson Junction.

0.64 Turn right (north) at Wisegarver Junction.

0.70 Continue straight (north) at Griffith Junction.

0.80 Turn left (north) at Jarrett Junction.

1.02 Turn right (east).

1.06 Founders Cabin.

1.12 Turn right (north).

1.32 Turn left (north) at Johnson Junction.

1.45 Footbridge.

1.60 Water crossing.

1.70 Turn right (east).

1.81 Pond; continue straight (east).

2.05 Arrive back at the trailhead.

25 Old Military Trail

Perry Lake Trail is a 29-mile hiking trail that was the second trail in Kansas designated as a National Recreation Trail, in 1978. The trail skirts the edge of the eponymous lake for a majority of its 29 miles, traveling through oak-hickory woodlands and over rolling hills and open fields. Its distance makes it an excellent backpacking trail; however, numerous sections are also ideal day hikes. The Old Military Trail area is one of the main trailheads for Perry Lake Trail and provides access to two of the best day hike sections of the entire loop.

Start: Old Military Trailhead

Elevation gain: 906 feet to 1,020 feet; 633 feet total elevation gain

Distance: 7.2 miles out and back

Difficulty: Moderate to difficult

Hiking time: About 3 hours

Seasons/schedule: Open year-round; best in the fall

Fees and permits: None

Trail contact: US Army Corps of Engineers, Perry Lake Project Office, 10419 Perry Park Dr., Perry 66073; (785) 597-5144; www.nwk .usace.army.mil/Locations/DistrictLakes/Perry-Lake/

Dog-friendly: Yes, on leash

Trail surface: Natural

Land status: Perry Lake (US Army Corps of Engineers)

Nearest town: Ozawkie, 4 miles to the west; Oskaloosa, 8 miles to the east

Maps: USGS Ozawkie, KS; trail map available online and at the trailhead

Other trail users: None

Special considerations: Ticks and spiderwebs are abundant April to September.

Amenities: None at trailhead; toilets and water at nearby campgrounds

Maximum grade: 18%; no sustained elevation gains, rather multiple short but steep inclines, as the trail is near the lakeshore

Cell service: Adequate to above average at the trailhead and on the trail

Finding the trailhead: From KS 92 east of Ozawkie, head south on Ferguson Road for 1.3 miles; turn west into the parking area for Old Military Trail. GPS: N39°12.828' / W95°25.003'

Trail conditions: The trail is superbly waymarked with blue blazes on trees and signs. There are very few intersecting trails or roads, making navigation simple. Multiple streams cross the trail; however, they are dry most of the year. Poison ivy and ticks are common in summer, as are spiderwebs across the trail. Hiking poles are helpful due to the rugged, rocky terrain and potentially muddy sections. The trail receives moderate to heavy foot traffic.

The Hike

The dam that created Perry Lake was constructed to control flooding downstream of the Delaware and Kansas Rivers. In 1968, the US Army Corps of Engineers reached an agreement with the Kansas Parks and Resources Department on land usage, creating Perry State Park. The Corps also manages trails and campgrounds around the lake, which has become one of the premier outdoor recreation spots in Kansas.

The Old Military Trailhead is one of several for Perry Lake Trail.

Perry Lake Trail, also known as Old Military Trail, is a 29-mile trail around the lake. The trail often follows along or near the shore of the lake, although in places it heads away from the lake into the surrounding woodland. Some intrepid hikers tackle the entire trail in one day; others use the Old Military Trail Campground Slough Creek and Longview Park areas to break their hike into shorter, more manageable sections. Several sections are excellent for day hikes, as explained below.

The Old Military Trail area is one of the main access points for Perry Lake Trail. Two excellent day hikes originate from this trailhead: one heading west toward Old Quarry Road (mile 11) and another heading east, following the Little Slough Creek to Kiowa Road (mile 18). Both hikes are 3.5 miles one way. The latter receives less usage and thus can be more overgrown. The hike described here is the west section to Old Quarry Road.

This hike is very easy to navigate thanks to blue blazes and the lack of intersecting trails. Navigationally, head west from the Old Military Trailhead for 3.5 miles until reaching a road. You can continue west and then south on the trail along the lakeshore or turn around and return to the trailhead. If you are looking for a shorter hike, there is a bench a little more than 2 miles from the trailhead, which would make the round-trip just under 4.5 miles. The trail here, and around the entire lake, is regularly maintained. However, some areas can become overgrown in summer, especially sections of the trail that are not regularly used. Additionally, April to September might not be pleasant for those who dislike spiderwebs and ticks, as they are abundant during these

Old Military Trail

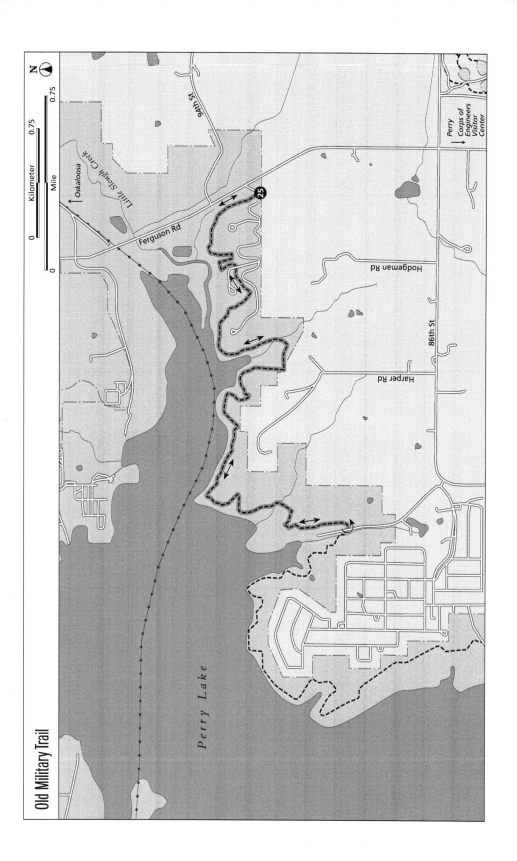

N

Kilometer
0   0.75   0.75

Mile
0   0.75

Oskaloosa

Little Slough Creek

94th St

Ferguson Rd

25

Hodgeman Rd

Harper Rd

86th St

Perry Lake

Perry
Corps of
Engineers
Visitor
Center

The trail is mostly shaded, but sections pass through open clearings.

months. Take extra precautions if you hike during these months, both for yourself and any dogs you hike with. Coming across a tick nest can be a very unpleasant experience for you or your furry companions.

Additional hikes: If you are looking for additional hiking at Perry Lake, there are several great options that make it one of the best hiking destinations in Kansas. The trail east from the Old Military Trailhead to Kiowa Road, also known as Section 3, is a favorite of park staff. Another park staff favorite is Section 4, which passes through the Topeka Audubon Society Sanctuary; this section can be accessed at the Ferguson Road Trailhead. Thunder Ridge Trail is a 2.5-mile loop in the Slough Creek Area with interpretive signage. There is a self-guided brochure available that provides children fun and educational information about Kansas ecosystems. The Delaware Marsh Trail is a 1.75-mile loop around the marsh. Dogs are allowed off-leash on this trail.

Miles and Directions

0.00 Start at the trailhead and head northwest.

0.51 Footbridge.

0.74 Cross an abandoned road and continue west.

1.53 Water crossing.

2.15 Bench. (Option: Turn around here for a shorter hike.)

3.60 Reach Old Quarry Rd; turn around and return to the trailhead.

7.20 Arrive back at the trailhead.

26 George Latham Trail

Clinton Lake, due to its proximity to Lawrence and I-70, is an outdoor recreation hot spot. If you want a quieter experience in nature, Woodridge Primitive Park is an excellent option. The George Latham Trail explores a wooded peninsula on the west end of the lake, with fifteen hike-in campsites that are perfect for a quiet weekend getaway. The short distance and multiple campsites make this trail an excellent one for children and adults new to backpacking.

Start: Woodridge Primitive Park
Elevation gain: 882 feet to 1,020 feet; 308 feet total elevation gain
Distance: 4.19-mile loop
Difficulty: Moderate
Hiking time: About 2 hours
Seasons/schedule: Open year-round
Fees and permits: None
Trail contact: Clinton Project Office, US Army Corps of Engineers, 872 N 1402 Rd., Lawrence 66049; (785) 843-7665; nwk.usace.army.mil/Locations/District-Lakes/Clinton-Lake/
Dog-friendly: Yes, on leash
Trail surface: Natural
Land status: Woodridge Primitive Park (US Army Corps of Engineers)

Nearest town: Lawrence, 17 miles to the east
Maps: USGS Clinton, KS; trail map available on the park website
Other trail users: Mountain bikers
Special considerations: Numerous small clearings along the trail make excellent camping spots, but the Corps asks that people use only preexisting, permanent campfire rings.
Amenities: Drinking water, vault toilet, primitive campsites with fire rings
Maximum grade: 8%; no sustained steep inclines, rather multiple ups and downs as the trail follows the edge of the lake
Cell service: Adequate on most of the trail, although tree cover may limit service on sections of the trail

Finding the trailhead: Woodridge Primitive Park is on the west shore of Clinton Lake. From the intersection of CR 1023 and CR 458, head east on North 1250 Road. Turn north on East 350 Road, then east onto Woodridge Road to access the trailhead campground. GPS: N38°55.573' / W95°26.124'

Trail conditions: The trail is excellently waymarked with blue hiker signs attached to trees. There are few intersecting trails, so navigation is straightforward. The campsites are marked with posts. The trail can become overgrown in summer, and ticks and spiderwebs can be a nuisance.

The Hike

If you are looking to get away from the trappings of modern society, a weekend at Woodridge Primitive Park will scratch that itch. The park is home to one of the best primitive camping experiences in Kansas. Not only are there a variety of campsites, both at the trailhead and along the 4.19-mile George Latham Trail, they are all free to use. Amenities are basic at the trailhead: a vault toilet at the trailhead, drinking water (the hand pump may be disabled, so bring your own supply just in case), fire rings,

George Latham Trail is a National Recreational Trail.

Woodridge Primitive Park is on the west end of Clinton Lake.

and picnic tables. The fifteen hike-in campsites along the trail have fire rings but no access to water, unless you hike off-trail to the lake to filter water.

There are two access points to George Latham Trail: one on the north end of the campground near the toilet and the other on the south end. Most hikers use the south trailhead and hike the loop counterclockwise, and the hike-in campsites are numbered accordingly. Navigation is simple: Just follow the singletrack footpath that is adorned with blue hiker markers affixed to trees. The only intersecting trails are ones leading to the campsites., social trails that lead to the lakeshore, or game paths.

The trail travels mostly along the wooded shore of Clinton Lake. Your first view of the lake is near camp 5 after 0.6 mile. The next mile, from camp 5 to camp 12, heads northeast, following close to the lakeshore. If you are hiking with several people and tents, camps 8 and 9 at the 0.75-mile mark are located next to each other. After camp 12, the trail heads northwest along the end of the peninsula. You'll hike along the edge of a hay meadow before reaching camp 13.

The roughest section of the trail is from near camp 13 until returning to the north trailhead at the campground. There are multiple inclines and declines as the trail follows right alongside the lakeshore on the northern end of the peninsula. If you are the first hiker of the day, you will be running into numerous spiderwebs

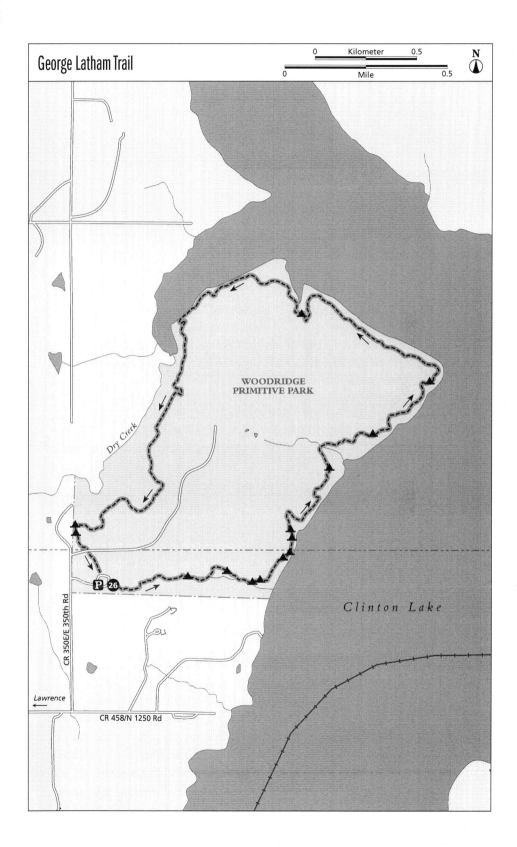

George Latham Trail

WOODRIDGE
PRIMITIVE PARK

Dry Creek

Clinton Lake

CR 350E/E 350th Rd

Lawrence

CR 458/N 1250 Rd

P 26

that stretch across the narrow trail. If these bother you, wear a bug net around your head for a more comfortable morning hike. The bench at 2.92 miles marks the end of lakeshore hiking as the trail heads south, climbing steadily back toward the trailhead. Once you arrive at camps 14 and 15, you will have only a few hundred more feet to hike. Cross the old service road, the last landmark on the trail, to return to the trailhead near the toilets.

Additional hiking: George Latham Trail is the best but not the only hiking trail on Clinton Lake. The Smokehouse Trail is a 2-mile loop at Bloomington Park on a large peninsula on the lake's south shore. The trail was damaged during flooding but had been restored as of August 2023. Much like the George Latham Trail, the Smokehouse Trail will likely be overgrown in sections during summer, and spiderwebs will be ever present. Clinton State Park, located on the north shore of the lake, has a 25-mile trail system that is popular with mountain bikers but also welcomes hikers. The trails are singletrack dirt paths with mile markers painted red, white, or blue. The red trail is 2 miles and the blue trail is 9 miles, with the white trail the longest at 14 miles. The Prairieview Nature Trail is a 0.75-mile-long self-guided nature trail located opposite the Coneflower Campground. Sanders Mound Trail is a 1-mile trail that has significant erosion issues and may be impossible to navigate if not closed entirely.

Miles and Directions

0.00 Start at the trailhead and head right (east).

0.30 Camp 1.

0.32 Camp 2.

0.40 Camp 3.

0.44 Camp 4.

0.59 Camp 5.

0.70 Camp 6.

0.76 Camps 8 and 9.

1.00 Bench.

1.10 Camp 10.

1.19 Footbridge.

1.39 Camp 11.

1.70 Camp 12.

2.38 Camp 13.

2.92 Bench.

3.51 Bench.

4.01 Camps 14 and 15.

4.09 Cross the road and continue south.

4.19 Arrive back at the trailhead.

27 Baker Wetlands

More than 11 miles of trails explore the Baker University Wetlands, one of the most beautiful places in the Sunflower State. The 927-acre natural habitat is a paradise for bird-watching—278 species have been identified here—and plant enthusiasts, who can try to identify all 487 species. The variety of trails, all well maintained and marked, allow an inclusive nature experience for all visitors.

Start: Near the south entrance of the Discovery Center

Elevation gain: 815 feet to 827 feet; 30 feet total elevation gain

Distance: 4.1-mile loop

Difficulty: Easy

Hiking time: 1.5–2 hours

Seasons/schedule: Open daily year-round, dawn to dusk

Fees and permits: None

Trail contact: Baker University Wetlands, 1365 N 1250 Rd., Lawrence 66046; (785) 594-4700; www.bakeru.edu/history-traditions/the-wetlands/

Dog-friendly: Yes, on leash (dogs not allowed on the boardwalks)

Trail surface: Crushed rock, natural (grass), and boardwalks

Land status: Baker University Wetlands and Discovery Center

Nearest town: Lawrence

Maps: USGS Lawrence East, KS; trail map available on the website

Other trail users: Mountain bikers

Special considerations: Bikes and dogs are not allowed on the boardwalk. Please do not collect items and remove them from the park.

Amenities: Restrooms and water when the Discovery Center is open

Maximum grade: Mostly flat trail with very little elevation change

Cell service: Excellent

Finding the trailhead: Baker University Wetlands is immediately south of KS 10/South Lawrence Trafficway. From US 59, turn east onto North 1250 Road, which is just south of KS 10. Continue east to the Discovery Center.

From West 31st Street, head south on Michigan Street/East 1350 Road. After crossing over KS 10, reach the Discovery Center. The trailhead is in the southeastern corner of the parking lot. GPS: N38°55.213' / W95°14.893'

Trail conditions: The trails are exceptionally well maintained and marked. There is a trail map displayed at the parking area. The grass trails will be damp in the morning.

The Hike

The Baker Wetlands Discovery Center, opened in 2015, features a large display area, a research lab, and classroom space. The wetlands were originally used to teach agriculture to Haskell Institute students. Since being turned into a nature preserve, the wetlands, wet meadows, and prairie have slowly been restored. Despite the fact that they are artificially sustained, the wetlands are incredibly beautiful and provide habitat for 278 species of birds, 98 other vertebrate species, and 487 plant species.

Only foot traffic is allowed on the boardwalks.

More than 4 miles of trails wend through wetlands along the Wakarusa River.

The 11-mile trail system allows hikers to follow specific loops, like the one described here, or wander the trails at their own leisure. While this description recommends a specific route, it is also recommended to leave your mobile phone and other distractions behind and walk the trails with binoculars in hand and your senses open to discovery. If the Discovery Center is open, step inside to ask for recommendations and learn about the wetlands; otherwise, begin on the south side of the building and explore the boardwalk.

Once you've made a loop of the boardwalk, head southeast on the Diagonal Trail, also called the Green Loop on the trail map. This trail bisects the main wetland area diagonally, hence the name. Just before reaching the 1-mile mark, you will reach an alternative trailhead near North 1200 Road/East 1400 Road. Naismith Creek also joins the Wakarusa River here as the trail crosses the creek. Head east along the southern edge of the West Virgin Wet Meadow, with the wooded Wakarusa River on your right to the south.

As you hike east, there are several options to cut this loop shorter by heading north. We will continue heading east, crossing Mine Creek shortly after the 1.5-mile mark of the hike. The far eastern section of Baker Wetlands receives less foot traffic than near the Discovery Center, so be prepared to spot wildlife here. After crossing

Baker Wetlands

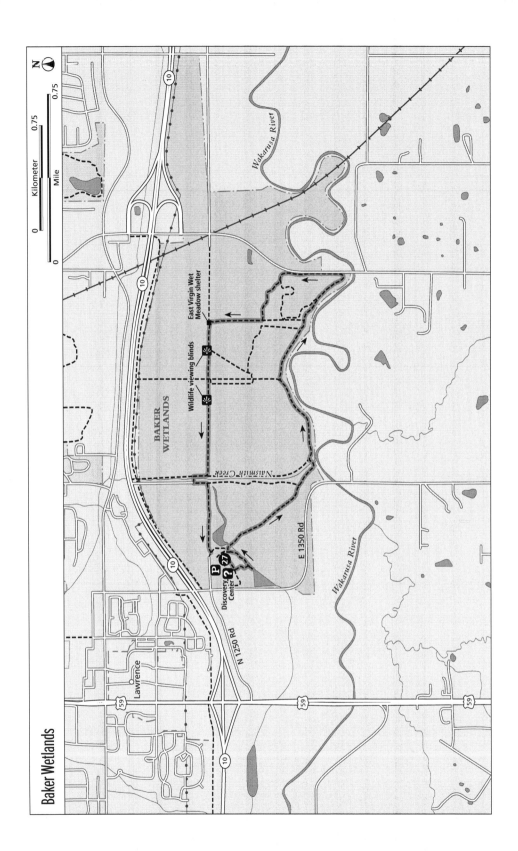

Mine Creek, the trail bends to head southeast until it reaches East 1500 Road, where it heads north, running parallel to the road for just 0.5 mile.

At the 2.30-mile mark, the trail becomes a beautiful boardwalk through the Night Heron Shallows. The boardwalk ends when it reaches Mine Creek Trail; turn north onto the trail until reaching the shelter at the northwestern corner of East Virgin Wet Meadow. The last mile is a straight shot west along the gravel road. There are two excellent viewing blinds along the trail that overlook the wet meadows; both are worth spending some time in to bird-watch and contemplate the beauty of Baker Wetlands.

If you want to visit another nature center, the Prairie Park Nature Center (lawrenceks.org/lprd/ppnc/) is located nearby in the southeastern part of Lawrence. The 100-acre preserve has wetlands, woodlands, and prairie, as well as a 5-acre lake. There are walking trails and a wide offering of environmental and recreation programs for the public.

Miles and Directions

0.00 Start at the south entrance to the Discovery Center and head south on Boardwalk Loop Trail.

0.06 Turn left (south) onto the boardwalk.

0.14 Turn right (south) to reach a viewpoint, then return to this junction and continue east.

0.32 Turn right (southeast).

0.45 Footbridge.

0.55 Bench and viewing platform.

0.81 Continue straight (southeast).

0.93 Keep left to continue east.

0.97 Reach a junction with three trails; take the middle trail to continue east.

1.40 Continue straight (east). (Bailout: Turn right/north then left/west to return to the trailhead.)

1.66 Continue straight (southeast).

1.82 Continue straight (southeast).

1.98 Bench.

2.33 Turn right (northwest) onto the boardwalk.

2.55 Turn right (north).

2.69 Continue straight (north).

2.80 Turn left (west) at the East Virgin Wet Meadow shelter.

3.00 Viewing blind.

3.10 Continue straight (west).

3.20 Viewing blind.

3.56 Turn right (north).

3.62 Turn left (west) and cross the footbridge over Naismith Creek, then turn left (south).

3.72 Turn left (west).

4.10 Arrive back at the trailhead.

28 Bull Creek Loop

Totaling 2,060 acres, Big Bull Creek Park is the largest in the Johnson County Parks & Recreation District system. A short, paved loop is accessible for all visitors, while singletrack trails create an extensive system totaling more than 7 miles. The trails explore the timbered ravines along Big Bull Creek and are a quieter alternative to some of the more congested trails in the Kansas City area.

Start: Restrooms near the parking lot

Elevation gain: 1,003 feet (at trailhead) to 1,027 feet; 240 feet total elevation gain

Distance: 6.0 miles out and back

Difficulty: Moderate due to length and sections of trail with rocks and tree roots

Hiking time: About 3 hours

Seasons/schedule: Open daily, dawn to dusk

Fees and permits: None

Trail contact: Johnson County Parks & Recreation District, 7900 Renner Rd., Shawnee Mission 66219; (913) 438-7275; www.jcprd.com/Facilities/Facility/Details/Big-Bull-Creek-Park-101

Dog-friendly: Yes, on leash

Trail surface: Natural; some sections are very rocky or have tree roots protruding from the dirt.

Land status: Big Bull Creek Park (Johnson County Parks & Recreation)

Nearest town: Gardner, 6 miles to the northeast

Maps: USGS Edgerton, KS; USGS Gardner, KS; and USGS Antioch, KS; trail map available on the park website

Other trail users: Mountain bikers and equestrians

Special considerations: Trails may be closed due to muddy conditions; please respect trail closures to prevent trail degradation. Call ahead ([913] 204-0204, ext. 25) for trail closures during wet weather.

Amenities: Restrooms and water at the parking lot

Maximum grade: 5%

Cell service: Adequate to above average at the trailhead and on the trails

Finding the trailhead: From I-35, take exit 202 and head north on Sunflower Road. After 0.7 mile, turn right (east) into Big Bull Creek Park. GPS: N38°45.481' / W94°59.951'

Trail conditions: The well-maintained trails are well-marked at all major junctions. Some sections of the trail are rocky and/or have tree roots protruding from the dirt. Also, some sections of trail are narrow singletrack, so be aware of mountain bikers. Trails will be closed if they are muddy. There are several water crossings. Ticks and poison ivy may be present.

The Hike

Big Bull Creek Park was inaugurated in 2018, becoming the largest park in the Johnson County Parks & Recreation District system. Big Bull Creek is far enough away from Kansas City to be considered Johnson County's "backcountry." The trails are much quieter than popular parks in the metropolitan area like Shawnee Mission Park.

Bull Creek Trail passes through an Osage orange hedgerow.

There is a paved trail that loops around the picnic shelters and playground. It begins near the parking area and is accessible to wheelchairs and strollers. The rest of the trails at Big Bull Creek Park are rugged singletrack paths of packed dirt. Rocky terrain and tree roots make the hiking difficult, as do the constant elevation changes. Horseshoe Loop connects to the paved trail near its southwestern and northwestern corners. Take Horseshoe Loop on the southwestern corner of the paved trail. The trail heads west, weaving through a fun maze of Osage orange trees until reaching the edge of the St. Columbine Cemetery. Here the trail heads north and descends into the Big Bull Creek watershed.

When you reach Junction B, take Quarry Loop if you want the challenge of the most difficult section of the Big Bull Creek trails. Quarry Loop heads north, then back south before heading east along Big Bull Creek. This section is the lowest of the trails, coming close to Martin Creek on several occasions. You'll be mistaken if you think you are in the Pacific Northwest—you are still in Kansas despite the mossy rocks and evergreens.

After 2 miles of hiking, the trail reaches a pond and Big Bull Creek itself; the trail is high above the creek, however. As the creek bends south, so does the trail. Continue south, passing three trail markers (E, F, and G) until reaching trail marker H. You can continue on the trail south, going underneath I-35, to reach Coyote Run. These are equestrian trails south of the interstate that lead to a group campsite. Instead, take the hairpin turn to head north along the easiest section of Big Bull Creek Loop. The trail runs higher above the first half of the loop, mostly still under tree cover but coming close to the edge of the woods, with fields to the west. Turn west onto the northern section of Horseshoe Loop to return to the paved trail and parking area.

Additional hikes: Located west of Big Bull Creek Park near Baldwin City, historic Black Jack Battlefield has approximately 2.5 miles of nature and prairie trails near a grave site and the historic Pearson House. Black Jack Battlefield was the site of one of the first battles of the Civil War and has been designated a National Historic Landmark. The trails may be overgrown and difficult to follow, but the site is worth a visit for those interested in history. Hillsdale State Park, south of Big Bull Creek Park on the southern end of Hillsdale Reservoir, has miles of multiuse trails. The Saddle Ridge trail system has nearly 50 miles of equestrian trails that are also open to hiking. There is also a nature trail near the US Army Corps of Engineers visitor center on the southeastern edge of the reservoir.

Miles and Directions

0.00 Start next to the restrooms and head east on the paved trail past the picnic shelters.

0.10 Turn right (south).

0.17 Turn left (west) onto a dirt singletrack.

0.40 St. Columbine Cemetery.

0.54 Continue straight (north).

0.66 Turn right (north) onto Quarry Loop.

0.94 Reach a fork and keep left (northwest).

0.96 Water crossing.

1.62 Water crossing.

2.20 Junction C; keep left (east).

2.30 Junction D; keep left (southeast).

2.38 Junction E; keep left (east).

2.71 Reach a junction and keep left (east).

3.07 Junction G; turn left (south).

3.30 Junction H; turn sharply right to head north on Bull Creek Loop.

3.58 Junction F; continue straight (north).

3.87 Reach a junction and keep left (northwest).

4.23 Junction E; continue straight (northwest).

4.32 Junction D; turn left (southwest) at the pond.

4.65 Junction C; keep left (west).

5.46 Junction A; turn right (west) onto Horseshoe Loop.

5.83 Turn left (south) onto the paved trail.

5.89 Turn right (west) to return to the parking lot.

6.00 Arrive back at the restrooms.

Mountain bikes are allowed on the trail, so keep your pet leashed.

Bull Creek Loop

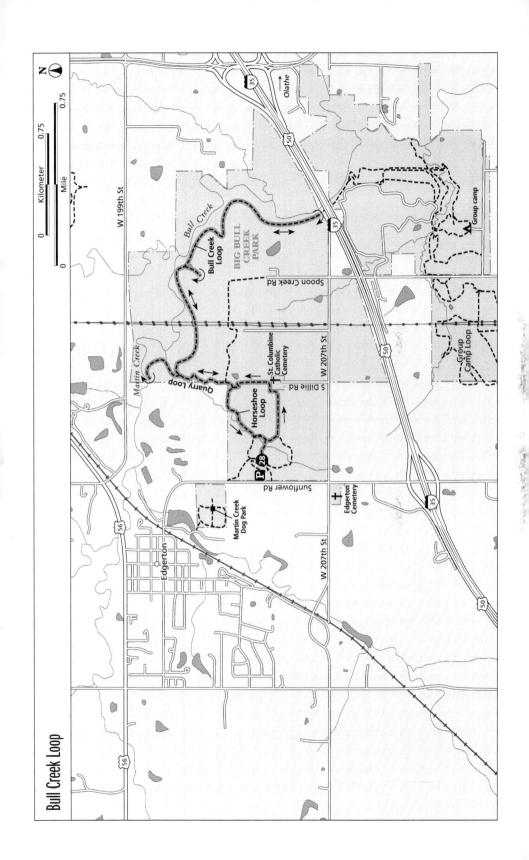

29 Kill Creek Trail

Kill Creek Park's location just to the west of the Kansas City metropolitan area makes it a perfect getaway for a weekday-evening stroll or a long weekend hike on its 12 miles of multiuse trails. The southern segment of the paved Kill Creek Streamway Trail begins in the park and is an excellent accessible trail that continues on to Olathe. The Russell and Helen Means Observation Tower and a prairie observation deck are excellent vantage points for bird-watching.

Start: Northwest corner of parking lot at Shelter #1
Elevation gain: 810 feet to 948 feet; 151 feet total elevation gain
Distance: 3.04-mile loop
Difficulty: Easy
Hiking time: About 1.5 hours
Seasons/schedule: Mar 1–Oct 31, 5 a.m.–11 p.m.; Nov 1–Feb 28, 7:30 a.m.–8 p.m.
Fees and permits: None
Trail contact: Kill Creek Park, 11670 Homestead Ln., Olathe 66061; (913) 204-0204, ext. 5; jcprd.com/Facilities/Facility/Details/Kill-Creek-Park-28
Dog-friendly: Yes, on leash
Trail surface: Paved and natural

Land status: Kill Creek Park (Johnson County Parks & Recreation)
Nearest town: De Soto, 7 miles to the north
Maps: USGS De Soto, KS; trail map available on the park's website
Other trail users: Mountain bikers
Special considerations: Call (913) 204-0204, ext. 25, or check the website (jcprd.com/696/Rainouts-Temporary-Closures closures) for trail closures.
Amenities: Restrooms at the parking lot
Maximum grade: 6%; the only significant incline is a gentle gain of approximately 80 feet over the final 0.5 mile.
Cell service: Reliable throughout the park

Finding the trailhead: From KS 10 and Kill Creek Road, head south on Kill Creek Road for 2.7 miles. Turn right (west) onto West 115th Street, then after 0.5 mile turn left (south) onto South Homestead Lane. After 0.2 mile, turn right (west) onto Access Road and continue for 0.6 mile. Turn right (west) into the parking lot. GPS: N38°54.893' / W94°58.461'

Trail conditions: The well-maintained, well-marked trails are a mix of paved, crushed rock, and natural surface. The trails receive heavy traffic, so avoid hiking with headphones or earbuds so you can hear mountain bikers and other trail users.

The Hike

Kill Creek Park is nestled along the wooded creek that gives the park its name. There are more than 12 miles of trails for mountain biking and hiking, as well as equestrian trails. There is also a 1.5-mile paved trail, accessible for wheelchairs and strollers, that is perfect for walking, running, and bicycling. The trails are not the only draw to the park; the large lake is great for fishing and boating, and the small fishing pond is an idyllic fishing hole. The numerous picnic shelters in the park are popular for family and group outings.

Kill Creek Trail is a level forest trail.

Prairie observation deck.

This is also an excellent birding destination—the observation tower and prairie observation deck offer great vantage points for viewing grassland species. The Russell and Helen Means Observation Tower takes its name from the former landowners, who donated more than 300 acres to the county for public use.

The 12-mile trail system allows visitors to hike as far or as short as they like. Most of the trails are woodland trails, while a few sections follow the edges of prairie. The hike described in "Miles and Directions" creates a simple yet challenging loop of slightly more than 3 miles, as there are a few stream crossings to manage. If you want to add distance to this hike, there are opportunities in the northwestern corner of the park, where trails weave through the forest. There is also a hiking/biking trail that is accessed via the paved trail on the west side of the park. This out-and-back hiking trail follows the course of Kill Creek.

Additional hikes: Kill Creek Park is connected to one of the two segments that make up Kill Creek Park Streamway Park. The southern segment goes through Kill Creek Park itself and then leaves the park to follow Kill Creek south to West 135th Street in Olathe. The northern segment—not connected to the southern segment—begins near Lexington Avenue in De Soto and winds south of KS 10 along Kill Creek. The two segments total almost 9 miles and are paved, making them excellent

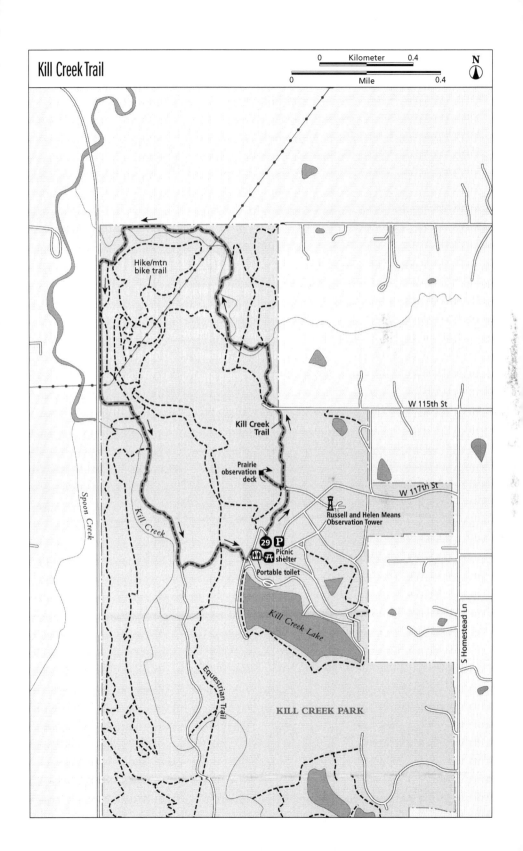

Kill Creek Trail

0 Kilometer 0.4

0 Mile 0.4

N

Hike/mtn
bike trail

Kill Creek
Trail

W 115th St

Prairie
observation
deck

W 117th St

Russell and Helen Means
Observation Tower

29 P

Picnic
shelter

Portable toilet

Spoon Creek

Kill Creek

Kill Creek Lake

Equestrian Trail

S Homestead Ln

KILL CREEK PARK

accessible options for enjoying the Kill Creek Area. Lexington Lake Park, located west of De Soto on KS 10, is a 465-acre park featuring a 27-acre lake. There is an accessible, paved 1.6-mile path around the lake, in addition to 9 miles of singletrack trails for hiking and mountain biking. The Emerald Loop is a popular route that has some difficult sections on the north half of the loop. Get a trail map on the park's website (jcprd.com/Facilities/Facility/Details/Lexington-Lake-Park-39).

Miles and Directions

0.00 Start at the northwest corner of the parking lot and head north on the paved trail.

0.03 Turn right (northeast) onto Prairie Hiking Trail.

0.16 Keep left (west).

0.19 Continue straight (west) toward the prairie observation deck.

0.26 Prairie observation deck.

0.38 Turn left (north).

0.60 Turn left (west) onto a gravel trail.

0.73 Streambed.

0.81 Water crossing.

0.83 Reach Junction D; turn left (west).

0.89 Continue straight (west).

0.94 Water crossing.

1.09 Water crossing.

1.19 Junction E; keep left (northwest).

1.53 Streambed.

1.66 Turn right (east).

2.00 Turn left (east) onto Kill Creek Trail.

2.15 At a bench, turn right (south).

2.67 Turn left (northeast) at a junction with a bench.

2.91 Turn left (north). (Option: Turn right/south to hike a loop around the lake.)

2.94 Turn right (east).

3.04 Arrive back at the parking lot.

30 Olathe Prairie Center

Olathe Prairie Center is an island of remnant and restored prairie in an urban sea. The wildflowers, native grasses, and clear air will reinvigorate you after a hike on its trails. Wildflower enthusiasts will find a variety of species to identify, including the endangered Mead's milkweed, which flowers in late May and early June. A branch of Cedar Creek with limestone bluffs passes through the prairie center.

Start: Parking lot near the intersection of South Cedar Niles Road and West 135th Street
Elevation gain: 915 feet to 1,037 feet; 230 feet total elevation gain
Distance: 2.83-mile loop
Difficulty: Easy
Hiking time: 1–1.5 hours
Seasons/schedule: Open daily year-round, dawn to dusk
Fees and permits: None
Trail contact: Olathe Prairie Center, 26325 W 135th St., Olathe 66061; (785) 273-6740; ksoutdoors.com/KDWP-Info/Locations/Museums-and-Nature-Centers/Olathe-Prairie-Center
Dog-friendly: No

Trail surface: Gravel roads and mowed grass paths
Land status: Olathe Prairie Center (Kansas Department of Wildlife & Parks)
Nearest town: Olathe
Maps: USGS De Soto, KS
Other trail users: None
Special considerations: There are no public buildings, and public access is restricted to trails and a few gathering areas.
Amenities: Pit toilets
Maximum grade: 11%; two notable inclines, both with approximately 50–70 feet of elevation gain
Cell service: Reliable on the entire trail

Finding the trailhead: From I-35, take exit 215 and head north on South Harrison Street. Turn left (west) onto KS 7. After 1 mile, turn right (north) onto South Lone Elm Road/South Parker Street, then turn left (west) onto West 143rd Street/West Dennis Avenue. After 3 miles, turn right (north) onto South Cedar Niles Road. GPS: N38°52.979' / W94°53.426'

Trail conditions: The trails are a mix of mowed grass, gravel, and natural surface. They are well maintained, but there are no trail markers. The trails receive moderate traffic.

The Hike

The primary goal of the Olathe Prairie Center is as a reserve for native plants, but it also serves as an oasis of nature in the densely populated Kansas City metropolitan area. Every season of the year offers different ways to connect with nature. Spring brings wildflowers such as spiderwort, Carolina anemone, and wild strawberry. Endangered Mead's milkweed can be found here; come in late May or early June to see it blooming. Aster and goldenrod bloom in late summer, marking the coming of fall, when the bluestem grows to 6 feet or taller.

The main trail at the Olathe Prairie Center is 2.83 miles, although there are additional trails mowed through the prairie so hikers can extend their hikes. Leave

Cedar Creek crossing.

Prairie Center Pond.

the parking area from its southwest corner and continue in the direction toward the pond. Fishing is allowed at the pond, so if you are an angler, don't forget to bring your rod and other equipment. Follow the trail on the pond's northern end, then turn north to descend toward the lowest point on the hike. Depending on the water level and recent precipitation, you may be able to cross the stream with little trouble and dry shoes. If the water is higher, take your time; the worst that can happen is you'll have to hike the rest of the trail with wet socks.

After 0.25 mile, turn left to head south through the prairie. You will pass a trail on your right that leads to an alternative trailhead in the northwestern corner of the reserve. When you reconnect with the gravel trail at a bench, turn right onto the gravel trail to continue south. The next mile will take you under tree cover as you head east, back toward the pond. There will be two more water crossings before you reach the pond, but much like the first crossing, they are easily managed. When you reach the picnic area on the western side of the pond, take the trail that heads southeast along the wooded southern edge of the pond, with prairie on your right. As you approach South Cedar Niles Road, turn north at an oak tree. If you hike in June, you will pass a very large patch of wild prairie rose. Continue heading north until reaching the parking lot.

Olathe Prairie Center

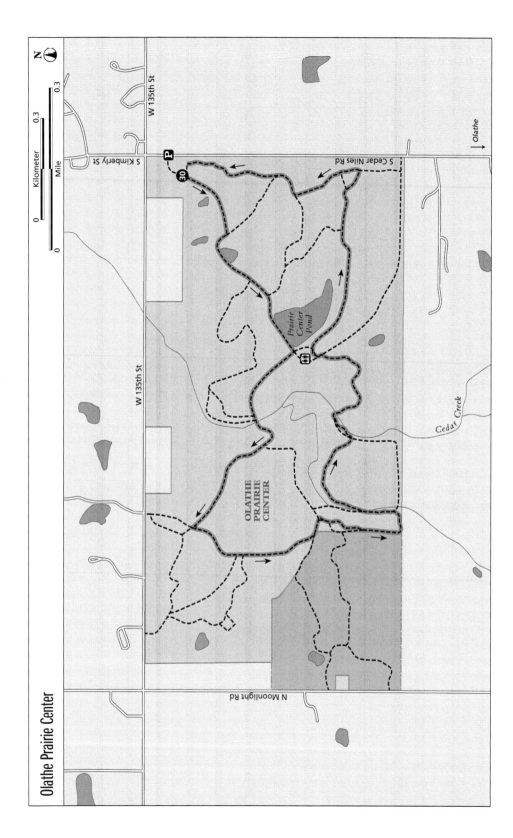

ERNIE MILLER PARK AND NATURE CENTER

The Ernie Miller Park and Nature Center has 3 miles of nature trails through tallgrass prairie, upland meadows, and bottomland forest. The stream offers exploration of aquatic life, while the nature center has year-round interpretive programming for all ages and a gift shop. Dogs are not allowed on the trails; however, the nature center and its trails are an excellent family-friendly place to explore and learn about nature.

Additional hikes: Cedar Niles Park, located less than 1 mile to the northeast of the Olathe Prairie Center, has a paved trail and singletrack hiking/biking trails. The park gets its name from the cedar forest and Little Cedar Creek, which passes through the park. The paved trail is 4 miles one way; the natural-surface Columbine Loop is around 4.5 miles.

Miles and Directions

0.00 Start at the gate and head south on the gravel road.

0.28 Continue straight (southwest).

0.45 Turn right (north).

0.62 Water crossing.

0.70 Continue straight (north). (Option: Turn left/southwest for a shortcut.)

0.92 Turn left (south).

1.03 Continue straight (south).

1.23 At a bench, turn right (southwest) onto the gravel trail.

1.50 Water crossing.

1.79 Water crossing.

2.00 Turn left (northwest).

2.42 At an oak tree, turn left (north).

2.47 Continue straight (north).

2.56 Turn right (northeast).

2.83 Arrive back at the parking lot.

31 South Shore Trails

Shawnee Mission Park is the most-visited park in the state of Kansas, thanks to its large size (1,655 acres) and location in the heart of the Kansas City metropolitan area. There are 10 miles of multiuse trails on the north shore; however, the 5 miles of trails on the south shore are hiker-only. Both sets of trails are busy, but if you are looking for a quiet escape on tranquil forest trails, head to the south shore.

Start: Parking lot for Shelter #10
Elevation gain: 878 feet to 966 feet; 223 feet total elevation gain
Distance: 4.27-mile loop
Difficulty: Moderate
Hiking time: 1.5-2 hours
Seasons/schedule: Open daily year-round, dawn to dusk
Fees and permits: None
Trail contact: Shawnee Mission Park, 7900 Renner Rd., Shawnee 66219; (913) 204-0204, ext. 20; jcprd.com/facilities/facility/details/Shawnee-Mission-Park-14
Dog-friendly: Yes, on leash
Trail surface: Paved and natural

Land status: Shawnee Mission Park (Johnson County Parks & Recreation)
Nearest town: Shawnee
Maps: USGS Olathe, KS; trail map available on the park website
Other trail users: None
Special considerations: None
Amenities: Restrooms and water at the parking lot
Maximum grade: 6%; the biggest incline is roughly 80 feet over less than 0.5 mile.
Cell service: Adequate to above average on the majority of the trails; tree cover may limit coverage

Finding the trailhead: From I-435, take exit 5 and head south on Renner Road. After 1 mile, turn west onto West 79th Street, then turn immediately south onto Barkley Drive. After 0.5 mile, turn north into the parking lot for Shelter #10. The trailhead is located at the parking lot for Shelter #10. GPS: N38°58.753' / W94°47.272'

Trail conditions: The trails are well maintained. There are no trail markers, and while it would be difficult to get lost, it is not out of the question. Follow a GPX track or get the map off the park's website if you have concerns about navigation. The trail receives heavy foot traffic.

The Hike

Shawnee Mission Park is perhaps the most popular park for outdoor recreation on the Kansas side of the KC metropolitan area, not only due to its location but also because of the variety of activities the park offers. The park's size, nearly 1,700 acres, occupies a substantial chunk of the metro area. The 120-acre lake is the centerpiece and focal point, as swimming at the beach and boating on the lake are popular weekend activities. There are numerous picnic areas, playgrounds, a 44-acre off-leash area for dogs, and events throughout the year.

For hikers, there are more than 10 miles of trails on both the north and south sides of the lake. There are both paved and natural-surface trails in the park. Since Shawnee

The trails on the south shore of Shawnee Mission Lake are hiker-only.

Shawnee Mission Lake.

Mission Park is the busiest park in the entire state of Kansas, it is hard to escape the crowds for a serene experience in nature. The paved trails receive the most traffic, although even the natural-surface trails are busy. The trails on the northern side of the lake are the most popular, as they are open to both hikers and bikers. All combined, the northern trails total 10 miles of hiking and biking. The advantage of the trails on the southern shore of Shawnee Mission Lake is that they are only open to hikers. The described hike comes in at just under 4.5 miles, but if you add the West Loop via the Connector Trail, you can hike more than 5 miles without worrying about bikers coming around a blind bend.

This hike begins at the parking lot for Shelter #10. Head north on a paved trail, passing the large, covered shelter, toward the Walnut Grove recreation area. Turn west, cross a small stream, and find the access point for the East Loop Trail; enter the trail and keep right to head northwest. The trail runs above a small creek—a popular and excellent place to explore with children, as the water does not run very deep. After nearly 0.75 mile, the trail reaches Shawnee Mission Lake and heads west for the next 0.25 mile and then south for roughly 0.5 mile until it reaches the junction with the Middle Loop. There are good views of the lake from this section of the hike. The trail has been relatively flat until now and continues to be for the next 0.5 mile until

South Shore Trails

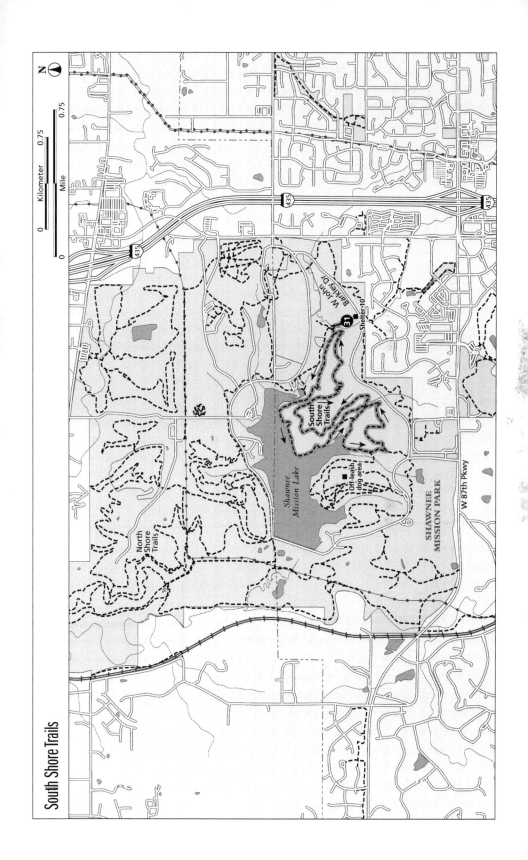

OVERLAND PARK ARBORETUM AND BOTANICAL GARDENS

The popular Overland Park Arboretum and Botanical Gardens is located south of Overland Park off US 69. The botanical gardens feature 1,700 plant species, with 6 miles of paved and wood chip hiking trails open to visitors. Most of the trails wander along and near the wooded Wolf Creek. The prairie south of the creek is open to off-trail exploration.

reaching the 2-mile mark. The trail heads south and climbs just under 100 feet as it heads south, away from the lake.

The 2-mile mark is the junction of Middle Loop and Connector Trails, which, as its name suggests, connects the East and Middle Loops with the West Loop Trail. If you hike both West Loop and Connector Trails, it will add almost 1.5 miles to this hike. To continue following the described hike, turn left (northeast) to remain on Middle Loop. The trail heads through upland forest, away from the lakeshore, until reaching the access point and paved trail leading to the parking area.

Additional hikes: While the trails at Shawnee Mission Park are excellent for hiking, other options in the area are quieter, but they come with caveats. The Hollis Renewal Center (holliscenter.org/hiking.html), located between the Kansas River and I-70, has more than 5 miles of trails that explore a hidden valley in Wyandotte County. The trails at this Christian retreat center are open to the public. Expect quiet trails, but some of the trails are overgrown in summer and thus prime woodland habitat for ticks, so prepare accordingly.

Miles and Directions

0.00 Start from the Shelter #10 parking lot and head north on the paved trail past the picnic shelter.

0.08 Keep left (northwest).

0.13 Continue straight (northwest).

0.27 Overlook of the creek.

1.55 Reach a fork and keep right (south), then cross a rocky stream.

2.08 Turn left (northeast). (Option: Continue straight/south to hike West Loop.)

2.38 Dry, rocky streambed.

2.61 Turn right (east), cross the stream, then turn right (southeast).

4.09 Turn right (east).

4.27 Arrive back at the parking lot.

Honorable Mentions

J Red Trail and Cedar Crest

Kaw River State Park and MacLennan Park sit adjacent to each other on the south bank of the Kansas River in the state capital. In fact, the governor's mansion, Cedar Crest, is located in MacLennan Park. Between the two parks, there are 11 miles of gravel and dirt trails along the forested river bluffs. Head deep into the trails on Red Trail to forget you are in the state capital right next to I-70.

Start: Trailhead on Governor's Lake Road
Elevation gain: 886 feet to 1,076 feet; 433 feet total elevation gain
Distance: 4.31-mile loop
Difficulty: Moderate
Hiking time: About 2 hours
Seasons/schedule: Open daily year-round, dawn to dusk
Fees and permits: None

Trail contact: Kaw River State Park, 300 SW Wanamaker Rd., Topeka 66606; (785) 273-6740; ksoutdoors.com/State-Parks/Locations/Kaw-River
Dog-friendly: Yes, on leash
Trail surface: Paved and natural surface trails (dirt and gravel)
Land status: Kaw River State Park and MacLennan Park (Kansas Trails Council)

Kaw River State Park and MacLennan Park.

Nearest town: Topeka
Maps: USGS Topeka, KS, and USGS Silver Lake, KS; trail map available online and at the park
Other trail users: Mountain bikers
Special considerations: Several parking areas provide access to the trail system in both parks.

Amenities: None
Maximum grade: 14%; two substantial climbs, both roughly 150 feet over less than 0.5 mile
Cell service: Reliable throughout the trail system

Finding the trailhead: Take exit 357A off I-70 in Topeka. Head north on Southwest Fairlawn Road, then turn west onto Southwest Cedar Crest Road. The trailhead is on the west side of Cedar Crest, the governor's mansion. GPS: N39°3.983' / W95°44.866'

   Trail conditions: The trails along the river are too rough for strollers and wheelchairs, although there are paved and level gravel trails around Cedar Crest. The trails receive heavy foot traffic.

K Lawrence River Trail

The Lawrence River Trail offers hikers and bikers almost 10 miles of trails on the wooded north bank of the Kansas River. Due to its location in Lawrence, the trail is very popular with both hikers and mountain bikers, who travel the trail in opposite directions.

Start: Lawrence Riverfront Park
Elevation gain: Minimal, as the trail follows the bank of the Kansas River.
Distance: 9-mile loop (there are several cutoffs to make the hike shorter)
Difficulty: Easy due to level terrain and ability to shorten the hike
Hiking time: About 3.5 hours
Seasons/schedule: Open daily year-round, dawn to dusk
Fees and permits: None
Trail contact: Lawrence Mountain Bike Club, PO Box 1963, Lawrence 66044; lawrence mountainbikeclub.org/lawrence-river-trails/
Dog-friendly: Yes, on leash
Trail surface: Natural (dirt)

Land status: North Lawrence City Park (maintained almost exclusively by the Lawrence Mountain Bike Club)
Nearest town: Lawrence
Maps: USGS Lawrence East, KS; trail map available online and displayed at the trailhead kiosk
Other trail users: Mountain bikers
Special considerations: Do not use the trails if they are muddy or your footprints leave a mark. Hikers travel counterclockwise; bikers go clockwise. Bikers must yield to hikers.
Amenities: None
Maximum grade: No significant, sustained inclines
Cell service: Adequate

Finding the trailhead: Going north on Massachusetts Street from downtown, take the first right (east) over the bridge onto Elm Street. Follow Elm to 8th Street. Turn right (south) onto 8th, and cross over the levee. There is a parking lot between the levee and the Kansas River. GPS: N38°58.318' / W95°12.964'

   Trail conditions: The trail is well maintained and marked. Due to the trail's popularity with mountain bikers, hikers must be aware of their surroundings; do not hike with headphones or

Lawrence River Trail.

earbuds so that you can hear approaching bikers. Hikers and bikers must travel the trail in opposite directions. Poison ivy, ticks, and insects are present. The trail receives heavy traffic.

∟ KU Field Station Trails

There are 5 miles of public nature trails at the University of Kansas Field Station, a research site located 15 minutes from downtown Lawrence. The Henry S. Fitch Nature Trail is named for a professor who lived and worked on the site from 1948 until 2009. The Fitch Trail connects to the adjacent Roth Trail and the paved Rockefeller Trail, which ends at the Kaw River Valley Overlook, offering spectacular views of the area.

Start: 2055 East 1600 Road, Lawrence
Elevation gain: 876 feet to 1,073 feet; 197 feet total elevation gain
Distance: 5 total miles of trails
Difficulty: Moderate due to overgrown trails
Hiking time: 2–3 hours
Seasons/schedule: Open daily year-round, dawn to dusk

Fees and permits: None
Trail contact: Kansas Biological Survey and Center for Ecological Research, (785) 864-1500; biosurvey.ku.edu/field-station-trails; email: biosurvey@ku.edu
Dog-friendly: No
Trail surface: Natural and gravel
Land status: University of Kansas Field Station

Henry S. Fitch Nature Trail.

Nearest town: Lawrence to the south

Maps: USGS Midland, KS; maps of full trail system installed at each trailhead

Other trail users: None

Special considerations: Rockefeller Trail is accessible to individuals who use wheelchairs.

Amenities: None

Maximum grade: 14%; Rockefeller Trailhead is 150 feet higher in elevation than Roth Trailhead; there are several inclines on Fitch Trail.

Cell service: Adequate, although may be limited under tree cover

Finding the trailhead: From I-70, take exit 204 in north Lawrence. Head north on US 59/US 40 for 0.4 mile, then turn east onto US 40/US 24. After 0.6 mile, turn north onto East 1500 Road. Continue for 2 miles, then turn east onto North 2000 Road. Turn north onto East 1600 Road after 1 mile and continue for 0.6 mile to the parking area at the Roth Trailhead. GPS (Roth Trailhead): N39°2.320' / W95°12.423'

Trail conditions: The trails are natural and receive minimal maintenance; be prepared for overgrown trails. There is poison ivy present, and ticks and insects are problematic April to October. Fitch Trail is well marked. The trails receive light traffic.

M Wyandotte County Lake Loop Trail

A 10.4-mile hike with more than 1,000 feet of elevation gain in the middle of a metropolitan area is surprising, to say the least. If you live in the Kansas City metro, you don't have to drive far for an epic hike. There are options for those who prefer a shorter hike. Keep in mind that navigation is difficult due to numerous trails and lack of waymarking.

Start: South end of the lake near the park headquarters

Elevation gain: 762 feet to 983 feet; 1,322 feet total elevation gain

Distance: 10.4-mile loop

Difficulty: Difficult due to distance, elevation gain, and navigation issues

Hiking time: 5 or more hours

Seasons/schedule: Open daily, 6 a.m.–10 p.m.

Fees and permits: None

Trail contact: Wyandotte County Lake Park, 701 N 7th St., Kansas City 66101; (913) 573-5311; www.wycokck.org/My-Neighborhood/Wyandotte-County-Lake-Park

Dog-friendly: Yes, on leash

Trail surface: Natural

Land status: Wyandotte County Lake Park (Wyandotte County Parks & Recreation)

Nearest town: Kansas City

Maps: USGS Wolcott, KS, MO; park and trail map available by contacting Wyandotte County Parks & Recreation

Other trail users: Mountain bikers and equestrians

Special considerations: Avoid using the trails when they are muddy to prevent trail degradation.

Amenities: Restrooms at the trailhead

Maximum grade: 23%; numerous inclines and declines, including one climb of 200 feet over less than 0.5 mile

Cell service: Adequate, although may be limited under tree cover

Finding the trailhead: From I-435, take exit 16 and head east on Donahoo Road. After 0.6 mile, Donahoo Road becomes Hurrelbrink Road; continue for 1 mile. Turn right (southeast) onto West Drive, then turn right into the parking lot at Shelter House 2. GPS: N39°9.019' / W94°47.335'

Trail conditions: The trail is not waymarked, making navigation difficult. Using a GPS device to follow a track is highly recommended. Avoid the trail after rain, as it will be muddy.

Wyandotte County Lake Loop Trail.

Osage Cuestas and Ozark Plateau

"We're not in Kansas anymore." If there is anywhere in Kansas where Dorothy's famous phrase rings true, it is in southeastern Kansas. The Osage Cuestas and Ozark Plateau, while within Kansas territory, share more in common with the state's southern neighbor of Oklahoma and eastern neighbor of Missouri. The Osage Cuestas region, encompassing almost all eastern Kansas south of the Kansas River, gets the latter half of its name from the Spanish "cuesta," meaning hill or cliff. The east-facing ridges rise 200 feet above the surrounding landscape. The first half of the region's name comes from the Midwestern Native American tribe of the Great Plains. The Osage were forced from Kansas to Oklahoma in the nineteenth century. Some of the best hiking in the entire state of Kansas can be found in the Osage Cuestas. The Elk River Hiking Trail is one of the most challenging backpacking trails in the Midwest, while the nearby Table Mound Trail in Elk City State Park is the author's choice for the best hike in the Sunflower State. Cross Timbers State Park includes several trails, the highlight being Ancient Trees Trail, with some of the oldest trees in Kansas in a beautiful post oak forest. As of 2023, the title of newest state park in Kansas belongs to Lehigh Portland State Park, former site of the largest cement company in the United States. The hiking and mountain biking trails have been extremely popular since their opening in 2016. Finally, Schermerhorn Park, located on the Ozark Plateau, takes hikers to the entrance of a cave that is home to several rare and endangered species of salamanders.

Elk River Hiking Trail.

32 Badger Creek North Trail

While popular with mountain bikers, Badger Creek North Trail is an excellent hiking trail through the riparian woodland along Badger Creek. The wooded trail is rugged, rocky, and quiet. Essentially a mountain bike trail, the trail is free-flowing narrow singletrack, but the large rock outcroppings entice hikers and bikers alike.

Start: Badger Creek North Trailhead on Badger Creek Road
Elevation gain: 978 feet to 1,050 feet; 220 feet total elevation gain
Distance: 3.59-mile loop
Difficulty: Moderate due to rocky, rugged terrain
Hiking time: About 2 hours
Seasons/schedule: Trails closed during firearms deer season and part of the archery deer season
Fees and permits: None
Trail contact: Fall Lake Project Office, US Army Corps of Engineers, 2453 Lake Rd., Fall River 67047; (620) 658-4445; www.swt.usace .army.mil/Locations/Tulsa-District-Lakes/ Kansas/Fall-River-Lake/
Dog-friendly: Yes, on leash

Trail surface: Natural (dirt, rocks)
Land status: Fall River Lake (US Army Corps of Engineers)
Nearest town: Eureka, 30 miles to the northwest
Maps: USGS Fall River Lake, KS; trail map displayed at the trailhead kiosk
Other trail users: Mountain bikers
Special considerations: In addition to trail closures during firearms deer season and part of the archery deer season, discretion is advised during the spring wild turkey season, as hunters may be present.
Amenities: None
Maximum grade: 7%; multiple inclines between 25 and 50 feet in elevation change
Cell service: Weak coverage due to tree cover

Finding the trailhead: From Eureka, head east on US 54 East/East River Street. After 2.5 miles, turn south onto KS 99 and continue for 13 miles. Turn east onto US 400; after 7.5 miles, turn north onto Lake Road. Continue on Lake Road for 4.5 miles. After crossing the Fall River Lake dam, turn north onto Badger Creek Road. Continue for 2.6 miles to the small parking area at the trailhead. GPS: N37°41.309' / W96°3.763'

Trail conditions: The trails are generally in good condition, but vegetation typically grows over sections during the summer. The trail receives light to moderate traffic.

The Hike

The Badger Creek Trail system comprises two trails along the eponymous creek, one to the west and the other on the east side of the creek. The trails are just north of Fall River Lake, a popular outdoor recreation spot for bikers, hikers, hunters, anglers, and campers. There are several campgrounds around the lake, making the area popular and busy during the summer and holiday weekends.

Badger Creek North Trail begins by heading north via a narrow dirt singletrack that is often overgrown in summer. Very shortly after leaving the trailhead, keep right

The trails meander through the Badger Creek watershed.

North Trail is one of two Badger Creek trails.

to continue north to hike the trail in a counterclockwise direction. The trail eventually widens out and becomes cleaner with less vegetation growing over the trail, although it will narrow again. You will want to wear long pants, even in summer, to protect against ticks. The trail is entirely underneath the tree canopy, so while you won't be getting bombarded by the sun, it will be humid.

The trail crosses several dry creek beds, rock outcroppings, and large boulders. As you head north you will see a trail to the west on your left. Continue on the same trail to prevent creating unwanted shortcuts and erosion; if you want to cut your hike short, simply turn around. Badger Creek runs parallel to the trail on your right (east). Eventually the creek will be to the north of the trail, and at this point it bends on itself to begin heading south. The trail requires little navigation, as there are no intersecting trails. Shortcuts and spur trails are marked, so keep your eyes open for them. Also, do not wear earbuds or headphones as you hike so that you can hear bikers approaching or coming from behind. Since this is an easy trail to navigate, immerse yourself in the woodnotes and birdsong of the forest.

The trail meanders south for over 0.5 mile before it heads west at the 1.6-mile mark. It is easy to mistake the dry creek beds in this section as the trail, so pay attention to where the singletrack leads ahead of you. Around the 1.75-mile mark, the trail

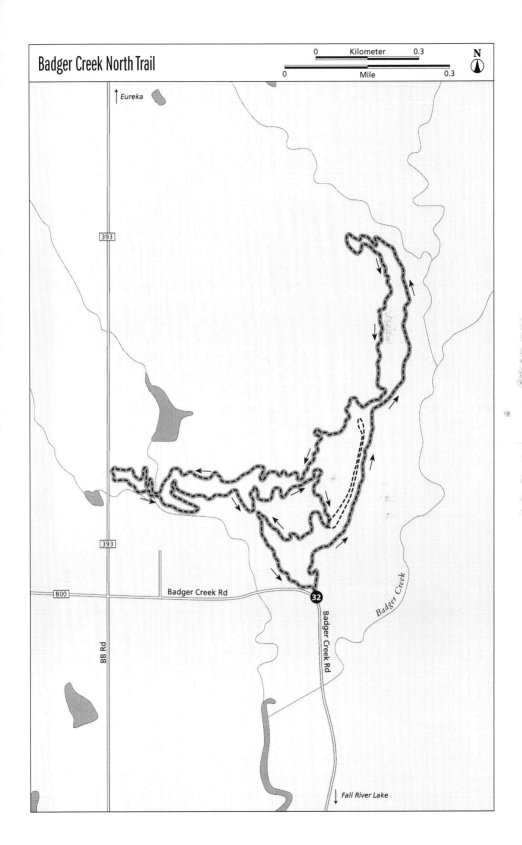

Helpful trail markers indicate shortcuts and bypasses.

crosses over a dry creek bed several times, so it's important not to confuse the creek bed with the trail and wander off-trail. After heading west for more than 0.5 mile, the trail bends on itself once again to head east.

After 3 miles, the trail begins to head south back to the trailhead. Shortly after, there is an option to take a loop north and then back south. If you want to add more mileage to your hike, take this route; otherwise veer right (southwest) at the bypass arrow at 3.11 miles. You will reach the picnic table you passed when you began the hike before reaching the trailhead.

Additional hike: Just south of the trailhead on Badger Creek Road is the trailhead for Badger Creek South Trail. This narrow loop trail heads north and then south on the east side of the Badger Creek watershed, totaling 4.4 miles. It is also popular with mountain bikers.

Miles and Directions

0.00 Start from the trailhead and head north.

3.11 Veer right (southwest), indicated by the bypass arrow on a sign nailed to a tree.

3.55 Turn right (south) at the picnic table.

3.59 Arrive back at the trailhead.

33 Ancient Trees Trail

Interesting rock formations make Ancient Trees Trail attractive, but it is the trail's namesake that truly makes this hike impressive. The trail meanders through an ancient forest of post and blackjack oaks, with interpretive signage along the trail dating some of the oldest trees. This is a wonderful family hike to explore the Cross Timbers region of southeastern Kansas.

Start: Trailhead west of the pay station at the entrance to the Toronto Point Area
Elevation gain: 923 feet to 991 feet; 72 feet total elevation gain
Distance: 0.96-mile loop
Difficulty: Easy, although uneven trail surface in sections may be challenging for some hikers
Hiking time: About 1 hour
Seasons/schedule: Open daily year-round, dawn to dusk
Fees and permits: Daily or annual vehicle permit required, purchased at the park office or online
Trail contact: Cross Timbers State Park, 144 Hwy. 105, Toronto 66777; (620) 637-2213; ksoutdoors.com/State-Parks/Locations/Cross-Timbers
Dog-friendly: Yes, on leash
Trail surface: Natural

Land status: Cross Timbers State Park (Kansas Department of Wildlife & Parks)
Nearest town: Toronto, 7 miles to the north
Maps: USGS Toronto, KS; park map available online
Other trail users: None
Special considerations: Trail best completed counterclockwise. As of July 2023, the southern end of the official loop was impassable and a shortcut had been created.
Amenities available: Water just south of the pay station and restrooms in Cross Timbers Campground
Maximum grade: 9%; the only incline of note is a 50-foot climb over almost 0.25 mile at the end of the loop.
Cell service: Adequate, although may be limited by tree cover

Finding the trailhead: From Toronto, head east on East Main Street. Turn south onto South Point Road and continue for 1.2 miles. The trailhead and small parking area are next to the RV dump station. GPS: N37°46.755' / W95°56.642'

Trail conditions: As of July 2023, the southern end of the loop was impassable due to a fallen tree and the trail disappearing into overgrown brush. An alternative shortcut connected to the loop, allowing hikers to return to the trailhead.

The Hike

Ancient Trees Trail is the only hiker-only trail in Cross Timbers State Park. The park gets its name from a region that covers Texas, Oklahoma, and a small portion of southeastern Kansas. There are many theories about the name but no consensus. The first recorded use of the name dates to 1716, by Spanish explorers. The ancient forest of post and blackjack oaks, in addition to sandstone rock formations and the Toronto Reservoir, make this state park popular with outdoor recreationists.

Ancient Trees Trail passes through a post and blackjack oak forest.

A rock shelter along the trail.

The trailhead for Ancient Trees Trail is marked by a sign, making it easy to find next to the pay station at the entrance to the state park's Toronto Point Area. You will have to descend a dozen stone steps at the beginning of the trail. Although the trail is short and has minimal elevation gain, the rocky and uneven trail surface will pose difficulties for people with mobility issues. The beauty of the forest can distract you, so make sure you pay attention to where you are stepping to avoid tripping over a rock or tree root.

This hike is not only a beautiful forest trail, it is also very informative. Numerous interpretive panels along the trail explain the natural history of the Cross Timbers region, the local flora and fauna, and of course information about the oldest trees along the trail. Some of the trees described by the panels are not immediately next to the trail, so take your time at each panel to find the corresponding tree. The trees were dated in 1982 by University of Arkansas Tree-Ring Laboratory scientists, who analyzed the tree rings of twenty-six post oaks in the forest. Fourteen of the old-growth oaks are visible from the trail, which was created after the scientists completed their study.

The trail is easy to follow thanks to trail markers along the way. After heading north for 0.5 mile, the trail turns to head south. You will reach a natural rock shelter after 0.75 mile. Imagine how many centuries this has been used by humans for shelter! As you continue heading south, you will pass a spur trail that connects to the

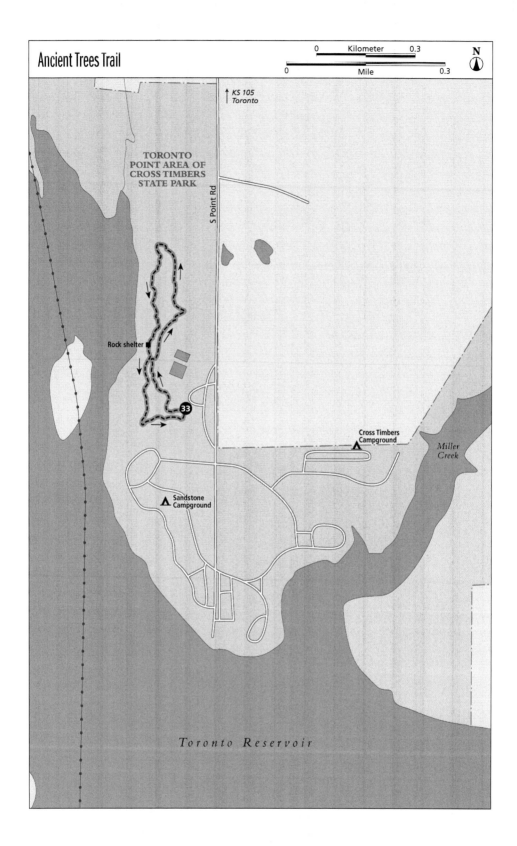

Ancient Trees Trail

0   Kilometer   0.3

0   Mile   0.3

N

↑ KS 105
Toronto

**TORONTO
POINT AREA OF
CROSS TIMBERS
STATE PARK**

S Point Rd

Rock shelter ■

33

Cross Timbers
Campground

*Miller
Creek*

▲ Sandstone
Campground

Toronto Reservoir

The trailhead is next to the pay station at the Toronto Point Area entrance.

original trail back to the trailhead. As of July 2023, the southern end of the loop was impassable. There were signs, but the trail had become overgrown and blocked by fallen trees. The section has been in disrepair for so long that the spur trail has become worn. The diversion is not marked, but it not difficult to find the spur trail and your way back to the trailhead.

Additional hikes: Chautauqua Hills Trail is another hiking opportunity in Cross Timbers State Park. Unlike Ancient Trees Trail, it is open to both hikers and mountain bikers. Intrepid hikers can complete the entire 11-mile loop, while a shorter 1.5-mile loop allows a more leisurely hike. Campsites along the trail provide backpacking opportunities. Find the main trailhead east of Osage Plains Campground. An alternative trailhead on Coyote Road allows quicker access to the second half of the loop. The Overlook Trail at Woodson Cove offers a challenging 1.25-mile hike with sandstone outcroppings, steep ravines, and spectacular views of the Toronto Reservoir. Two trails, Blackjack and Oak Ridge, at the Holiday Hill Area are additional hiking options.

Miles and Directions

0.00 Facing the trailhead sign, take the trail on the right to head northwest.

0.69 Rock shelter.

0.84 Turn left (northeast).

0.96 Arrive back at the trailhead.

34 Elk River Hiking Trail

"We're not in Kansas anymore." Even though the Elk River Hiking Trail is indeed in Kansas, you will be repeating Dorothy's famous saying while hiking the best hiking trail in the Sunflower State. The 15-mile point-to-point hike is one of the most underrated backpacking trails in the United States and one of the most challenging trails in the Midwest.

Start: The East Trailhead, West Trailhead, and Oak Ridge Public Use Area are the only access points.

Elevation gain: 777 feet (lowest) to 911 feet (highest); 977 feet total elevation gain

Distance: 15 miles point to point

Difficulty: Difficult due to length, lack of access points, and rugged terrain

Hiking time: 6 hours, minimum

Seasons/schedule: Open daily, year-round

Fees and permits: None

Trail contact: Elk City Lake Project Office, 19065 Cherryvale Pkwy., Cherryvale 67335; (620) 336-2741; www.swt.usace.army.mil/Locations/Tulsa-District-Lakes/Kansas/Elk-City-Lake/

Dog-friendly: Yes, on leash

Trail surface: Natural

Land status: Elk City Lake (US Army Corps of Engineers)

Nearest town: Independence, 9 miles to the southeast

Maps: USGS Elk City, KS, and Table Mound, KS 2018; trail map available on the website and at access points

Other trail users: None

Special considerations: Backcountry camping is allowed at campsites along the trail.

Amenities: Camping

Maximum grade: 15%; the steepest climb is 100 feet over 0.33 mile near the east trailhead. There are multiple inclines and declines throughout the trail's length.

Cell service: Adequate to weak

Finding the trailhead: To reach the East Trailhead from Independence, head west on US 160/US 75. Turn north onto 3325 Road and continue for 1 mile. Turn west onto CR 4600, then turn immediately north onto CR 3300. Continue for 2 miles until CR 3300 becomes Table Mound Road; continue another 0.4 mile. Keep left (west) onto CR 5050. Cross the dam, then turn west at the Elk City Fish & Wildlife Office to reach the East Trailhead.

    East Trailhead GPS: N37°16.916' / W95°48.017'

    West Trailhead GPS: N37°16.077' / W95°54.046'

    Oak Ridge Public Use Area GPS: N37°15.571' / W95°51.640'

    Trail conditions: The trail is well marked with blue blazes, but it is recommended to follow the trail using a GPS device.

The Hike

Do not let the distance or lack of access points discourage you—a 3-mile day hike on the Elk River Hiking Trail is just as rewarding as hiking the entire trail. Obviously, if you hike the entire length, or even hike back after completing the trail in one direction, you will feel immense satisfaction having tackled one of the most challenging

This is not your typical Kansas prairie trail.

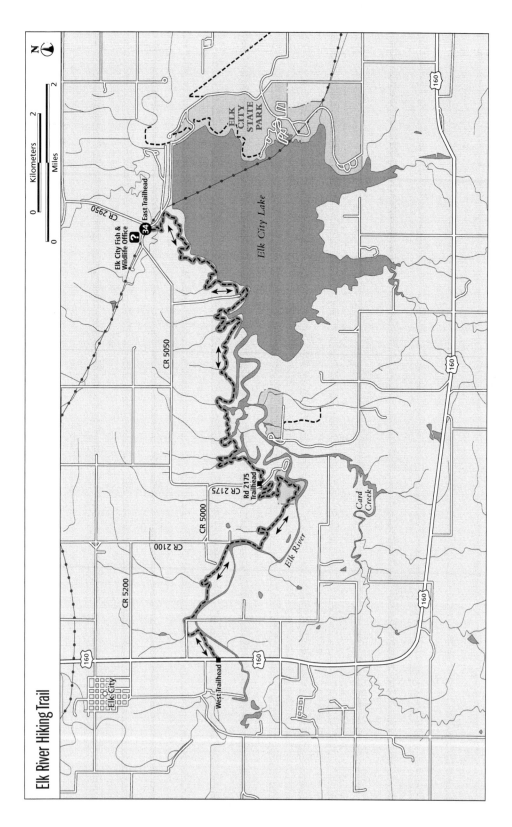

Elk River Hiking Trail

hikes in the Midwest. But if your time is limited, or you just are not up to taking on the entire trail, a short day hike of any distance will leave an indelible impression after experiencing one of Kansas's natural wonders.

If you start from the East Trailhead, you will climb 100 feet over 0.33 mile before reaching a section with incredible rock formations. You do not need to worry about navigation, as the trail is excellently waymarked with blue blazes. Although the trail can become overgrown in stretches during the summer, it receives enough foot traffic that most of the trail is relatively clean. After 0.5 mile, the trail nears the dam that created Elk City Lake. Here the trail heads west along the north shore of the lake, passing underneath limestone overhangs and by immense boulders; you will have to squeeze through a few of the rock formations as well as scramble over others. This is definitely not a gentle hike through the Kansas tallgrass prairie, so wear sturdy footwear and bring at least 1 liter of water for every 4 miles that you hike.

If you plan to camp, make sure you pitch your tent at one of the several disturbed sites along the trail. There are several campsites before and after the Oak Ridge Public Use Area, which is more than 10 miles from the East Trailhead. There are a few campsites close to the East Trailhead, while a longer hike is required to reach the first campsites from the West Trailhead. Smart hikers stash water, food, and other supplies at the Oak Ridge Public Use Area to lessen the weight in their backpacks. There are plenty of secluded places to hide your supplies, but most people are respectful of other hikers and do not disturb their caches.

Additional hikes: There are several trails at nearby Elk City State Park on the eastern end of Elk City Lake. Timber Ridge Trail, located on the south shore of Elk City Lake, is not on state property but is open to hiking. This trail is part of the US Army Corps of Engineers land around the lake. The 2.5-mile loop also takes hikers through oak-hickory forest with impressive rock formations. The trailhead is located in the Card Creek recreation area on Road 4600.

Miles and Directions

0.00 Start at the East Trailhead.

10.50 Oak Ridge Public Use Area.

15.00 Arrive at the West Trailhead.

35 Table Mound Trail

While Elk River Hiking Trail gets the accolades as the best backpacking trail in Kansas, Table Mound Trail might be the best trail in Kansas—period. It is a perfect day hike for trekkers looking for a challenge but do not want to hike double-digit miles. While the rugged terrain on the north end of this out-and-back presents challenges, overall this is the perfect trail for novice hikers looking to challenge themselves.

Start: Timber Road Area
Elevation gain: 800 feet to 978 feet; 394 feet total elevation gain
Distance: 5.38 miles out and back
Difficulty: Moderate due to rugged terrain
Hiking time: About 3 hours
Seasons/schedule: Open daily, year-round
Fees and permits: Daily or annual vehicle permit required, purchased at the park office or online
Trail contact: Elk City State Park, 4825 Squaw Creek Rd., Independence 67301; (620) 331-6295; ksoutdoors.com/State-Parks/Locations/Elk-City
Dog-friendly: Yes, on leash
Trail surface: Natural (dirt, rocks)
Land status: Elk City State Park (Kansas Department of Wildlife & Parks)

Nearest town: Independence, 5 miles to the southeast
Maps: USGS Table Mound, KS, 2018; park map available online
Other trail users: None
Special considerations: The trailhead at the Elk City Lake Scenic Overlook is another starting option and does not require a daily or annual vehicle permit.
Amenities: Toilets and water at the Timber Road Campground and the scenic overlook
Maximum grade: 21%; steepest section is a 100-foot climb over 0.2 mile after crossing CR 3300. The rest of the trail is relatively even, with slight inclines and declines.
Cell service: Adequate, although may be limited by tree cover

Finding the trailhead: From Independence, head west on US 160/US 75. After 3 miles, turn right (north) onto 3325 Road. Turn left (west) onto CR 4600, then take the next right (north) onto CR 3300. Continue north for 1.5 miles, then turn left (west) onto Squaw Creek Road. Follow the signs for Timber Ridge Campground to reach the Table Mound Trailhead. GPS: N37°15.521' / W95°46.748'

Trail conditions: The trail is well marked and well maintained. It receives heavy traffic, so the trail is clean and easy to follow. The section around the scenic overlook requires scrambling over large boulders and rock formations; sturdy footwear is recommended.

The Hike

Overall, Table Mound Trail is a straightforward trail, with only one section that might be confusing navigationally. Beginning at the scenic overlook trailhead does not require a state park entry permit; however, this option will leave the steepest climb at the end of your hike, when you will likely be tired. The trail from the Timber Road Area follows a wide doubletrack and gently but steadily climbs as it meanders around the steep bluffs high above Elk City Lake on its eastern shore. There is a steep descent

Table Mound Trail attracts rock climbers as well as hikers.

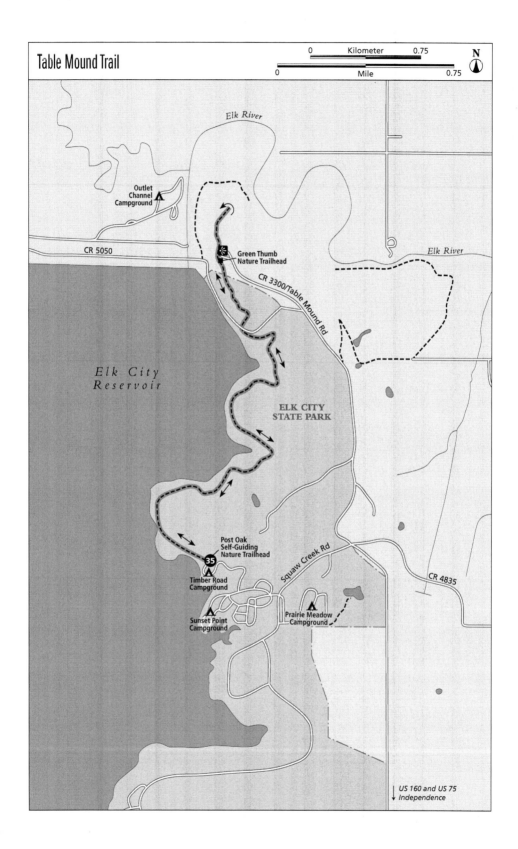

Table Mound Trail

0   Kilometer   0.75

0   Mile   0.75

N

Elk River

Outlet
Channel
Campground

CR 5050

Green Thumb
Nature Trailhead

CR 3300/Table Mound Rd

Elk River

Elk City
Reservoir

ELK CITY
STATE PARK

Post Oak
Self-Guiding
Nature Trailhead

35

Timber Road
Campground

Squaw Creek Rd

CR 4835

Sunset Point
Campground

Prairie Meadow
Campground

US 160 and US 75
Independence

into a drainage at the hike's 1-mile mark. The trail quickly climbs out of the drainage and then has a few ups and downs until reaching CR 3300.

This is the steepest section of the hike. The trail climbs 100 feet over less than 0.25 mile. Once you get to the end of the climb, you will have the option of either turning left at the 2.10-mile mark to stay on Table Mound Trail or continuing straight briefly and then turning left (west) onto the Post Oak Self-Guiding Nature Trail at 2.12 miles. Either option is fine, but both are recommended. The lower Table Mound Trail follows the most scenic and fun section of the trail, as it requires you to scramble over large boulders and underneath incredible rock formations. Post Oak runs parallel to Table Mound, heading northwest atop the bluff toward the scenic overlook.

Once you reach the scenic overlook, find the Table Mound Trailhead at the northern end of the parking area. You will need to scramble down a slot in the rocks and then hike around the bluff to follow Table Mound southeast through a maze of boulders and rock formations. This area is popular with rock climbers. Once you return to the junction of Post Oak and Table Mound Trails, the remaining hike is an enjoyable descent back to Timber Road on the same trail you hiked earlier.

Additional hikes: Adjacent to the Table Mound Trailhead is the trailhead for the Green Thumb Nature Trail. This 1-mile hiker-only loop has two wooden boardwalks and interpretive panels that describe the local flora and fauna. The state park describes the hike as moderately strenuous, requiring uphill hiking. There is a spectacular view of Elk City Lake at the top of the hike. Leashed pets are welcome. The Osage Bike Trail is a 3-mile wheelchair-accessible trail open to both hikers and bikers.

Miles and Directions

0.00 Start at the Timber Road Trailhead.

1.01 Veer left (north) down into a drainage.

2.03 Cross CR 3300 and continue northeast (uphill).

2.12 At the end of the climb, turn left (northwest) onto Post Oak Self-Guiding Nature Trail.

2.40 Post Oak Self-Guiding Nature Trailhead.

2.45 Table Mound Trailhead.

2.65 Scramble down the slot in the rocks.

3.25 Turn right (south) and hike downhill.

3.32 Cross CR 3300 and continue south.

5.38 Arrive back at the trailhead.

36 Tallgrass Heritage Trail

Located in the heart of the Osage Cuestas region, Tallgrass Heritage Trail takes hikers through prairie and woodlands on the south shore of Melvern Lake. The trail is split into two sections: The first follows a developed trail through woodland along the shore of Melvern Lake; the second takes hikers across open prairie with fabulous views north of Melvern Lake. Hikers wanting a shorter trek can do either section as an out-and-back hike.

Start: Arrow Rock Park Campground
Elevation gain: 1,045 feet to 1,106 feet; 482 feet total elevation gain
Distance: 8.29 miles out and back
Difficulty: Moderate due to length
Hiking time: About 3.5 hours
Seasons/schedule: Open daily year-round, dawn to dusk
Fees and permits: None
Trail contact: Melvern Lake Project Office, US Army Corps of Engineers, 31051 Melvern Lake Pkwy., Melvern 66510; (785) 549-3318; www.nwk.usace.army.mil/Locations/District-Lakes/Melvern-Lake/
Dog-friendly: Yes, on leash
Trail surface: Gravel and natural (mowed grass)

Land status: Melvern Lake (US Army Corps of Engineers)
Nearest town: Lebo, 15 miles to the southwest
Maps: USGS Lyndon, KS, USGS Waverly NW, KS, USGS Osage City SE, KS, and USGS Lebo, KS; trail brochure available on the website
Other trail users: Mountain bikers
Special considerations: Snakes are common around Melvern Lake. Poison ivy is also present.
Amenities: Restrooms and water at Arrow Rock Park Campground
Maximum grade: 10%; multiple short inclines of 50 feet or less
Cell service: Adequate to above average

Finding the trailhead: From I-35, take exit 155 and head north on US 75. After 4 miles, take the KS 276 exit and head west on KS 276. After 1 mile, turn right onto South Fairlawn Road. South Fairlawn Road turns slightly left and becomes Arrow Rock Parkway. After 0.5 mile, turn left (west) to stay on Arrow Rock Parkway. Arrow Rock Park Campground is at the end of the road. GPS: N38°29.447' / W95°45.632'

Trail conditions: The trail from Arrow Rock Park Campground is a wide, gravel path that follows the lake until reaching the recreation area on the east end of Arrow Rock Park. There are no trail markers, but it is easy to follow. The prairie section of the hike also has no markers, but the mowed grass trail is also easy to follow. The trail receives light to moderate traffic.

The Hike

The first 2.21 miles of Tallgrass Heritage Trail follow a developed trail along the south shore of Melvern Lake. After arriving at the entrance to Arrow Rock Park on South Fairlawn Road, the trail heads east through open prairie toward Coeur d'Alene Park. If you would rather not hike the full 8.29 miles, the 4.42-mile out-and-back from

The first 2.21 miles of the trail follow the shore of Melvern Lake.

Arrow Rock Park to South Fairlawn Road is a pleasant, shady hike. The 3.88-mile out-and-back from South Fairlawn Road to Coeur d'Alene Park has no shade but unobstructed views to the north of Melvern Lake.

There is no information at the trailhead in Arrow Rock Park; the easiest place to begin is on the east side of the shower house near the fee station. The mowed grass trail heads northeast, passes a pond, then becomes a developed gravel trail that meanders along the south shore of Melvern Lake under the shade of trees. Several footpaths lead to the lakeshore along this section of the trail, so if you want to spend the day on a secluded "beach" on the lake, Tallgrass Heritage Trail is your best access.

After more than 1 mile of hiking northeast, you will pass a picnic table as you approach a recreation area on the east end of Arrow Rock Park. The trail heads south here, following a mowed grass trail. You can also follow the park roads south. Continue heading south as the trail enters another wooded area, where you will soon reach the entrance to Arrow Rock Park. This is an excellent spot to turn around if you want a shorter hike; otherwise, continue east through the open prairie. You will lose the shade of the woods but gain unobstructed views of Melvern Lake to the north. This section is also 1.94 miles, so once you reach the fee booth and entrance to Coeur d'Alene Park, you will have hiked 4.15 miles. The return to Arrow Rock Park is via the same trail that you have just hiked.

Tallgrass Heritage Trail

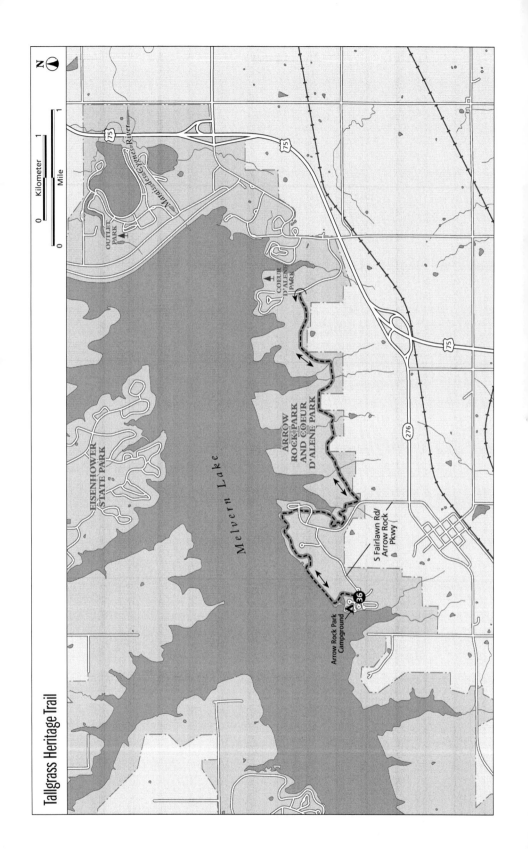

Arrow Rock Park Campground.

Additional hikes: The US Army Corps of Engineers has long-term goals to connect Tallgrass Heritage Trail with the trail system at Outlet Park. This would create more than 10 miles of connected trails at Melvern Lake. The current trail system at Outlet Park has 3 miles of trails, including a 0.5-mile paved accessible trail. The oxbow can be explored via a 2-mile gravel trail. The River Bottom Nature Trail is a primitive trail located in the northeast corner of the park. Besides being the eastern trailhead of Tallgrass Heritage Trail, Coeur d'Alene Park also has two additional hiking trails: the short Overlook Trail and the 0.5-mile Breakwater Trail that provides access to the lake.

Miles and Directions

0.00 Start behind the shower house and head northeast.

0.90 Bench.

1.50 Cross the road and continue south.

2.21 Turn left (northwest) onto a mowed trail through the prairie. (Bailout: Turn around to return to the trailhead at Arrow Rock Park Campground.)

4.15 Fee booth at Coeur d'Alene Park; turn around and head west to return to Arrow Rock Park.

8.29 Arrive back at Arrow Rock Park.

37 Wolf Creek Trails

The trails at Wolf Creek Environmental Education Area provide a quiet experience in several eastern Kansas ecosystems. Prairie Lake Trail leads to a viewing blind overlooking the northern end of Wolf Creek Reservoir, where a pair of bald eagles have nested since 1994. The Kansas Nature Trail meanders through woodland and prairie. Eagle Nest Tower provides excellent views of the surrounding landscape.

Start: Parking area on the northside of 17th Road Northeast; the Silo Trailhead (Eagle Nest Tower), the trailhead for all three trails, is 0.1 mile north of the parking area.
Elevation gain: 1,089 feet to 1,127 feet; 79 feet total elevation gain
Distance: 2.79 miles over three loops
Difficulty: Easy for Prairie Lake and South Pond Trails; moderate for Kansas Nature Trail due to more-difficult trail finding
Hiking time: 1.5–2 hours
Seasons/schedule: Open daily year-round, dawn to dusk
Fees and permits: None
Trail contact: Wolf Creek Nuclear Operation Cooperation, 1550 Oxen Ln., PO Box 411, Burlington 66839; (620) 364-4141

Dog-friendly: Yes, on leash
Trail surface: Natural
Land status: Wolf Creek Environmental Education Area
Nearest town: Burlington, 7 miles to the south
Maps: USGS New Strawn, KS; trail map displayed at a kiosk at Eagle Nest Tower/Silo Trailhead
Other trail users: Mountain bikers
Special considerations: There is no water source at the trailhead or on the trail system.
Amenities: Restrooms near the parking area
Maximum grade: 4%; very few inclines of note
Cell service: Adequate

Finding the trailhead: From Burlington, head north on US 75. After 4.7 miles, turn east onto 17th Road Northeast. Continue east for 1 mile and turn north into the parking area. GPS: N38°16.490' / W95°43.042'

   Trail conditions: Prairie Lake and South Pond Trails are relatively clean, wide, and devoid of vegetation. Kansas Nature Trail is more wild, and the northern portions can be overgrown in summer, making navigation more difficult. The trails receive light foot traffic.

The Hike

There are three loops at Wolf Creek Reservoir Educational Area that, when combined, total nearly 3 miles. Eagle Nest Tower, also known as the Silo Trailhead, is the trailhead for all three trails. It is accessed by hiking north along the doubletrack gravel road from the parking area, passing the restrooms and a dinner bell that was placed here in honor of Alton and Avis Phillips, who cared for this land before the power plant was built.

   Before reaching the Silo Trailhead, the trail passes a large barn to the west of the trail, which is used to store equipment to manage the land as well as other materials.

Eagle Nest Tower at the Silo Trailhead.

Kansas Nature Trail is more wild and overgrown than the other trails.

The Silo Trailhead, or Eagle Nest Tower, is shortly after the barn. A kiosk at the junction of the three trails displays the trail map. The tower is a silo that has been converted into a wildlife observation tower, with stairs leading up to the top. The tower is closed to the public when barn owls are nesting inside.

The beauty of the Silo Trailhead as the access point for all three loops is that it allows hikers to do one, two, or all three. If you are looking for just a short, leisurely hike with payoff, Prairie Lake Trail is the best option. The trail is crushed rock, so while you may be able to get a stroller or wheelchair on the path, it will likely be bumpy. The trail is wide and clean, so you shouldn't need to worry about ticks (unlike on Kansas Nature Trail). In about 0.25 mile, you will reach a viewing blind overlooking the northern end of Wolf Creek Reservoir. This is an excellent spot to watch bald eagles during the winter. The return to Silo Trailhead is about 0.33 mile.

If you want to add some distance to your hike, the Kansas Nature Trail is the best option. Be prepared, however, for tall grass and some navigational difficulties. Kansas Nature Trail follows a mowed path, so unless the grass has been mowed recently, you will likely be hiking through shin-high grass. The grass is taller in lower-lying areas, and after crossing a footbridge at 0.82 mile and a bench at 1.14 miles, the trail heads north into upland prairie with shorter grass. At 1.2 miles, the trail heads northeast

Wolf Creek Trails

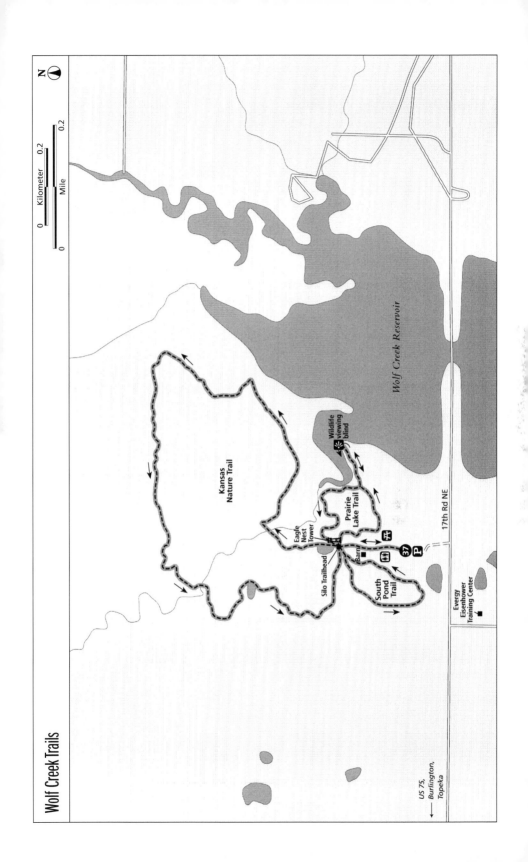

through a wildlife food plot, so it is possible you will be rewarded with wildlife sightings. The trail turns west at the 1.3-mile mark and follows an Osage orange hedgerow that borders a field to the north. This section has the tallest grass on the trail, which can be hard to follow in places. Continue heading west and the trail will reappear. You will enter a clearing at 1.6 miles, then enter a wooded area. There are a couple of trails through the woods. After crossing the bridge over the stream at 1.8 miles and the footbridge at 1.9 miles, keep left (southeast). Follow this trail back to the Silo Trailhead, where you can connect to South Pond Trail. This is the easiest, and least scenic, of the three trails on the western side of Wolf Creek Reservoir.

Additional hikes: There are additional trails on the eastern side of Wolf Creek Reservoir. Continue east on 17th Road Northeast, then turn north after crossing the bridge over the reservoir. If the gate is locked, park next to it and hike to the trailhead. Marsh Island Trail is a 0.4-mile loop south of the trailhead, while Woodland Deer Trail crosses wetland and woodland ecosystems on the nearly 1-mile loop.

Miles and Directions

0.00 Start next to the dinner bell and head north.

0.08 Barn.

0.11 Silo Trailhead; turn right (east) after the kiosk onto Prairie Lake Trail.

0.31 Reach a fork and keep right (east) toward the bird-viewing blind.

0.39 Bird-viewing blind.

0.67 Reach Eagle Nest Tower; turn right (west), then right (northwest) onto Kansas Nature Trail.

0.82 Footbridge.

1.14 Bench.

1.53 Bench.

1.81 Bridge over stream.

1.90 Footbridge.

2.28 Silo Trailhead; turn right, then immediately right (southwest) onto South Pond Trail.

2.49 South Pond viewing blind.

2.60 Barn.

2.67 Silo Trailhead; turn right (south) at the information kiosk to return to the parking lot.

2.79 Arrive back at the dinner bell.

38 Eastern Trailhead Loop

The 14-mile trail system at Lehigh Quarry Lake, known as Lehigh Portland Trails, has been extremely popular with mountain bikers and hikers since they were opened to the public in 2016. In 2023, Lehigh Portland became the newest state park in Kansas. While it will take several years for the state park infrastructure to be completed, the trails are open and lead to impressive rocky cliffs overlooking Lehigh Quarry Lake, the former site of the largest cement company in the United States.

Start: Eastern trailhead off Nebraska Road
Elevation gain: 961 feet to 991 feet; 66 feet total elevation gain
Distance: 2.15-mile loop
Difficulty: Easy due to short distance and minimal elevation gain
Hiking time: About 1 hour
Seasons/schedule: Open daily year-round, dawn to dusk
Fees and permits: None
Trail contact: Thrive Allen County, 9 South Jefferson Ave., Iola 66749; (620) 365-8128; www.lehightrails.com; email: info@thriveallencounty.org
Dog-friendly: Yes, on leash

Trail surface: Gravel and natural
Land status: Lehigh Portland State Park (Kansas Department of Wildlife & Parks)
Nearest town: Iola
Maps: USGS Iola, KS; trail map available on the website
Other trail users: Mountain bikers
Special considerations: There are no amenities at the trailheads, but nearby Iola has services.
Amenities: None
Maximum grade: 4%; generally level trail with minimal inclines
Cell service: Reliable

Finding the trailhead: From US 169 east of Iola, take the US 54 exit and head east. After 0.3 mile, turn south onto 1800th Street/Rock Creek Road. After 0.5 mile, turn west onto Nevada Road and continue for 0.5 mile. Turn south onto 1700 Street, and after 0.5 mile driving south, turn west onto Nebraska Road. After 0.5 mile, reach the parking area at the intersection of Nebraska Road and 1600th Street. GPS: N37°54.447' / W95°23.451'

Trail conditions: The trails are well maintained but not waymarked; bring a map or follow a GPX track for easier navigation. The trails receive moderate to heavy foot traffic.

The Hike

On April 19, 2023, Governor Laura Kelly established Lehigh Portland as the twenty-eighth state park in Kansas. The project was years in the making, driven by Thrive Allen County. Before attaining state park status, the park thrived as a hiking and biking destination on the south side of the town of Iola. The Iola Portland Cement Company operated the largest cement plan in the United States at the site until 1970. Thrive Allen County and numerous volunteers developed the extensive trail system that was opened in 2016. The state park infrastructure will include a welcome center and cabins; activities will include swimming, fishing, and hiking and biking the trail system.

Forest track on the eastern shore of Lehigh Quarry Lake.

The rocky bluffs of Lehigh Quarry Lake.

While outdoor enthusiasts will have to wait for the state park developments to be completed, the public can still visit Lehigh Portland to hike the prairie and woodland trails. There are more than 14 miles of trails, from wide gravel to natural-surface singletrack. Like many areas popular with mountain bikers, hikers can be overwhelmed by the maze of trails. However, it is often best to just wander these trails without a specific route in mind and encounter any number of interesting things along the way.

If you are interested in a short hike with great views along the rocky cliffs of Lehigh Quarry Lake, head to the trailhead on the east side of the lake; there is a small parking area located just off Nebraska Road. Several trails branch off from the kiosk; take the wide, gravel trail heading directly south. Take the first right turn to head west toward the lake. Continue straight past the first trail on your left, then pay attention for a spur trail at 0.2 mile to leave the wide gravel trail and enter the woods. As you approach the lake, turn south at the "South Loop/Location SL 50" trail sign. The trail winds through the forest—you'll be playing limbo with the spiderwebs—before reaching a clearing after 0.5 mile.

The trail heads southeast atop the high, rocky cliffs overlooking Lehigh Quarry Lake. While the cliffs are a man-made relic of the cement company, they are nonetheless impressive. At the 0.7-mile mark, the singletrack South Loop, on which you have

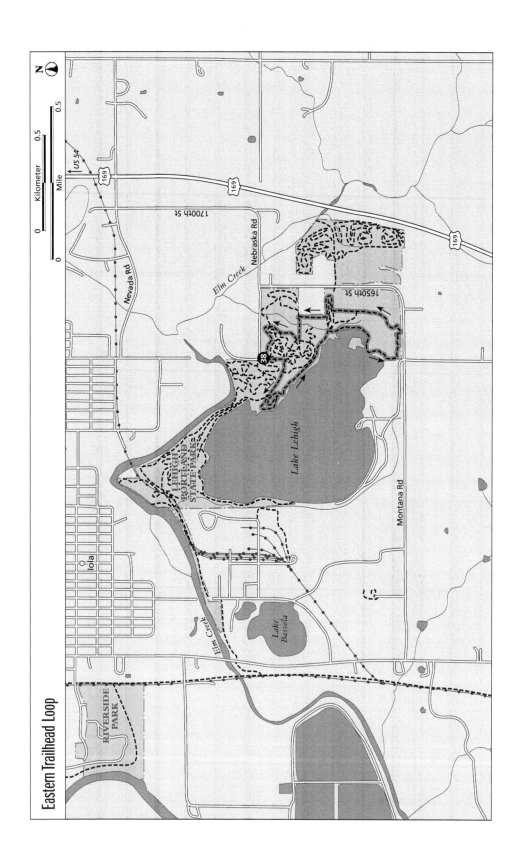

Eastern Trailhead Loop

been hiking, nears the wide gravel East Loop. If you find yourself on East Loop, find a way back onto South Loop to continue heading southeast along the top of the cliffs. Shortly after, at 0.82 mile, a spur trail leads downhill toward the lakeshore. Continue south, following the trail along the cliffs, where it bends to head west at the 1-mile mark. When South Loop approaches Montana Road, it turns to head east and then north along the edge of woodland and prairie.

You will reenter the more heavily forested area at 1.55 miles. There are numerous winding mountain bike trails in this section. Make sure you pass Hobo Camp before returning to the eastern trailhead. There is an abandoned camper and other interesting equipment to explore.

The Lehigh Portland Trails website (lehightrails.com) is an excellent resource. There are trail maps and photo tours of the individual trails, both the wide gravel trails and the singletrack natural-surface trails. These are very helpful to get an idea of what the trails look like and also to build several different routes combining the various trails.

Miles and Directions

0.00 Start from the trailhead and head south on the trail to the right of the kiosk.

0.08 Turn right (northwest).

0.12 Continue straight (northwest).

0.20 Leave the wide trail onto a narrow footpath heading northwest.

0.28 Turn left (south) at the "South Loop/Location SL 50" trail sign.

0.58 Picnic shelter.

0.70 If you find yourself on the wide gravel trail, keep right to find the singletrack along the cliffs.

0.82 Turn left (northeast), then right (south). (Option: Turn right/southwest to follow a spur trail to the lakeshore, then return to this junction.)

0.84 Turn right (southwest).

1.14 Keep left (southeast).

1.47 Continue straight (north).

1.55 Turn right (east) onto South Loop.

1.60 At the fork marked by the "Location SL 13" trail sign, keep left (northeast).

1.70 Turn right (north).

1.80 Turn left (west).

1.85 Hobo Camp.

1.88 Turn right (north) onto East Loop.

2.15 Arrive back at the trailhead.

39 Prairie, Creek, and Nature Trails

One of the best hikes in the state for history buffs, the trails at Mine Creek Civil War Battlefield State Historic Site are an underrated gem. Mine Creek was the site of a major Civil War battle and key Union victory. The interpretive signage describes not only the history of the area but also the local flora and fauna. The prairie and woodland trails are an excellent way to spend an afternoon.

Start: Prairie Trail south of the visitor center
Elevation gain: 830 feet to 864 feet; 75 feet total elevation gain
Distance: 3.9-mile loop
Difficulty: Easy due to level terrain
Hiking time: 1.5–2 hours
Seasons/schedule: Open daily year-round, dawn to dusk
Fees and permits: None
Trail contact: Kansas Historical Society, 20485 K 52, Pleasanton 66075; (913) 270-4217; kshs.org/p/mine-creek-civil-war-battlefield/19567
Dog-friendly: Yes, on leash
Trail surface: Natural (grass and dirt)

Land status: Mine Creek Civil War Battlefield State Historic Site (Kansas State Historical Society)
Nearest town: Pleasanton, 4 miles to the north
Maps: USGS Pleasanton, KS; trail map displayed on a panel outside the visitor center
Other trail users: None
Special considerations: Visitor center open 10 a.m.–5 p.m., Wed–Sat
Amenities: Restrooms and water when visitor center is open
Maximum grade: 2%; flat and level trail
Cell service: Reliable service at the trailhead and on the trails

Finding the trailhead: From Pleasanton, head south on US 69 for 2.3 miles. Take the KS 52 exit toward Mound City and head west. After 1 mile, turn south into the visitor center parking area. GPS: N38°8.685' / W94°43.386'

Trail conditions: The trails are well-maintained and well-marked. They may be muddy after recent rains, so avoid hiking to prevent trail degradation. The trails receive light to moderate traffic.

The Hike

Mine Creek Civil War Battlefield holds an important place in Kansas history. The visitor center has excellent information about the battle and the history of the area; check the website (kshs.org/p/mine-creek-battlefield-plan-your-visit/11877) for open hours. The trails, open year-round from dawn to dusk, also provide plenty of historical information on interpretive signs located around the visitor center and on the trails.

The battle took place on October 25, 1864, on the banks of Mine Creek. The creek is just south of the visitor center. It was one of the largest cavalry battles in the Civil War. Despite being outnumbered 7,000 to 2,500, the Union forces were victorious. After the battle, the Union brigades followed the Confederates

Mine Creek Battlefield includes prairie and woodland trails.

into Missouri, Arkansas, and the Indian Territory, effectively securing Kansas for the Union.

Prairie Trail is a 1-mile loop that begins south of the visitor center. Facing south, take the trail on the left. Hike for nearly 0.5 mile before reaching a fork; the left fork leads to a Confederate memorial in the woods. Continue on Prairie Trail heading west, then north to reach the junction with Creek Trail. You can head back to the visitor center via Prairie Trail, but the hike into the woods on Creek Trail is worth the effort.

Creek Trail is a 1.5-mile loop that stays on the north side of Mine Creek. After crossing a short footbridge over a small stream, take the left fork at 0.85 mile to follow the trail southeast. This trail will take you into the woods to reach the bank of Mine Creek at 1.4 miles. There is a panel describing the chaotic scene during the battle as Confederate troops crossed the creek. Continue northwest on the trail as it follows Mine Creek on your left. Be careful of the poison ivy along the trail.

Reach the junction of Creek and Nature Trails at 1.85 miles. Once again you have the option to return to the visitor center via Creek and Prairie Trails. If you feel up for it, continue south onto Nature Trail and cross Mine Creek. Nature Trail meanders along the southern bank of Mine Creek in two interlocking loops that total 1.25

Turkey vultures.

Three-toed box turtle.

miles. The trail can be extremely muddy after recent rains, so turn back to avoid trail degradation. As you hike, look for pawpaw trees in the forest understory. If you visit in September, you may be lucky to see the largest edible fruit indigenous to the United States. The far eastern point of Nature Trail reaches the other side of the Mine Creek crossing that you saw at the 1.4-mile mark. The far western point of Nature Trail is another trailhead that gives direct access to Nature Trail. As you head back to the visitor center, look for scissor-tailed flycatchers on Prairie Trail.

ST. PHILIPPINE DUCHESNE MEMORIAL PARK

Located 14 miles northwest of Mound City, St. Philippine Duchesne Memorial Park is a 450-acre Catholic retreat center. The center is the former St. Mary's Sugar Creek Mission, the tragic end of the Trail of Death. In 1838, 900 Potawatomi from the Great Lakes region were forced to walk to the mission in southeastern Kansas. More than 40 died along the way, and more than 600 died during the mission's ten-year existence. There are 2 miles of woodland trails open to the public.

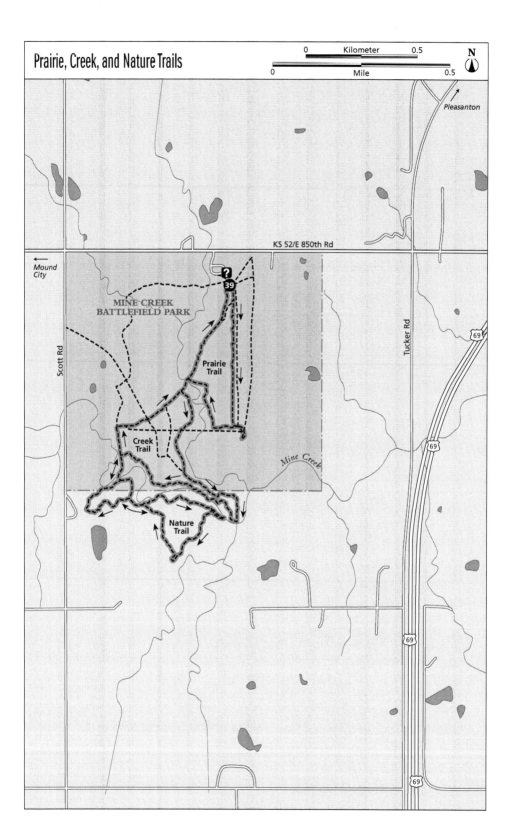

Prairie, Creek, and Nature Trails

0 — Kilometer — 0.5

0 — Mile — 0.5

N

Pleasanton

KS 52/E 850th Rd

Mound City

?
39

MINE CREEK
BATTLEFIELD PARK

Prairie
Trail

Creek
Trail

Nature
Trail

Mine Creek

Scott Rd

Tucker Rd

69

69

69

69

Miles and Directions

0.00 Start at the Battlefield Trails panel, south of the visitor center, and head south on Prairie Trail.

0.44 Reach a fork: Left (southeast) leads to the Confederate memorial; Prairie Trail continues right (southwest).

0.50 Confederate memorial.

0.80 Turn left (south) onto Creek Trail. (Bailout: Turn right/north to return to the visitor center on Prairie Trail.)

0.85 At the fork, keep left (southeast) onto Creek Trail.

0.98 Bench.

1.40 Mine Creek.

1.85 Turn left (south) onto Nature Trail. (Bailout: Turn right/north to continue on Creek Trail to return to the visitor center.)

1.88 Cross the footbridge over Mine Creek.

1.93 Reach a bench and turn left (east) to follow Timber Loop.

2.02 Keep left (east).

2.07 Keep left (east).

2.30 Reach a fork; continue straight (southeast); after 200 feet reach the Mine Creek crossing. Then return to this junction and turn left (south).

2.35 Mine Creek crossing.

2.81 Keep left (west).

2.87 Keep left (west).

3.03 Turn right (north).

3.17 Keep left (south) and cross the footbridge.

3.25 Continue straight (south) on Creek Trail.

3.55 Continue straight (northeast).

3.59 Continue straight (north).

3.90 Arrive back at the visitor center.

40 Schermerhorn Cave

Schermerhorn Park includes 1 mile of trails along Shoal Creek in the "Kansas Ozarks," an area known for karst limestone formations such as sinkholes, bluffs, and caves. Schermerhorn Cave is home to some of the rarest animals found in the Sunflower State. The cave entrance is closed to protect endangered salamanders, but a level trail leads to a platform to view the cave's entrance and the impressive limestone bluff.

Start: Trailhead northeast of the Shoal Creek Picnic Area
Elevation gain: 849 feet to 920 feet; 115 feet total elevation gain
Distance: 1.0-mile loop
Difficulty: Easy
Hiking time: About 1 hour
Seasons/schedule: Open daily year-round, dawn to dusk
Fees and permits: None
Trail contact: Southeast Kansas Nature Center, 3511 S Main St. (KS 26), Galena 66739; (620) 783-5207; ksoutdoors.com/KDWP-Info/Locations/Museums-and-Nature-Centers/Southeast-Kansas-Nature-Center
Dog-friendly: Yes, on leash

Trail surface: Natural
Land status: Schermerhorn Park and Southeast Kansas Nature Center (Kansas Department of Wildlife & Parks)
Nearest town: Galena, 2 miles to the north
Maps: USGS Baxter Springs, KS
Other trail users: None
Special considerations: The cave entrance is blocked with a steel gate to protect the habitat and the resident bats from white nose syndrome. Only the twilight zone of the cave can be seen from a platform at its entrance.
Amenities: Restrooms and water at the nature center and picnic area on Shoal Creek
Maximum grade: 9%
Cell service: Adequate to above average

Finding the trailhead: From Galena, head south on South Main Street toward West 6th Street. After 2.3 miles, turn left (east) onto Denny Drive to reach the Southeast Kansas Nature Center. The trailhead is in the north end of the park. GPS: N37°2.696' / W94°38.399'

Trail conditions: While the trails are not waymarked, they are well maintained and easy to follow. The trails receive moderate foot traffic.

The Hike

Schermerhorn Park takes its name from a wealthy landowner who donated land on Shoal Creek to the town of Galena for the purpose of a city park. The Works Progress Administration (WPA) built the stone structures in the park in the 1930s and 1940s. Today, Shoal Creek is a popular spot for local residents to cool off in the summer. The main attraction of the park, however, is the 0.5-mile-long Schermerhorn Cave.

The cave is home of some of the rarest animals in Kansas. Dark-sided, cave, and graybelly salamanders, all on the Kansas endangered list, find refuge in the cool and damp spring that flows through the cave. The entrance to the cave is gated to protect the endangered species as well as resident bats. The cave is typical of this corner of the Sunflower State, known as the "Kansas Ozarks." The karst limestone formations

The trails at Schermerhorn Park total 1.0 mile.

Schermerhorn Cave

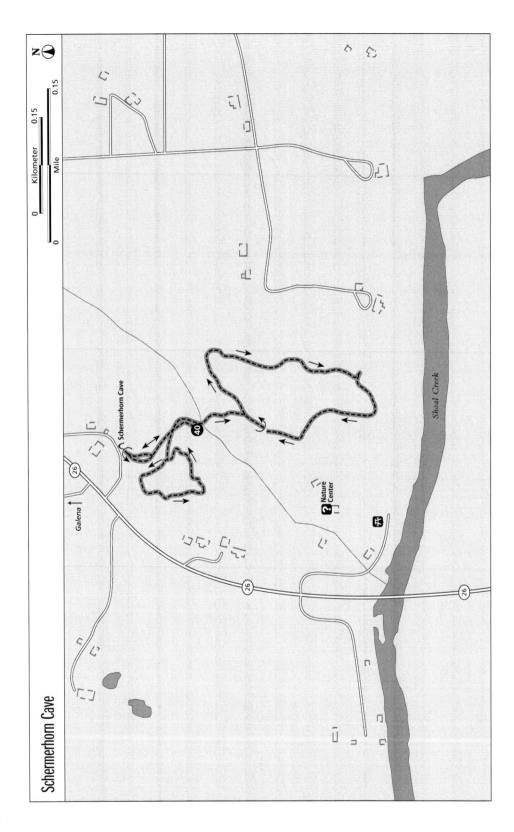

include caves, bluffs, sinkholes, and other interesting geological features not found in the rest of the state. The Southeast Kansas Nature Center is housed in a historic Scout cabin on the hill above Shoal Creek. The nature center has exhibits about the unique Ozark Plateau ecosystem and offers environmental classes and workshops.

The trail to Schermerhorn Cave is located north of the nature center at the end of a park road. The trailhead provides access to both Cave Trail and Grassland Trail. Cave Trail is a short, level trail leading to a platform where you can view the cave entrance and the impressive limestone rock formations. The steel gate prevents people from entering the cave to protect the rare salamanders as well as resident bats. The cave is 0.5 mile deep and about 2 feet high.

After viewing the cave, you can turn west and climb a hill to follow the short Grassland Trail loop back to the trailhead.

There are two additional trails south of the Cave and Grassland trailhead. Once you reach the parking area, continue past the amphitheater to find the trailhead for Roosa Trail. You can combine Roosa and Lucas' Lookout Trails, both leading through oak-hickory forest, with the park road to create a 0.5-mile loop.

Miles and Directions

0.00 Start from the trailhead and head northeast.

0.15 Schermerhorn Cave.

0.20 Turn left (west) onto Grassland Trail.

0.25 Keep right (north).

0.40 Turn right (east).

0.50 Turn right (south).

0.55 Cross the park road and parking area, and continue south onto Roosa Trail.

1.00 Reach the park road and continue northeast toward the parking area.

Honorable Mentions

N Marais des Cygnes Trails

Ten miles of trails on six established trails take hikers through bottomland hardwood forests, wetlands, and prairie at the Marais des Cygnes National Wildlife Refuge. The habitats found here are uncommon in the rest of the state. Spend a day exploring several trails, and don't forget to bring your binoculars for excellent bird-watching.

Start: Multiple trailheads (see GPS on page 243)
Elevation gain: Variable, depending on the trails hiked
Distance: 10 total miles of trails
Difficulty: Easy
Hiking time: Variable, depending on the trails hiked
Seasons/schedule: Open daily year-round, dawn to dusk
Fees and permits: None
Trail contact: Marais des Cygnes National Wildlife Refuge, 24141 KS Hwy. 52, Pleasanton 66075; (913) 352-8956; fws.gov/refuge/marais-des-cygnes
Dog-friendly: Yes, on leash
Trail surface: Natural (grass and dirt)
Land status: Marais des Cygnes National Wildlife Refuge (US Fish & Wildlife Service)
Nearest town: Pleasanton, 4 miles to the southwest
Maps: USGS Pleasanton, KS, and USGS Worland, MO, KS; as of May 2023, trail maps displayed on panels at three trailheads (Forest, Mosaic, State Line Pond)
Other trail users: None

Marais des Cygnes National Wildlife Refuge.

Special considerations: Hunting is permitted, so dress (blaze orange) and plan accordingly. If you go off-trail, which is permitted, make your presence known during hunting season.

Amenities: None
Maximum grade: Variable, depending on trail
Cell service: Adequate to weak coverage

Finding the trailhead: Marais des Cygnes National Wildlife Refuge is south of KS 52 and east of US 69. To access the various trailheads, enter the GPS coordinates below into a GPS device.

GPS (Woodland Ridges Trail): N38°12.472' / W94°39.517'

GPS (Forest Trail): N38°14.435' / W94°38.408'

GPS (Mosaic Trail): N38°12.955' / W94°38.059'

GPS (Turkey Foot Lake Trail): N38°12.913' / W94°37.473'

GPS (State Line Pond Trail): N38°13.848' / W94°36.752'

GPS (East Mine Creek Trail): N38°11.656' / W94°36.789'

Trail conditions: The trails are generally easy to follow. They follow mowed paths or gravel roads. Off-trail hiking is permitted, but be aware of poison ivy, ticks, insects, and hunting seasons.

◯ Casaletto Loop

Casaletto Loop winds through riparian woodlands, wetlands, and grasslands along a tributary of Cow Creek. Several coal pit ponds in the park are open to fishing. A portion of the trail system is ADA accessible, while more challenging trails take hikers along ridges created by open-pit mining.

Wilderness Park, near Pittsburg.

Start: 907 West McKay Street, Frontenac

Elevation gain: Variable, depending on route

Distance: More than 4 total miles of trails

Difficulty: Easy

Hiking time: Variable; about 2 hours if you hike all the trails

Seasons/schedule: Apr–Oct, 7 a.m.–8 p.m.; Nov–Mar, 8 a.m.–5 p.m.

Fees and permits: None

Trail contact: City of Pittsburg; www.pittks.org

Dog-friendly: Yes, on leash

Trail surface: Natural (gravel and dirt)

Land status: Wilderness Park (City of Pittsburg)

Nearest town: Pittsburg

Maps: USGS Pittsburg, KS; trail map displayed at the trailhead kiosk

Other trail users: Mountain bikers

Special considerations: Bikers must yield to hikers; however, be aware of your surroundings and don't hike with headphones.

Amenities: None

Maximum grade: Variable, depending on route

Cell service: Adequate

Finding the trailhead: From Pittsburg, head north on US 160. Turn west onto West McKay Street. After 0.5 mile, turn south into the Wilderness Park parking area. GPS: N37°27.294' / W94°42.806'

Trail conditions: The trails can be overgrown in the further sections of the park. Ticks and insects are abundant in warmer months. The trail system can be confusing, so take a picture of the map at the trailhead kiosk and follow a track on a GPS device. Trails will be muddy and possibly submerged after heavy rain.

Hike Index

THE TEN ESSENTIALS OF HIKING

American Hiking Society

American Hiking Society recommends you pack the "Ten Essentials" every time you head out for a hike. Whether you plan to be gone for a couple of hours or several months, make sure to pack these items. Become familiar with these items and know how to use them. Learn more at **AmericanHiking.org/hiking-resources**

1. Appropriate Footwear

6. Safety Items (light, fire, and a whistle)

2. Navigation

7. First Aid Kit

3. Water (and a way to purify it)

8. Knife or Multi-Tool

4. Food

9. Sun Protection

5. Rain Gear & Dry-Fast Layers

10. Shelter